LATIN AMERICAN REVOLUTIONARY POETRY

POETRY

POESIA REVOLUCIONARIA LATINOAMERICANA

LATIN AMERICAN REVOLUTIONARY POETRY

A bilingual anthology
Edited and with an
Introduction by
Robert Márquez

POESIA REVOLUCIONARIA LATINOAMERICANA

Monthly Review Press
New York and London

Library of Congress Cataloging in Publication Data
Márquez, Robert, comp.
    Latin American revolutionary poetry.
    1. Revolutionary poetry, Latin American. I. Title. II. Title:
Poesía revolucionaria latinoamericana.
PQ7084.M28   861   73–90079
ISBN 0–85345–321–7

First Printing

Monthly Review Press
62 West 14th Street, New York, N.Y. 10011
21 Theobalds Road, London WCIV 8SL

Manufactured in the United States of America

Acknowledgments

I would like to take this opportunity to express my sincerest thanks to the many people who, in one form or another, collaborated in the preparation of this volume. I am especially indebted to Susan Lowes of Monthly Review Press, and to Bobbye Ortiz, Associate Editor of *Monthly Review*, for their usual support and encouragement, and to the several translators whose work appears in these pages. I would also like to thank my *compañero* David Arthur McMurray, whose reading and commentary are as much appreciated as his fine translations.

To these I must add the name of Arnaldo Orfilia Reynal, Director of Siglo XXI Editores, Mexico, whose generous gift of the now out-of-print *Muros de luz* by Marco Antonio Flores, and general graciousness, deserving of more proper acknowledgement, are very much appreciated. My thanks, finally, to Trudy Pax for sharing with me her collection of the work of Thiago de Mello and for making it possible for me to contact the poet directly.

I also take this opportunity to join with the publishers in acknowledging the sources of the poems included in this anthology and in expressing our gratitude for permission to reprint material.

Our largest debt is to the Casa de Las Américas, Havana, Cuba, from whose various editions the work of the following poets is reproduced: Juan Gelman (*Poemas*, 1968), Víctor García Robles (*Oíd, mortales*, 1965), Pedro Shimose (*Quiero escribir, pero me sale espuma*, 1972), Ernesto Cardenal (*Poemas*, 1967), Javier Heraud (*Poe-*

mas, 1967), Roque Dalton (*El turno del ofendido*, 1963; *Taberna y otros lugares*, 1969), Antonio Cisneros (*Canto ceremonial contra un oso hormiguero*, 1968), Carlos María Gutiérrez (*Diario del cuartel*, 1970), and Otto René Castillo (*Poemas*, 1971). Enrique Lihn's poem "Europeos" appeared in the journal *Casa de Las Américas*. We are also indebted to the Unión Nacional de Escritores y Artistas de Cuba (UNEAC), the publisher of Nancy Morejón's *Richard trajo su flauta y otros argumentos* and of David Fernández Chericián's *La onda de David*.

Acknowledgement is due to *El corno emplumado* (Mexico) in which Donald Gardner's translation of Ernesto Cardenal's "La hora cero" and the anonymous Colombian poet's "Colombia masacrada" first appeared, and which also published "Condecoración y ascenso" by Jorge Enrique Adoum, "Sin título" and "Siete y cincuenta y cinco" by Edmundo Aray, and Tim Reynold's translation of "Viudo del mundo" by Otto René Castillo.

For permission to reprint copyrighted material, our thanks to:

Enrique Molina and Ediciones Sunda (Buenos Aires), for "Hue," "Información," and "Hueco nocturno" from *Monzón napalm*, copyright © 1968 by Ediciones Sunda.

Nicolás Guillén and the University of Massachusetts Press for "Crecen altas las flores," "Ángela Davis," "Lectura de domingo," and their respective translations from *Man-Making Words: Selected Poems of Nicolás Guillén*, copyright © 1972 by Robert Márquez and David Arthur McMurray; and to Nicolás Guillén and Monthly Review Press for "Tengo" and its translation from *Patria o Muerte: The Great Zoo and Other Poems by Nicolás Guillén*, copyright © 1972 by Robert Márquez.

9

For
el compañero Presidente
Salvador Allende Gossens,
Pablo Neruda,
and the many thousands gone
in memoriam

For
Jari, Lan, Beví,
Ayrín, y las dos Iris
nuevamente

Índice

Argentina

Enrique Molina   36

   Hue   38
   Información   46
   Hueco nocturno   48

Juan Gelman   50

   Los ojos   52
   Epocas   54
   Argelia   56
   Historia   58

Víctor García Robles   60

   Sepa lo que pasa a lágrima viva y
     con malas palabras   62

Bolivia

Pedro Shimose   80

   Sueño de una noche de verano   82
   Epigrama pequeñoburgués superacademi-
     correalista   84
   El conde Drácula sale de inspección   86

Contents

Introduction   25

Argentina

Enrique Molina   36

     Hue   39
     Information   47
     Night Watch   49

Juan Gelman   50

     Eyes   53
     Epochs   55
     Algiers   57
     History   59

Víctor García Robles   60

     Know Ye What Happens Amidst Copious
     Tears and with Four-Letter Words   63

Bolivia

Pedro Shimose   80

     A Midsummer Night's Dream   83
     A Petty-Bourgeois Suracademicrealistic
     Epigram   85
     Count Dracula on an Inspection Tour   87

Brasil

Thiago de Mello   88

   Os estatutos do homem   90
   Canção do amor armado   98

Chile

Enrique Lihn   104

   Europeos   106

Anónimo   112

   Bandos marciales   114

Colombia

Anónimo   120

   Colombia masacrada   122

Cuba

Nicolás Guillén   154

   Crecen altas las flores   156
   Tengo   164
   Ángela Davis   168
   Lectura de domingo   172

Roberto Fernández Retamar   176

   Epitafio de un invasor   178
   Es bueno recordar   180

Brazil

Thiago de Mello   88
    The Statutes of Man   91
    Song of Armed Love   99

Chile

Enrique Lihn   104
    Europeans   107

Anonymous   112
    Proclamations   115

Colombia

Anonymous   120
    Colombia Massacred   123

Cuba

Nicolás Guillén   154
    The Flowers Grow High   157
    I Have   165
    Angela Davis   169
    Sunday Reading   173

Roberto Fernández Retamar   176
    Epitaph for an Invader   179
    We Do Well to Remember   181

Es mejor encender un cirio que maldecir
    la oscuridad   182
Seria bueno merecer este epitafio   184

David Fernández Chericián   188

    Sección de anuncios clasificados   190
    Respecto del Tercer Mundo   192
    Una canción de paz   194

Nancy Morejón   200

    Los Aqueos   202
    Freedom Now   206

La República Dominicana

Pedro Mir   208

    Amén de mariposas   210

Ecuador

Jorge Enrique Adoum   232

    Condecoración y ascenso   234
    Pasadología   240

El Salvador

Roque Dalton   242

    Sobre dolores de cabeza   244
    OEA   246
    Karl Marx   248
    Dos guerrilleros griegos: un viejo y
        un traidor   250

It's Better to Light a Candle than
    to Curse the Darkness   183
It Would Be Nice to Deserve This Epitaph   185

David Fernández Chericián   188

  Classified Section   191
  On the Third World   193
  A Song of Peace   195

Nancy Morejón   200

  The Achaeans   203
  Freedom Now   207

Dominican Republic

Pedro Min   208

  Amen to Butterflies   211

Ecuador

Jorge Enrique Adoum   232

  Medals and Promotion   235
  Pastology   241

El Salvador

Roque Dalton   242

  On Headaches   245
  OAS   247
  Karl Marx   249
  Two Greek Guerrillas: An Old Man and
    a Traitor   251

Guatemala

Otto René Castillo   252

    Informe de una justicia   254
    Revolución   260
    Intelectuales apolíticos   264
    Viudo del mundo   270

Marco Antonio Flores   272

    De la cárcel   274
    De la madre   282
    Habana 59   286

Haiti

René Depestre   288

    Minerai noir   290
    Confession   294

México

Juan Bañuelos   296

    En Vietnam las púas gotean nubes
      de corderos   298
    Perros   300
    Fusil, hoja que conmueve a todo el árbol   304

Nicaragua

Ernesto Cardenal   312

    Salmo 48   314
    Salmo 36   318
    Salmo 5   322
    La hora cero   326

Guatemala

Otto René Castillo   252

    Report of an Injustice   255
    Revolution   261
    Apolitical Intellectuals   265
    Widowed of the World   271

Marco Antonio Flores   272

    On Jail   275
    Mother   283
    Havana 59   287

Haiti

René Depestre   288

    Black Ore   291
    Confession   295

Mexico

Juan Bañuelos   296

    In Vietnam the Thorns Drip Clouds
      of Lambs   299
    Dogs   301
    A Gun, the Leaf That Moves the Entire Tree   305

Nicaragua

Ernesto Cardenal   312

    Psalm 48   315
    Psalm 36   319
    Psalm 5   323
    Zero Hour   327

Anónimo 364

La cortina del país natal 366

Perú

Antonio Cisneros 368

Karl Marx Died 1883 Aged 65 370
In Memoriam 374
Crónica de Chapi, 1965 378

Arturo Corcuera 386

Fábula de Tom y Jerry 388
Fábula del Lobo Feroz 390
Cow-boy y fábula de Buffalo Bill 392

Javier Heraud 394

Alabanza de los días
destrucción y elogio de las sombras 396
Palabra de guerrillero 398
Arte poética 400

Puerto Rico

Pedro Pietri 402

Obituario puertorriqueño 404

Iván Silén 424

Los he mandado a llamar 426
Voy a escriber un poema 430
A veces estoy aburrido 436

Anonymous   364

    The Curtain of the Native Land   367

Peru

Antonio Cisneros   368

    Karl Marx Died 1883 Aged 65   371
    In Memoriam   375
    Chronicle of Chapi, 1965   379

Arturo Corcuera   386

    Tom and Jerry: A Fable   389
    Fierce Wolf: A Fable   391
    Cowboy and Fable of Buffalo Bill   393

Javier Heraud   394

    In Praise of Days
       Destruction and Eulogy to Darkness   397
    A Guerrilla's Word   399
    Ars Poetica   401

Puerto Rico

Pedro Pietri   402

    Puerto Rican Obituary   405

Iván Silén   424

    I sent for you   427
    I am going to write a poem   431
    I am sometimes bored   437

21

Iris M. Zavala   440

   Duelo I   442
   Nunca conoceré tu rostro   444
   Palabras y palabras   446

Uruguay

Mario Benedetti   448

   Con permiso   450
   Holocausto   454
   Quemar las naves   456
   Contra los puentes levadizos   460

Carlos María Gutiérrez   470

   Condiciones objetivas   472
   03:15 AM / − 4°   474
   Cartilla cívica   478
   Piedra blanca sobre piedra blanca   484

Venezuela

Edmundo Aray   496

   Sin título   498
   Siete y cincuenta y cinco   500
   Esto leo a mi hija   504

Iris M. Zavala   440

 Lament I   443
 I'll never know your face 445
 Words words   447

Uruguay

Mario Benedetti   448

 With Your Permission 451
 Holocaust   455
 Burning the Ships   457
 Against Drawbridges 461

Carlos María Gutiérrez   470

 Objective Conditions 473
 3:15 A.M. / −4°   475
 Voting Instructions   479
 White Stone on White Stone 485

Venezuela

Edmundo Aray   496

 Untitled   499
 Seven Fifty-Five   501
 I Read This to My Daughter 505

Introduction

Latin American poets in this century have been steadily abandoning the strictly hermetic narcissism of the ivory tower tradition whose largest debt is to the nineteenth century romantics, and are turning with increasing insistence to an exploration of poetry's sources in the reality of an ethos, in the commonplace, the "antipoetic" and rhetorically unadorned. Simultaneously, they are turning to a progressively more unambiguous denunciation of the continent's neocolonial status. This trend, which the work of the younger poets included in this anthology extends and continues, is another dimension of, and a testimony to the artist's growing commitment to, the larger struggle for national liberation whose first major victory was the triumph of the Cuban Revolution. The roots of this change in perspective reach back to the avant garde movements of the twenties and thirties—surrealism, indigenism, afrohispanism[1]—and, for our immediate contemporaries, to the imposing figures of César Vallejo, Pablo Neruda, and, still more recently, Nicanor Parra.

Neruda and Vallejo, after their youthful initiation in the waning *modernista* movement, were both nourished and sustained by the surrealist experiment. They found in its iconoclasm, originality, and innovative spirit, in its language and techniques, a vehicle for expressing the nature

---

[1] We should add to this list the *négritude* of Aimé Césaire and other francophone poets, as well as Brazil's particular version of Modernism and the work of Carlos Drummond de Andrade.

25

of their specific malaise: for Neruda, the insecurity and almost metaphysical anguish of being surrounded by a material universe moving, like all things mortal, inexorably to ruin; for Vallejo, the existential torment of life in a world ruled by the absurd—chance, death, injustice, alienation from one's confrères—where, faced with the absurd, one is condemned to endure the further agony of an unspecified guilt and one's own insufficiency.

Then, combining the lyrical with the prophetic and even the apocalyptic in the wake of the Spanish Civil War, Neruda and Vallejo turned from the metaphoric obscurity of the surrealists and the narrow confines of a purely private pain to the public role, the more ecumenical vision, of the militant troubadour whose poetry defines and shapes at the same time that it mirrors and speaks to the spirit of a people. Their eventual membership in the Communist Party was not incidental but an intrinsic part of a radical change of outlook whose necessary corollary was the persistent struggle to forge a language, esthetically rigorous, that would be ever more consistent with their revolutionary convictions and their role as "people's poets." Neruda immediately discarded the mournful pessimism and metaphysics of the *Residence on Earth* (1925–1935) for the militancy and epic grandeur of the monumental *Canto general* (1940–1950). With a rhetorical sweep that echoes Walt Whitman, and an originality all its own, the *Canto* celebrated the landscape, history, and peoples of *nuestra América*. It set the precedent for Neruda's later work, and also for the progressive simplification of language which reaches an apogee in the limpidity and accessibility of the *Elementary Odes* (1954). Vallejo's sympathy and identification with human suffering, in particular that of the poor and hungry, intensified and deepened with his recognition of its origins in the social and economic structure. The source of this identification was equally in his intuitive perceptions and emotional makeup, and it is this profoundly *ethical* note,

26

this *visceral* authenticity, with its atmosphere of semi-colloquial familiarity and lingering melancholy, which has found an echo in poets as diverse as Carlos María Gutiérrez, Juan Gelman, and Pedro Shimose; its influence among the younger generation of poets seems destined to increase rather than diminish.

The impact of Neruda's extraordinarily prolific output was more thoroughly literary and not without its "paralyzing" and creatively antagonistic dimensions.[2] His poetry, joined to the inevitable proliferation of imitations his vast production inspired, eventually led to a "reaction" that became identified with the anti-poetry of Nicanor Parra and was actually a search for a new, more current, and ostensibly less rhetorical idiom. Negative in impulse, irreverent, corrosive in their humor, direct, skeptical, flat of tone, Parra's *Poems and Anti-Poems* (1954) encouraged a self-consciously *prosaic* verse. This in turn suggested the *conversational* poetry (already implicit in Vallejo's work) that is in a sense the obverse side of the coin but which Roberto Fernández Retamar, one of its most accomplished practitioners, considers more positive. "Conversational poetry," he argues, "tends to be grave but not solemn, and [in contrast to the anti-poet's threatening cynicism] . . . tends to affirm its beliefs, which are on the one side political and in some other cases are even religious, as in the case of Ernesto Cardenal."[3] It is these two poetic modes, Retamar continues, which are the direct antecedents of Latin America's most recent poetry and of the realism that is its most salient characteristic, "a realism enriched by the achievements . . . of the poetry that has been written during the

---

[2] See, for example, Mario Benedetti, "Vallejo y Neruda: dos modos de influir," in the author's *Letras del continente mestizo* (Montevideo: Editorial Arca, 1967).

[3] "Antipoesía y poesía conversacional en América Latina," in *Panorama de la actual literatura latinoamericana* (Havana: Casa de Las Américas, 1969), p. 262.

27

last forty or fifty years." [4] It is this realism, with all its radically objectivistic immediacy, that the reader will find in the work of our anonymous Colombian poet, for instance, and that, despite individual differences of theme and style, is most typical of a majority of the poems brought together here.

Literary influences and antecedents notwithstanding, these poems are equally a response to the nature of specific conditions; written against the background of contemporary Latin American history and the global movement for change, they reflect the impact of events. Their context is imperialism—concrete and intolerably continuing. It is the systematic economic, cultural, and human despoliation which has threatened the area's very existence since the "Discovery," and by which the ruling elites of the United States and Latin America, the force of arms their ultimate weapon, maintain their present hegemony.[5] Moved by their refusal to accept the immutability of this state of affairs, and by the pseudo-sovereignty of national governments and bodies like the Organization of American States (OAS), these poets' themes are suggested by that refusal and the vicissitudes of struggle:

---

[4] Ibid.

[5] The case of Puerto Rico is at once representative and painfully unique. Like Cuba, it was taken from Spain by conquest in 1898. It was declared a Commonwealth by an act of the U.S. Congress on July 25, 1952, when, in the jargon of the empire, it became "a free associated state" of the United States. The island's singular status as a classic colony brings it under the exclusive and nearly absolute economic and political control of the United States. The transformation of the native population into a cheap labor force (and of the native bourgeoisie into a class of middlemen for imperialism), of the island itself into a military outpost, a tourist playland, a market for expensive North American goods, rigidly subordinated to the metropolitan priorities so typical of classic colonialism, have already led to the exodus (as a result of low wages, high unemployment, and the general uncertainty affecting the poor) of one-third of the people to mainland ghettos. The island is thus particularly vulnerable to the encroachments of Yankee cultural imperialism, which threatens it with the loss of its own identity.

they range from the military intervention, assassination, arbitrary detention, torture, and general poverty typical of reactionary regimes protected by foreign interests, to an indictment of Yankee cultural imperialism and the ideology of white supremacy, to, in a more positive vein, the eulogy of those, like Sandino, Camilo Torres, and Che, who died fighting to realize their vision of a more just society. The poets fully recognize the existence of a larger confraternity of suffering, and their work reflects their solidarity with liberation struggles throughout the Third World and in the United States itself. The more intimate themes of love and family, for example, are set against the backdrop of this broader canvas. These poems are history as considered and experienced by Caliban.[6] They seek to break through at the same time that they condemn the ideological camouflage and monopoly of information of the status quo. "To give the lie to the AP and the UPI," Cardenal tells us, "is also the poet's mission."

The importance of Cuba is crucial. The First Free Territory in the Americas, the first socialist republic in the hemisphere, and the first Latin American country to provide equitably for the general welfare of all its people, Cuba stands as an example, serves as a catalyst and a

---

[6] Caliban, the deformed slave of Shakespeare's last play *The Tempest* (and the author's anagram on the word cannibal, as the original inhabitants of the Americas "discovered" by Columbus were thought to be), is a metaphor for the relationship between the colonized and the colonizer and is now the symbol considered most appropriate to contemporary Latin America—and, indeed, the whole of the colonized world. "Our symbol . . . is . . . Caliban," writes Roberto Fernández Retamar. "This is something that we, the *mestizo* inhabitants of these same isles where Caliban lived, see with particular clarity: Prospero invaded the islands, killed our ancestors, enslaved Caliban, and taught him his language to make himself understood. What else can Caliban do but use that same language—today he has no other—to curse him, to wish that the 'red plague' would fall on him? I know of no other metaphor more expressive of our cultural situation, of our reality." See "Calibán," *Casa de Las Américas*, no. 68 (septiembre–octubre 1971), p. 131; translated in *The Massachusetts Review*, winter 1974.

goal. Its many achievements, in the face of counter-revolutionary attacks and a nearly total blockade, have shattered the myth of Yankee invincibility and challenged the apathy to which that myth gave rise, shaking the continent out of its complacency. As Mario Benedetti pointed out in a very perceptive recent essay,

> The Cuban Revolution did away with balances which appeared to be stable, with the routine resignation of certain sectors on the left; it did away, too, with the most accepted schema created or disseminated by the empire, destined for the neocolonial estates. Fundamentally, the Cuban Revolution showed our peoples that the picture of Latin American man offered by the empire was a caricature, a distortion that merely served its plunderous intentions.
>
> With the Cuban Revolution, then, there began a new, experimental, and imaginative way of moving ahead with an anti-imperialist politics.[7]

The Revolution's effect upon the literati was equally profound: there were suddenly new demands on the writer to interpret Latin American culture and reality, and to be ethically, as well as artistically, consistent. This stimulated and intensified the search for appropriate forms of expression. "Curiously," Benedetti continues,

> Latin American literature . . . also broke with the old molds, with the old rhetoric, with the old routine, and began enthusiastically to experiment. Just as politics was mixed with economics, art, and religion, the literary genres humbled themselves, and theater came in contact with journalism; the novel, with poetry; poetry with narrative and elements of testimony. Literature also made some assaults on the impossible, and its relative failure was not useless either, rather it opened the way to other, more successful experiments [*Hopscotch, One Hundred Years of Solitude*] . . .

---

[7] "El escritor latinoamericano y la revolución posible," *Casa de Las Américas*, no. 79 (julio–agosto 1973), p. 139.

30

and, even more recently, the novel-poem authored by Benedetti himself, *Juan Angel's Birthday*.

The Revolution, like the war in Vietnam, imposed itself on consciousness in every possible sphere; it is an implacable dividing line marking the end of an era in Latin American history, ushering in and representing a new epoch. In this sense, as Benedetti argues, "Novelists and poets, playwrights and essayists, are all (putative or natural, prodigal or parricidal) offspring of the Latin American revolution," and of the process set in motion by the *barbudos'* assumption of power. These particular poets are among those whose relationship to it is direct and openly acknowledged.

Cuba, finally, is a point of focus, a compelling cultural phenomenon no less than a political fact, and an encouragement to progressive intellectuals and revolutionaries throughout the continent and the Caribbean archipelago. Most of our poets have, at one time or another, visited, resided, and had their work published there, an act of solidarity and identification which, not incidentally, defies the attempt to isolate Cuba from the rest of Latin America. The island's own complementary efforts, moreover, are just as significant. Its extraordinary activity as a promoter, critic, and publisher of things Latin American has already sparked something of a renaissance, underscoring the importance of culture in the struggle for national liberation and transforming Havana into a publishing capital that—despite material limitations—commands a drawing power and prestige nearly equal to that of Mexico and Buenos Aires. This activity, seconded by journals like *Casa de Las Américas* and literary contests like those very important ones it sponsors annually in the various genres, provides another forum for some of the hemisphere's most commanding writers and thinkers. It also serves as a vehicle for the promotion and encouragement on a continental scale of the work of younger artists, and forms an inextricable part of a broader policy which seeks both to give concrete expression to Marti's concept of *nuestra América*, and to reintegrate Cuba more completely into its proper ambiance by shaking it loose, once and for all, from the cultural orbit and influence of Anglo-America. The success of this policy speaks for itself. It has already contributed significantly to the breakdown of regional insularity, to the creation of a wide international audience and perspective, and to the failure of the blockade. Based on the premise that, over and above specific particularities, the countries of Latin America share a common heritage and a common destiny, that they form a hemisphere-wide whole distinct from that of their common oppressor, it looks forward to the realization of that destiny in the liberation of the entire area. That these poets, for whom Cuba is a symbol and a sign, share that conviction, that vision, should be evident.

That they do not subscribe to the notion of a "pure" poetry somehow unblemished by the milieu and circumstance in which it is created is equally evident. I suspect Roque Dalton speaks for all of them when, dismissing the philosophical idealism that lends support to that notion, he says: "It is foolish even to argue with those who affirm that the social and humanist attitudes in poetry are, at the very least, extrapoetic elements. Foolish principally because such a discussion implies an *a priori* renunciation of the universality of poetry." [8] As for the artistic integrity, strength, quality, and impact of any individual poem or group of poems—that the reader will have to judge for himself. The principle, however, can hardly be denied. I heartily endorse it.

A Final Word

This collection, like all anthologies, suffers from the inevitable flaw inherent in the genre: it is neither strictly representative nor broadly comprehensive. To be either

---

[8] "Poesía y militancia en América Latina," *Casa de Las Américas*, nos. 20–21 (septiembre–diciembre 1963), pp. 18–19.

would, at the very least, require two volumes significantly larger than this one and, in addition to including the work of a number of other poets from each of the countries represented (not to mention those, like Panama and Honduras, which are not), would be even more prohibitively expensive. Quite possibly it would prove to be unmanageable and unreadable as well.

This anthology therefore presents the work of three different groups of poets who together represent a certain esthetic, thematic, ethical, and even "generational" continuity. There are those poets, like Nicolás Guillén, who were practically born with the century, whose work spans several decades, and who, like Guillén, have a long history of artistic and political dedication to the revolutionary cause. There are also the younger poets, like Roque Dalton, Enrique Lihn, Juan Gelman, and Ernesto Cardenal, who are just approaching or are just past forty and whose work began to appear in the late fifties and sixties. And finally, there are those still younger poets, like Nancy Morejón, Pedro Pietri, and Antonio Cisneros, who are just crossing over into their thirties and who, more often than not, have benefited from the experiences —the achievements and limitations—of their predecessors in their approach to and analysis of the issues which are the common concern of them all.

My concern is to expose the reader to a small range of contemporary Latin American poetry as written in the context of the broad struggle for national liberation and the achievement of a sovereign independence, simultaneously alerting him to the urgency and commitment that struggle compels.

Robert Márquez

Amherst, Massachusetts

33

LATIN AMERICAN REVOLUTIONARY POETRY

POESIA REVOLUCIONARIA LATINOAMERICANA

Argentina

Enrique Molina (1910–   ), artist and translator as well as poet, was born in Buenos Aires, Argentina. He traveled extensively as a merchant seaman before he published his first book, *Las cosas y el delirio*, in 1941. In 1953, with Aldo Pellegrini, he founded the short-lived surrealist journal *A Partir de Cero*. The journal became the vehicle for what the critic Jorge Timossi refers to as the "furious vitalism" of its founders. After a substantial career as an aestheticist "indifferent to . . . the social and political situation," Molina, on the evidence of the following poems, is clearly moving away from the isolationism of a strictly art for art's sake tradition and opening himself up to the impact of contemporary events and to themes, like the Vietnam war, more typical of the engagé poet. He nonetheless remains an unremitting sensualist, unwavering in his original allegiance to surrealism and its "furious vitalism."

The recipient of several poetry prizes—the Martín Fierro Prize (1941), the Buenos Aires Municipal Prize (1946, 1961), and the National Fund of Arts and Letters Prize (1962)—his published works include *Pasiones terrestres* (1946), *Costumbres errantes* (1951), *Amantes antípodas* (1961), *Las bellas furias* (1966), and *Monzón napalm* (1968). The following poems are taken from the latter.

Hue

Donde el Río de los Perfumes mueve sus ligeras llamas
    bajo la luna
y las mujeres cantan en su boca
y hunden sus rostros de ópalo vivo en sus muslos que
    reverberan entre címbalos
un antro dormido al esplendor de oscuras dinastías
emperadores de labios inmóviles y grandes testículos de
    oro
cuya bilis era el relámpago
cuya sombra es piedra labrada jardines y sueño
       He ahí
el destello perdido entre las columnas
dioses de máscaras de canela
y caderas lascivas
fantasmas de garras reales
un vértigo de mariposas
entre el templo la fortaleza y la noche
amantes descalzas y vendedores de las orillas
        uniendo en sus anillos
las ceremonias de la vida
entretejida urdimbre del hambre y el olvido
en tales almas
graznido de las aves de un mundo caliente
       la vieja ciudad sagrada
       los monasterios de mármol
construidos sobre cráneos de colibríes
y el río de seda arrastrando mercaderías frutas podridas
lenguajes y juncos de velas negras de cáñamo
       pomada de plumas
en los senos que pueblan el mercado en los brazos
impregnados por el sudor de la luz
como la floración animal de un sueño
en un lento espasmo
       Y de pronto

Hue

Where the Perfume River moves its slight flames beneath
    the moon
and the women sing at its mouth
and sink their living opal faces in their thighs that
    reverberate like cymbals
a sleeping cavern in the splendor of dark dynasties
emperors with immobile lips and huge testicles of gold
whose bile was the lightning
whose shadow was polished stone gardens and sleep
               Here is
the flash lost among the columns
gods with masks of cinnamon,
and lascivious thighs
phantoms with royal claws
a vertigo of butterflies
between the temple the fortress and the night
barefoot mistresses and seaside vendors
              holding in their rings
life's ceremonies
a warp intertwined of hunger and oblivion
in these copper chests
in these souls
birds croaking in a heated world
             the sacred old city
             the marble monasteries
built on the skulls of hummingbirds
and the river of silk dragging along trade goods rotten
    fruit
languages and junks with black hemp sails
             pomade of feathers
in the breasts that crowd the market in the arms
drenched in the sweat of the light
like the animal florescence of a dream
in a slow spasm

la rajadura ciega
ciudad arrasada hasta no quedar ni un bloque de piedra
    en sus mandíbulas
quemada viva como el bonzo en su súplica atroz
desnudo su flanco incandescente
llaga deforme entre tizones
salen de las raíces desde los arrozales
secretos
                esos hijos volcánicos
se aferran
                a una indomable arquitectura
 y entre el estallido de la sangre barridos de napalm y
    crimen
apostados sobre tumbas reales
exaltaron su propia muerte con una majestad salvaje
                desgarradura y convulsión
de esa rugiente maternidad de pólvora
            otra Hue ha nacido
—su doble de piedras impalpables—
muertos latentes en el aire
¡oh criaturas del monzón!
           resisten aún
entre las hendiduras violentas del muro
cubiertas de vísceras explosiones y carne vidriosa
tanta vena de sed
tanto verdor de aldeas que latían
vaciado gota a gota por la herida

Hue fantasma
hecha de sombras de cadáveres la obstinada
resistencia sin término
los pequeños hombres elásticos que ardieron en la roca
           el guerrillero
con su gran sol central que lo hace crepitar como el
    acantilado
           el guerrillero
cada vez más hundido en su siniestra ciénaga de plomo

And suddenly
the blind cleavage
a city leveled until not one block of stone remains in its
        jaws
burned alive like the Buddhist monk in his cruel plea
his incandescent flank naked
a deformed sore amid half-burned embers
they come out of the roots from the secret
rice fields
                those volcanic children
they cling
                to an indomitable architecture
and amid the burst of blood swept by napalm and crime
standing on royal tombs
they exalted their own death with a savage majesty
                laceration and convulsion
of that roaring maternity of gunpowder
                another Hue is born
—its double of impalpable stone—
latent corpses in the air
oh creatures of the monsoon!
                you resist
even from between the violent fissures in the wall
covered with viscera explosions and glassy flesh
so many thirsty veins
so much green of villages that breathed
emptying drop by drop from a wound

Hue a phantom
made from the shadows of cadavers the obstinate
unending resistance
the small elastic men who burned in the rock
                the guerrilla
with his great central sun that makes him crackle like the
        cliff
                the guerrilla
each time sunk deeper in his sinister swamp of lead

flagelo de adioses vigilia y súplica de mujer sola que se
    desvanece
en su patíbulo nocturno
cielo desenterrado o lejanía
ni caricia ni lengua devorante
tanta garganta rota entre los restos imperiales

        Hue defendida hueso a hueso
        Hue triturada Hue mortaja de sol
        Hue resistida hasta la última llama
        Hue de ojos de felino entre los inter-
           sticios del desastre
        Hue coagulada ahora en la memoria
                        verdosa
pesadilla en alguna charca tan triste del cielo
gato que llora a gritos sábana venenosa plato donde cae
    sangre
en vez de arroz
y el hombre que retorna con cabeza de moscas
y no comprende más ni el vino ni sus manos en la terrible
disección de la noche
        Hue de escalpelo
        Hue sin labios
        Hue silencio de sangre
tantos muertos
han defendido el río la semilla el pubis de flores de la
    lluvia
la trenza que se entreabre y deja ver los cálidos demonios
    de la piel
tanta lumbre de cabaña tan lejos
la huella de sandalias en la arena
la mujer lacia bajo la hoja del banano
        llena de espectros
otra Hue ondula entre la niebla
        de espejismo
Hue reverbera sobre el casco inflamado del "marine"
        (*recubierto de slogens formol*

a flagellant of good-byes vigils and pleas by a woman
    alone who faints
in her nocturnal brothel
disinterred sky or distance
without a caress or a devouring tongue
so many broken throats amid the imperial ruins

                    Hue defended bone by bone
                    Hue crushed Hue shroud of sun
                    Hue enduring until the last flame
                    Hue with feline eyes peering between the
                        intervals of the disaster
                    Hue coagulated now in the memory
                                        greenish
nightmare in some too sad pond in the sky
a cat who cries in screams poisonous blankets a plate
    where blood falls
instead of rice
and the man who returns with a head of flies
and understands no more not the wine nor his hands in
    the terrible
dissection of the night
                    Hue of the scalpel
                    Hue without lips
                    Hue silence of blood
so many dead
have defended the river the seed the pubes of flowers in
    the rain
the pigtail that half opens and lets us see the warm
    demons of the skin
so many lighted huts so far away
the trace of sandals in the sand
the flaccid woman under the leaf
                    of the specter-full banana tree
another Hue undulates in the mist
                    with its mirages
Hue a reverberation in the inflamed helmet of a marine

43

y vendas puedes ahora beber la lepra en tu gaseosa
             la gangrena)

Hue de estrellas que hierven como una nueva
constelación del cielo del infierno
Hue inviolable
donde el Río de los Perfumes gira lentamente alrededor de
    la luna

*(wrapped in slogans formaldehyde
and bandages now you can drink the leprosy in your soda
the gangrene)*

Hue of stars that boil like a new
constellation in the sky of hell
Hue inviolate
where the Perfume River turns slowly round the moon

[Translated by Robert Márquez]

Información

Metralla:
son ligeras costillas las que muerdes frágiles costillas de
    bambú palpitantes jaulas torácicas
donde un globo de sueños se llena de súbito de hormigas
un bello corazón rojo de la manigua torturada
esos terribles cetros de insania
a llamaradas entre los helechos

Es un nido de venas una garganta
donde corría el vino de unos cantos rituales el viento
    dulzón y denso del verano
de un país de arrozales y plumas
               las fornicaciones
como una urdimbre suspirante del trópico en la dulzura
    humana
de amantes entre la espuma lunar sobre sus sábanas de
    arena
ese lugar de flores usurpadas
de pájaros tatuados por el fuego
todo el horror desnudo de unos muertos que encienden en
    la sombra
una brasa humillada y vengadora

Information

Machinegun:
those are slight ribs you bite fragile ribs of bamboo
    heaving thoraxic cages
in which a globe of dreams is filled suddenly with ants
a beautiful red heart from the tortured jungle
those terrible scepters of insanity
flashing among the ferns

It is a nest of veins a throat
where ran the wine of a few ritual songs the dense and
    gentle wind of summer
in a country of rice fields and feathers
              the fornications
like a sighing weave from the tropics in the human
    sweetness
of lovers in the lunar spume on their blankets of sand
that place of usurped flowers
of birds tattooed by fire
all the naked horror of corpses igniting in the shade
a humiliated and vengeful wood

[*Translated by Robert Márquez*]

Hueco nocturno

Ahora puedes ver
a través de los mostradores contra los cuales los borra-
    chos farfullan
y con grandes gargantas y abdómenes hinchados bajo el
    algodón de la luz llena de humo de cigarro y vaho de
    bebidas
los comerciantes hunden y pinchan con un dedo paralí-
    tico las teclas
de la máquina registradora
a través de las parejas que esta noche hacen el amor y se
    entrelazan en largas flotaciones obscenas
a través del tráfico
y los muros rutilantes de neón y orgullo de inmundicias
los adoquines húmedos de los suburbios de Saigón
con una gota de sangre sobre ellos
donde la guerrillera de ojos de jaspe de furia del insomnio
    vigila en la noche
y espera

Night Watch

Now you can see
over the counters where drunks babble
and with big throats and swollen bellies under the cotton
    light of cigarette smoke and fumes of drink
the merchants sink and with a paralytic finger pinch the
    keys
on the register
through the couples who make love tonight and entwine
    in long obscene flotations
through the traffic
and the walls of flashing neon and pride of filth
the humid paving stones of Saigon's suburbs
with a drop of blood on them
where the *guerrillera* with eyes of jasper of fury of
    insomnia watches in the night
and waits

[*Translated by Robert Márquez*]

Juan Gelman (1930–   ), one of the most talented and original of the younger Argentine poets, left his studies in chemistry to dedicate himself to his poetry. A native of Buenos Aires, he became a member of the radical literary journal and publishing house *El Pan Duro*, which was founded in 1954. It was, by its own definition, "a group of poets receptive to many voices, united by aesthetic and ethical principles. We seek . . . to be revolutionary in form and content. We want to be in the real vanguard, the people's vanguard, which is as far from those who create a mere rhetoric as from those who only copy what is external in what the new transmits." Gelman later formed part of *La Rosa Blindada* group, founded in 1962, which was another attempt "to give the people the poetry they create daily." Involved in left movements since the late forties, Gelman has been imprisoned more than once for his political activities. He has worked as a journalist and has traveled in Latin America, Africa, and China. He refers to the latter as his "best apprenticeship."

For Gelman, "the struggle for a new poetry must always be understood as the struggle for a new culture." His poetry, in which the influence of Vallejo merges easily with his sympathy for the tango and the equally popular *lunfardo*, transmits the situation in contemporary Latin America by focusing on day-to-day reality and by cultivating a language in which understatement, laconic humor, a deceptive simplicity, and militancy all come together in verses of impressive intensity.

Among Gelman's many books of poetry are *Violín y otras cuestiones* (1956), *El juego en que andamos* (1959), *Gotán* (1962), and *Cólera buey* (1971). The poems that follow are taken from the Casa de Las Américas collection *Poemas* (1968), which includes selections from each of these works.

Los ojos

no sé quién soy o he sido sólo conozco mi desorden
pasé los años agotando obsesión tras obsesión
aprendí pocas cosas y vi cambiar al mundo
o escuché a los amantes besarse contra el mundo
o vivir y morir por la Revolución
y nada fue más bello
que mirarles los ojos al pie de sus balazos
al final de tan corto camino

Eyes

i don't know who i am or was i know only my chaos
i spent years consuming obsession on obsession
learned very little and saw the world change
or heard lovers kiss in defiance of the world
or live and die for the Revolution
and nothing was more beautiful
than looking in their eyes beside their bullet wounds
at the end of so short a road

[Translated by Elinor Randall and Robert Márquez]

Epocas

hemos debido estar gentísimos para quedarnos tan solos
lumumba usted y yo
una mañana cualquiera en medio de la historia
los senos de su mujer según recuerdo
son dos tambores desolados abiertos hacia el áfrica
o como pueblos entregados de balde al enemigo
usted medita y crece bajo el polvo
contrarias circunstancias
mataron a lumumba al héroe al gran cartero repartidor de
    buenas nuevas
como la dignidad como el honor
patricio escribe cartas
dice: es pesada la sangre que vierte la traición
dice: amen al enemigo en su cadáver odien a los amigos
    con amor
estas señales y otras estallan en su tumba lumumba gira
    en sombras
en paz con su gran congo en paz con sí como poquísimos
en paz con el pasado el presente el futuro los vientos las
    gaviotas en guerra con nosotros
no debemos huir mis pequeñitos yo nunca aprenderé a
    restar
quiero decir: a resignarme
odio tu gran cadáver lumumba ora por nosotros

Epochs

we must have nurtured multitudes to be left so alone
on a morning like any other in the midst of history
lumumba you and i
your wife's breasts as i remember
are two disconsolate drums open to africa
or like peoples freely surrendered to the enemy
you meditate and grow beneath the dust
contrary circumstances
killed lumumba the hero the great postman bringer of
    good news
like dignity like honor
patrice also writes letters
he says: the blood that treason sheds is sluggish
he says: love your enemy in his cadaver hate your friends
    lovingly
these signs and others burst in his grave lumumba turns
    in darkness
at peace with his great congo at peace with himself as are
    very few
at peace with the past the present the future the winds
    the seagulls at war with us
we mustn't run away my little ones i'll never learn to rest
i mean: resign myself
i hate your great cadaver lumumba pray for us

[*Translated by Robert Márquez and Elinor Randall*]

Argelia

ah dueños de la cólera del miedo y la venganza
y de la borrachera del amor absoluto
y de los horizontes quietos en la esperanza
y de todo lo vivo de todo lo que muere
qué bellos iban solos al frente de batalla
y con la compañía de un pueblo de congojas
y cómo manejan sus dudas sus cansancios
y cómo levantaban una pregunta roja
como sus dos derrotas de ayer y de mañana
y cómo renacían y cómo renacían
ah pueblos bellos solos pero no solos únicos
y dueños de la cólera del miedo y la venganza
y pueblos bellos solos como mujeres húmedas
quietos entre horizontes como una esperanza
la noche es dura y larga aquí toca sufrir
y medir y parir monstruos de la ternura
y almenar los testículos para sobrevivir
ah pueblos bellos solos la noche es larga y dura
ahora tiene el aroma de húmedas mujeres
cortadas a pedazos en argelia la dura
sus pedazos violentos duran como paredes
donde duran las frases del odio y la ternura
argelia tiene huesos podridos bajo tierra
que crecerán en huesos podridos todavía
húmedos de mujeres y pedazos violentos
que a lo mejor perdonan algún día algún día
y entre los tiros últimos y las últimas cóleras
y los últimos miedos en el cajón del áfrica
reventados y duros y largos bellos solos
se acostaban de nuevo los rostros de rimbaud

Algiers

O masters of rage and fear and vengeance
and of the drunkenness of an absolute love
and of all the horizons silent in their hope
and of all that is living of everything that dies
how beautifully they went to the battlefront alone
and in the company of an afflicted people
and how they managed their doubts their weariness
and how they raised a scarlet question
like their two defeats of yesterday and tomorrow
and how they were reborn and how they were reborn
O beautiful people alone but not alone uniquely
and masters of rage and fear and vengeance
and beautiful towns alone like humid women
silent in the midst of horizons like a hope
the night is harsh and long here one must suffer
and judge and give birth to monsters of tenderness
and crown the testicles with merlons to survive
O beautiful people alone the night is long and harsh
and has the smell of humid women
cut to pieces in algiers the harsh
those violent pieces endure like walls
where the graffiti of hate and tenderness endure
algiers has rotten bones beneath the ground
bones that will grow into the still-damp rotten
bones of women and violent fragments
that may some day some day forgive
and among the final shots and final rages
and final fears in the coffin of africa
crushed and harsh long alone and beautiful
the faces of rimbaud lay down again

[*Translated by Elinor Randall and Robert Márquez*]

Historia

Estudiando la historia,
fechas, batallas, cartas escritas en la piedra,
frases célebres, próceres oliendo a santidad,
sólo percibo oscuras manos
esclavas, metalúrgicas, mineras, tejedoras,
creando el resplandor, la aventura del mundo,
se murieron y aún les crecieron las uñas.

History

Studying history,
dates, battles, letters written on stone,
famous phrases, luminaries smelling of sanctity,
I see only dark, metallurgical,
mining, sewing, slaves' hands
creating the brilliance, the adventure of the world,
they died and their fingernails still grew.

[*Translated by Robert Márquez*]

Víctor García Robles (1933–   ) was born in Buenos Aires, Argentina, where he teaches primary school and is on the editorial board of the literary magazine *El escarabajo de oro*. He was one of the founders of its now defunct predecessor, *El grillo de papel*. Robles is especially at ease with the long narrative poem. His poetry merges literary (especially surrealist) language and culture with the popular speech and culture of the people; it is a response to the reality of contemporary Argentina.

His only book to date, *Oíd, mortales,* whose title is taken from the Argentine national anthem, was awarded the Casa de Las Américas prize for poetry in 1965. One of the judges who voted Robles the prize, the Chilean poet Nicanor Parra, was particularly impressed by his "chaotic and torrential power" and said of the following poem that "its extreme vulgarity borders on genius."

Sepa lo que pasa a lágrima viva
y con malas palabras

Ayer mientras escribía otro poema
se me caían las lágrimas
¿saben? se me caían de bronca,
escuchaba dentro de mi cabeza los pelotazos de la
    cancha,
el grito de los hinchas enardecidos,

entretanto iba escribiendo un poema
metía las manos en los bolsillos
buscando el último peso,

se me caían las lágrimas que daba lástima,

mientras pensaba en la huelga ferroviaria,
la movilización, el aumento del dólar,

estaba escribiendo otro poema,
no este panfleto, otro
donde según mi oficio de poeta
cantaba al ruiseñor del arcoiris
y a la estrella fugaz de la belleza,

sin embargo pensaba en otras cosas,
me temblaban las manos pensando en la guerra,
supónganse una bomba H en Buenos Aires,
qué quedaría de estas calles queridas,
de tantos pibes divinos,
de los mercados, los boliches, los árboles,
la temblorosa esquina para citar al amor.
Qué quedaría de nada . . .

Lloraba que daba pena
mientras los versos salían riéndose

Know Ye What Happens Amidst Copious Tears and with Four-Letter Words

Yesterday while I was writing a different poem
I kept crying
I was so mad, you know
& a ball kept whamming about my skull
while the players yelled

& while I kept working at the poem
I was digging thru my jeans
looking for that last dollar

crying so hard it was a shame

while I thought about the railstrike
& mobilization & inflation

I was writing a different poem,
not this broadside, another one
where doing my poet's job
I was singing to the rainbow's nightingale
& the fleeting star of beauty

thinking other things just the same
my hands shook considering the war
suppose an H-bomb hit Buenos Aires
what would be left of the streets I love
all those great kids
the stores, the bars, the trees
the shaky corner where you meet the girls
what would be left of anything?

I was crying so hard it was a shame
while my different poem laughed along
because people need a little confidence,

porque la gente necesita que le inspiren confianza,
necesita estar contenta, que la ayuden un poco,
por lo menos con un verso divertido . . .

bueno, viejo, yo lloraba como una magdalena,
fabricando estrofas según la regla de oro,

entretanto sentía que la radio hablaba de la democracia,
hinchaban las pelotas con la austeridad y con los
    préstamos,
por radio no dicen: Se indulta a los huelguistas
por radio no dicen: Las fuerzas armadas se dedican al
    contrabando
por radio no dicen: El presidente hace macanas,
lo están presionando,
traiciona el programa,
que salga y hable con el pueblo,
dígale al pueblo lo que pasa,
señor presidente, le aseguro
que el pueblo se juega si hace falta,
señor presidente, sin demagogia,
de usted dependen tantas cosas,
pero la radio no dice: Se aprobó la reforma agraria
por la radio no dicen los nombres de los presos políticos,
por la radio no dicen quién mató a Satanowsky y a
    Ingalinella,
por la radio no dicen una mierda,
meta boleros y preguntas y respuestas,

los diarios son lo mismo,
para qué carajo sirven los diarios,
nos engrupen sobre oriente
nos engrupen sobre occidente,
las revistas nos distraen con unas cuantas minas en
    pelotas;

ayer se me caían las lágrimas mientras estaba escri-
    biendo;

64

need cheering up, a helping hand
with maybe a funny line or two

So there I was, man, bawling like a baby
grinding out stanzas according to the Golden Rule

while I could hear the radio talking democracy,
busting my balls with talk about austerity & international
    loans
they never say: Strikers freed
the radio never says: The army is into contraband
the radio never says: The President is fucking up
he's being pressured
he's betraying the program
he should come out & talk to the people
tell them what's what,
Mr. President, I guarantee
the people will back you if you need them
no demagogy now, Mr. President,
a lot depends on you
but the radio doesn't say: Agrarian reform approved
the radio doesn't name political prisoners
the radio doesn't say who killed Satanowsky & Ingalinella
they don't say shit on the radio
just some *boleros* questions and answers

same story with the papers
what the fuck good are newspapers?
we're being had on the East
& being had on the West
& they fake us out with some bare-ass chicks

yesterday I was crying while I wrote

it's a crime, man, I kept thinking nonstop
we've all had it with this song & dance
the newspaperman was telling me:
This country's a crock of shit!

viejo, es una vergüenza, pensaba a todo vapor,
somos tantos los que estamos cansados de que siga la
    farra,
el diarero me decía:
¡Este país es una cagada!

Yo le retruqué:
¡No es verdad, el país
es tan bueno como cualquier otro!

Entonces me dijo:
¡El pueblo no vale un comino!

Y le porfié de nuevo:
¡Tenemos un pueblo
tan bueno como cualquier otro!

Medio enchinchado el diarero preguntó:
¿Entonces, qué corno pasa?

Sabe lo que pasa, le contesté,
y entonces me empezaron a caer las lágrimas,
sabe lo que pasa, le contesté
y entonces empecé a sentir que los versos civiles
me daban tremendas patadas en la mano
y me saltaban los sesos como un pistoletazo,
y daban tremendos tumbos brutales por mi sangre,
me hinché con todos los porros que nos han metido,
reventé de aguantar las viejas amarguras,
y entonces sentí que la radio hablaba boludeces
y que los diarios cobran su precio por boludeces

y me acordé del golpe de Uriburu,
de la semana trágica,
me acordé de Castillo y de Perón y la picana
y la Revolución Libertadora,
me acordé de la Operación Masacre y de los fusila-
    mientos,

I came back with:
That's not true, this country's
just as good as any other!

Then he said:
The people here aren't worth a damn!

And I hit him with:
We've got people
just as fine as any others!

Then what the fuck's wrong?
the newspaperman asked, getting red in the face

Know what's going on? I answered
& then I started to bawl
You know what's wrong? I answered
& then I began to feel a civil poetry
kicking enormously hard at my hand
& blowing my brains out like a gunshot
& brutally tumbling through my blood
& I was fed up with all the beatings we've had
& I blew up from holding in old bitterness
& I realized the radio was talking shit
& the newspapers are charging for their shit

& I remembered the Uriburu coup
& the Tragic Week
& I remembered Castillo & Perón & the cattle prods
& the Liberation Revolution
& I remembered Operation Massacre & the executions
& the dead in Cordoba & I remembered
the riddled bodies in May Day Square

& I kept crying harder
while I remembered continuism
& the electoral campaign and the people's choice

y de los muertos de Córdoba y me acordé
de los baleados en Plaza Mayo,

y cada vez las lágrimas caían más grandes,

mientras me acordaba del continuismo
y la campaña electoral y la elección del pueblo
y el ascenso del presidente que era la única esperanza
porque más o menos había luchado toda una vida,

y después me acordé lo que pasó con la Cade
y con la Ansec y con el Grupo Bemberg,
y me acordé de la compra del portaaviones,
el Artículo Veintiocho,
· la manifestación por la Enseñanza Laica,
las bombas de gases lacrimógenos,
y me acordé de todo a medida que los versos aparecían
    entre mis lágrimas,
me acordé de las grandes estancias que hay en la
    República,
(por ejemplo los latifundios que ahogan al pueblo de
    Tecka allá en el sur),

me acordé de todo,
Villa Miseria también es América,
el infierno en los yerbales,
(decían del Tigre Millán: Es cuchillero y curdela
el negro zaparrastroso),
me acordé de todo,

los contratos con la Loeb,
la huelga de los petroleros mendocinos,
las concesiones a la Shell y a la Standard Oil . . .

¡Puta!, me decía,
¡nos van a joder de lo lindo!

& the inauguration of a president who was our only
    chance
because he'd been a fighter all his life, more or less

then I remembered what happened with the CADE
& with ANSEC & with the Bemberg Group
& I remembered buying the aircraft carrier
Article Twenty-Eight
& the Demonstration for Secular Schooling
the tear-gas bombs
& I remembered everything while the poem materialized
    through my tears
& I remembered the great estates all over the country
(for instance the latifundia that are strangling the people
    of Tecka down south)

I remembered everything
the slums outside Buenos Aires are America too
& the infernal *mate* plantations
(they used to say of Tiger Millán: He's quick with the
    knife & a drunk
that dirty black bastard)
I remembered everything

the Wall Street contracts
the oil workers' strike in Mendoza
the Shell and Standard Oil concessions

Motherfuckers! I kept saying,
they're going to screw us but good!

I was bawling up a storm, brother,
still writing that jailed poem
& so messed up you would've freaked

Know what's going on?
You know what's wrong?

69

Caía cada lágrima, hermano,
mientras estaba escribiendo ayer ese poema entre rejas,
caía cada lágrima que daba miedo.

Sabe lo qué pasa,
sabe lo qué pasa,
dije, se da cuenta lo qué pasa,
piense, dije,

(el diarero no veía las lágrimas),

sabe qué pasa, grité,

(el diarero se tapaba los oídos,
dos o tres pelotudos se reían de mí),

Sabe qué pasa,
sabe, sabe qué pasa,

(venía corriendo hacia mí un enojado policía),

sabe qué pasa en este país,

(el policía me zarandeaba del brazo),

QUE LO ESTÁN CARNEANDO
QUE SE LO REPARTEN UNOS CUANTOS,
QUE LES IMPORTA UN PITO DE TODOS NOSOTROS,

sabe qué pasa,

QUE PIENSAN EXPRIMIRNOS HASTA LA
ÚLTIMA GOTA,
QUE PIENSAN ENGAÑARNOS HASTA EL ÚLTIMO
    MOMENTO,
QUE PIENSAN SEPARARNOS CON ESTUPIDECES,

I said, You know what's going on?
Dig it! I yelled

(the newspaperman couldn't see my tears)

Dig it! I bawled

(the newspaperman had plugged his ears
& a couple of assholes were laughing at me)

Know what's going on?
Dig it, do you know what's wrong?

(an infuriated cop was running at me)

You know what's going on in this country?

(the cop was twisting my arm)

THEY'RE BUTCHERING IT
THEY'RE SPLITTING THE TAKE AMONG A FEW
THEY COULD CARE LESS ABOUT THE REST OF US

Dig it!

THEY PLAN TO SQUEEZE US
TO THE LAST DROP
THEY'RE GOING TO CON US TILL
THE LAST MINUTE
THEY'RE GOING TO SPLIT US
APART WITH HALF-ASS ISSUES

Know what's wrong?
You know what's going on?
Dig it!

sabe qué pasa,
sabe qué pasa,
sabe,

(el policía me daba en la cabeza con el palo),

sabe qué pasa,

SON UNOS CUANTOS HIJOS DE UNA GRAN PUTA
QUE SE BURLAN DEL SOL Y DE LA TIERRA,
DE LOS AMORES,
DE LA ALEGRÍA,
de la honda negrura de los campos arados,
de las espigas necesarias, del pan y del asado,
no les importan las manos
de las mujeres y los pibes,

LOS PIBES ¡CARAMBA!

no las manos
oscuras del trabajo,

SON UNOS CUANTOS ASESINOS
SON UNOS CUANTOS LOCOS,
SON UNOS CUANTOS IMBÉCILES,
son unos pocos cretinos que operan con la banca,
que están bien escondidos,

sabe qué pasa,
sabe qué pasa,

(entonces me tiraron de un puntapié en el calabozo),

SON UNOS CUANTOS TURROS QUE NO QUIEREN A
    NADIE,
QUE NO TIENEN SANGRE,

(the cop was knocking my skull with his stick)

Know what's wrong?

IT'S A FEW MOTHERFUCKERS
LAUGHING AT THE SUN & THE EARTH
& LOVE
& JOY
laughing at the deep blackness of ploughed fields
at the wheat we need & the bread & the meat
they don't care about
kids' or women's hands

THE KIDS FOR CHRISSAKES!

or hands
blackened by work

IT'S A FEW MURDERERS
A FEW MANIACS
A FEW IMBECILES
it's a few cretins juggling credit
hidden away

Know what's going on?
Do you know what's wrong?

(at that point they kicked me into a jail cell)

IT'S A FEW BLOODLESS FUCKERS
WHO DON'T LOVE ANYBODY

WHO'RE GOING TO PAY FOR IT
ONE OF THESE DAYS

Know what's going on?
Do you know what's wrong?

QUE LA VAN A PAGAR UN DÍA DE ESTOS,

sabe qué pasa,
sabe qué pasa . . .

y seguían cayendo mis lagrimones
borroneando en el papel la tinta de las palabras.

Toda tormenta pasa como un cuerpo
fragante,
                          descubriendo
formas crecientes,
                          se desplaza
desgarrando el reposo, acude con la lluvia a peinar polvo,
con viento a dar distancias.

Algo así mi tormenta desde el sur,
tormenta de pasión, en rachas cálidas,
escabritando el mar sobre la tierra.

Opaco estoy a veces, ciudadano,
con una mano gris y un cráneo oscuro,
escuchando el reloj dentro del pecho,
la fecha en que apresé pájaros propios,
la luna que me dio cuerpo en la noche.

Pero a mi espalda, cuando se hace un grillo
todo el silencio de la tierra áspera,
a mi espalda, sin que
pueda impedirlo mirándome las uñas,
con un
tambor incontenible,
con ímpetu
de toros y charrúas
se pone el sur en pie, un sur de piedra,

a mi espalda nomás que va trajeada
de Buenos Aires impecable,

& big, whopping tears kept falling
blurring the ink of my words on the paper

Every storm comes through
like a fragrant body
                        uncovering
growing forms
                        moving on
rending sleep, combing dust
with the rain
increasing distances with the wind

Something like that my storm from the South
a passionate storm in tepid gusts
driving the sea upon the land

I get gloomy sometimes, citizen,
with a gray hand and a shadowy brain
listening to the clock in my heart
the time I caught birds of my own
the moon that bodied me forth in the night

But behind me, when the whole silence
of the harsh earth buzzes locust-like
& I can't restrain it by staring at my fingernails
the South, the stony South stands up
beating an unstoppable
drum
powered by vultures & bulls

behind my back, which is dressed in nothing less
than impeccable Buenos Aires
you can hear the savage bellowing of a season
scarcely contained by a fiber
of fury
crouched
with steely pumas & solitudes
at the edge of a deep, red cyclone

se oye el bramido bárbaro de un tiempo
apenas contenido en una fibra
de furia,
agazapado
con pumas de acero y soledades,
al borde de un ciclón rojo, profundo,
que va a arrastrar el cielo por la tierra,
deshilachando estrellas
urbanizadas,

de pronto todo en ira refrescante,
todo a caballo, en trompos repentinos,
a toda volanda,
dándose trompicones saludables,
creciendo sobre los diques rotos,

un galope de rostros y de manos
empuñando las cosas y la tierra,
tirando al aire los fantasmas,
por sobre mis espaldas
toda la sudestada del amor decidido,
desordenando
las preciosas cajitas,
las sonrisitas,
los chequecitos,

que de hombre y de polen calentará la tierra
indiferente,
                    rugiendo en la ternura,
abriendo las provincias,
                    colocando los ríos,
ordenando crecer rápidamente
los cereales, las carnes, los vellones . . .

Ay entonces, mis uñas soslayadas;
huía de mis camisas intocables,
pobre la raya de mi pantalón subordinado,

which is about to drag the sky down to the earth
unravelling urbanized
stars

everything suddenly refreshingly raging
everything on horseback, suddenly
spouting tornadoes
knocking about in a healthy way
swelling over broken dams

a mad gallop of faces & hands
grabbing at things & the earth
hurling ghosts into the air
up, over my shoulders
a full Southeaster of resolute love
scattering
exquisite little boxes
& smiles
& checkbooks

& how the indifferent earth will heat up
with pollen and men
                    roaring with tenderness
opening up provinces
                    ordering rivers
commanding grain & meat & wool
to grow quickly

So much for you, my careful fingernails
I'd have to flee my untouchable shirts
my poor creased & subordinate trousers
my lamentable lackeyed backbone

I'll have to put my shoulder to the wheel
& revise my heart in its hairy den
so it won't fly off like forgotten laundry

lamentable mi columna vertebral en su costumbre lacaya,

tendré que enderezarme a puro lomo,
revisar el pecho en su pelo cojudo
por que no vuele como ropa triste,
tendré que hacer pata ancha
porque van a pasarme por encima,

¡no van a darme tiempo de pensarlo!
Es una sudestada,
¡entiendan esto!

No va a quedar un muro
ni para muestra,
no va a quedar un odio
ni para sombra,

al fuego, al bronce, a la sangre indomable,
cualquier hombre,
toda mujer dejar las enagüitas,

hace falta ir a pie sobre caminos
de sol rajante,
hace falta empuñar lodo y pantanos,

formar el bosque en marcha,
la cordillera humana.

Toda tormenta, y ésta que se viene,
saca de cuajo como gran relámpago
a cualquiera que muera de rosa o señorío.

Así se da en la letra el bramadero,
así en salud ansiada;
así en revuelta,

en toro,

en adelanto.

I'll have to be really on my toes
or they'll pass over me

they won't give me a second to think about it!
It's a Southeaster,
can you dig it?

There won't be a wall left standing
not even as a sample
nor any hate
for the sake of a little shade

everybody to the fire, to bronze & untamable blood
every man
& every woman leave your fancy togs behind

it's time to walk
the sun-split roads, it's time
to get ahold of mud & swamps

to form a marching forest
a human mountain chain

Every storm including this one coming
wreaks havoc with those who dream of roses &
        seigniories
strikes like lightning, chars selfishness to the root

This is the way to talk about Bedlam
about the health we yearn for
about revolt
                & bullish strength
                & progress

[*Translated by Luis Ellicott Yglesias*]

Bolivia

Pedro Shimose (1940–) was born in Riberalta, Bolivia. After two years as a law student at the University of La Paz, he abandoned his studies to become a journalist and composer of popular music. By the time his first book of poems appeared in 1965 he had already won the National Prize for Poetry given by the Bolivian University Confederation; a year later he went on to win the first prize for poetry in the Floral Games of Sucre. *Triludio en el exilio* was followed by *Sardonia* (1967) and *Poemas para un pueblo* (1968). In 1972 Shimose won the Casa de Las Américas prize for poetry with his latest effort, *Quiero escribir, pero me sale espuma*, which was published in Havana that same year, and from which the poems included here are taken.

Shimose has lived in exile for the past several years and his poetry is filled with the pain of that exile as well as with the fury current conditions in his country inspire. His work shows the influence of César Vallejo, from whom he takes the title of his last book, and Nicolás Guillén. He shares with Vallejo the anguished vision of an exile and a revolutionary identification with the Indian and the poor. He shows a great sensitivity to the rhythm of his verse and, like Guillén, frequently uses words and images which, because clearly alien to the Bolivian setting, highlight the depth and consequences of the United States presence there. To this he adds a tone of self-assurance distinguished by its sharp and implacable irony.

Sueño de una noche de verano

Terminas de hurgar la mugre y la ceniza, de hacer los mandados,
de pelar papas, lavar, fregar, tirar la basura, etc.,
terminas de comer las sobras en un rincón de la cocina
y te escondes en tu cuarto,
te miras en un espejo roto,
te pintarrajeas los ojos, te maquillas,
escuchas radionovelas, miras fotorromances,
vas al cine del barrio a ver otra de Alain Delon,
juegas a ser estrella como la Marilyn o la Sofía,
te miras el ombligo,
te extasías mirándote el ombligo,
viajas por tu sombra con azaleas y gardenias,
caminas por tu cuerpo con minifaldas y ojeras,
piensas en el gordo de la Lotería,
te pintas las uñas sucias,
deletreas la predicción astrológica para mañana,
sueñas con tu príncipe azul,
con el hada madrina, con la varita mágica,
tú eres la chica de la zapatilla de cristal,
la del baile a medianoche con corceles que son ratones
y carrozas que son calabazas . . .
Mira ñatita, tú eres linda, pero
¡lávate las axilas y deja de hacer macanas
que te está llamando la patrona!

A Midsummer Night's Dream

You finish cleaning out the dust and the ashes, doing all
    the errands,
peeling the potatoes, washing, doing the dishes, throwing
    out the trash,
finish eating leftovers in a corner of the kitchen
and go hide in your room,
look at yourself in a shattered mirror,
daub your eyebrows, makeup,
listen to soap operas, glance through *True Romances*,
go to the local movie to see another Alain Delon,
play at being a star like Marilyn or Sophia,
look at your navel,
become ecstatic looking at your navel,
move over your shadow with azaleas and gardenias,
walk over your body with a miniskirt and sunken eyes,
imagine hitting the jackpot in the lottery,
paint your dirty nails,
spell out the astrological prediction for tomorrow,
dream about your prince charming,
about the fairy godmother, with the magic wand,
you are the girl with the crystal slipper,
the one at the midnight ball with horses that are mice
and coaches that are pumpkins . . .
Look *ñatita*, you're pretty, but
wash your underarms and stop the foolishness,
the mistress is calling!

[*Translated by Robert Márquez*]

Epigrama pequeñoburgués
superacademicorrealista

Después de impresionar a las muchachas con nuestro
    ingenio;
después de violar vestales y de escandalizar monjas;
después de quemar lirios, enterrar nubes e incendiar
    templos;
después de degollar vacas sagradas o asesinar dioses;
después de escribir sin mayúsculas y sin signos de
    puntuación;
después de atacar a la rosa y al rey Gustavo de Suecia;
después de dinamitar museos y bailar en los cementerios,
de perseguir la gloria y soñar que nos acostamos con ella;
después de pelear con dragones, imperios y quimeras,
de gemir por que publiquen nuestro nombre en los
    periódicos
y de reunirnos por la madrugada para derribar pirámides,
¿qué nos queda?

Un sillón en la academia
y una chequera.

A Petty-Bourgeois Suracademicrealistic Epigram

After having impressed young women with our genius,
ravaging vestal virgins and scandalizing nuns;
after setting fire to lilies, burying clouds, burning temples,
decapitating sacred cows and murdering gods;
after writing without capitals or punctuation,
attacking the rose and Gustave, King of Sweden;
after blowing up museums, dancing in graveyards,
chasing fame and dreaming we slept with her;
after fighting dragons, empires and chimeras,
crying to have our name published in the papers;
after meeting at dawn to bring down pyramids,
what's left?

A seat in the academy,
a checkbook.

[*Translated by Robert Márquez*]

El conde Drácula sale de inspección

Te despiertas, sediento, a medianoche.
Emerges de la tumba, bebes *whisky on the rock*,
chillas y aleteas,
vuelas por el país con los Boinas Verdes,
fundas el miedo, registras las ciudades,
allanas domicilios, saqueas librerías,
clausuras universidades, censuras la prensa,
abates la ternura, lees *El Pato Donald*,
persigues, encarcelas, interrogas y suspiras,
seduces a tus víctimas con mil voltios en los ojos,
les das el beso de la muerte y antes del alba
regresas al castillo,
                    te duchas y te afeitas,
desayunas con Frankestein, hojeas los periódicos,
bostezas
            y retornas a los reinos profundos
            de las tinieblas.

Count Dracula on an Inspection Tour

You wake up, thirsty, at midnight.
You emerge from your tomb, drink whiskey on the rocks,
shriek and spread your wings,
fly over the country with the Green Berets,
instill fear, search the cities,
break into homes, ransack bookstores,
close universities, censor the press,
humiliate tenderness, read *Donald Duck*;
you persecute, jail, interrogate, sigh,
seduce your victims with thousand-volt eyes,
give them the death-kiss and just before dawn
return to the castle,
                 take a bath, shave,
breakfast with Frankenstein, leaf through the papers,
yawn
         and retire to the deep kingdoms
              of the dark.

[Translated by Robert Márquez]

Brazil

Although the work of **Thiago de Mello** (1926–) is hardly known in this country, he is one of Brazil's more important contemporary poets and a member of the so-called Generation of '45, whose work started to appear immediately after the death of Mario de Andrade (1893–1945). De Mello began writing in a fiercely individualistic way but gradually moved on toward a less opaque, more all-embracing and communicative verse whose revolutionary fervor is tempered by an ummistakable gentleness.

De Mello, says the critic Alecu Amoroso Lima, writes "a verbally light, delicate, subtle poetry ever linked to a deep personal sentiment, which is lately becoming more and more open to the drama of the modern world."

De Mello's published works include *Silencio y palabra* and *Faz escuro mas eu canto*. The poems included here are taken from the recent anthology of his work, *Canção de amor armado*.

Os estatutos do homem
(Ato institucional permanente)

A Carlos Heitor Cony

ARTIGO I.
Fica decretado que agora vale a
  verdade,
que agora vale a vida
e que de maos dadas
trabalharemos todos pela vida verdeira.

ARTIGO II.
Fica decretado que todos os dias da
  semana,
inclusive as têrças-feiras mais cinzen-
tas,
têm direito a converter-se em manhãs
de domingo.

ARTIGO III.
Fica decretado que, a partir dêste
  instante,
haverá girassóis em tôdas as janelas,
que os girassóis terão direito
a abrir-se dentro da sombra;
e que as janelas devem permanecer, o
  dia inteiro,
abertas para o verde onde cresce a
  esperança.

ARTIGO IV.
Fica decretado que o homem
não precisará nunca mais
duvidar do homem.
Que o homem confiará no homem
como a palmeira confia no vento,
como o vento confia no ar,
como o ar confia no campo azul do
  céu.

The Statutes of Man
(A Permanent Act of Law)

For Carlos Heitor Cony

ARTICLE I.   It is hereby decreed
that now what counts is truth,
that now what counts is life
and that, hands joined,
we will all work for what life really is.

ARTICLE II.   It is hereby decreed
that every weekday,
even the grayest Tuesday,
has the right to become a Sunday morn-
ing.

ARTICLE III.   It is hereby decreed that, from now on,
there will be sunflowers on every win-
dowsill,
that sunflowers have the right
to blossom in the shade;
and that windows will be open all day
long
to the green in which hope grows.

ARTICLE IV.   It is hereby decreed that man
will never more doubt man.
That man will trust man
like the palm tree trusts the wind,
like the wind trusts the air,
like the air trusts the blue field of the
sky.

PARAGRAPH I. Man will trust man
as one child trusts another.

91

PARAGRAFO I. O homem confiará no homem
como um menino confia em outro
menino.

ARTIGO V.   Fica decretado que os homens
estão livres do jugo da mentiras.
Nunca mais será preciso usar
a couraça do silêncio
nem a armadura de palavras.
O homem se sentará à mesa
com seu olhar limpio
porque a verdade passará a ser servida
antes da sobremesa.

ARTIGO VI.   Fica estabelecida, durante déz séculos,
a prática sonhada pelo profeta Isaías,
e o lôbo e o cordeiro pastarão juntos
e a comida de ambos terá o mesmo
gôsto de outrora.

ARTIGO VII.   Por decreto irrevogável fica estabele-
cido
o reinado permanente da justiça e da
claridade,
e a alegria será uma bandeira generosa
para sempre desfraldada na alma do
povo.

ARTIGO VIII.   Fica decretado que a maior dor
sempre foi e será sempre
nao poder dar-se amor a quem se ama
e saber que é a água
que dá à planta a milagre da flor.

ARTIGO IX.   Fica permitido que a pão de cada dia
tenha no homem o sinal de seu suor.

ARTICLE V.   It is hereby decreed that men are free
of the yoke of lies.
No one will ever have to wear
the armor-plate of silence,
the weapon of words.
Man will sit at the table
with a pristine eye
for he will be served truth
before dessert.

ARTICLE VI.   The practice dreamed of by Isaiah the
prophet
is, for ten centuries, hereby decreed:
the wolf will pasture together with the
lamb,
and their food will taste no different
than before.

ARTICLE VII.   The permanent reign of justice and clar-
ity
is, by irrevocable decree, hereby estab-
lished,
and happiness will be a generous flag
forever waving in the people's soul.

ARTICLE VIII.   It is hereby decreed that the worst pain
always was and always will be
the inability to give love to a loved one
and knowing it is water gives the plant
the miracle of flowers.

ARTICLE IX.   Our daily bread is hereby allowed
to bear the trademark of man's sweat.
But, above all, it must always have
the warm taste of tenderness.

93

Mas que sobretudo tenha sempre
o quente sabor da ternura.

ARTIGO X.   Fica permitido a qualquer pessoa,
                a qualquer hora da vida,
                o uso do traje branco.

ARTIGO XI.   Fica decretado, por definição,
                que o homem é um animal que ama
                e que por isso é belo,
                muito mais belo que a estrêla da manhã.

ARTIGO XII.   Decreta-se que nada será obrigado nem
                    proibido.
                Tudo será permitido,
                inclusive brincar com os rinocerontes
                e caminhar pelas tardes
                com uma imensa begônia na lapela.

PARAGRAFO I.   Só uma coisa fica proibida:
                amar sem amor.

ARTIGO XIII.   Fica decretado que o dinheiro
                não poderá nunca mais comprar
                o sol das manhãs vindouras.
                Expulso do grande baú do mêdo,
                o dinheiro se transformará em uma
                    espada fraternal
                para defender o direito de cantar
                e a festa do dia que chegou.

ARTIGO FINAL.   Fica proibido o uso da palavra liber-
                    dade,
                a qual será suprimida dos dicionários
                e do pântano enganoso das bôcas.
                A partir dêste instante

ARTICLE X.   Every person is hereby allowed,
                  at any time in life,
                  to wear his Sunday best.

ARTICLE XI.   It is hereby decreed that man,
                  by definition, is an animal that loves
                  and so is beautiful, more beautiful than
                      any morning star.

ARTICLE XII.   Be it decreed that nothing
                  will be ordered or forbidden.
                  All things will be permitted,
                  including playing with a rhinoceros
                  and walking in the afternoon
                  with an immense begonia in the lapel.

PARAGRAPH I.   Only one thing will be forbidden:
                  to love and feel no love.

ARTICLE XIII.   It is hereby decreed that money
                  will no longer be able to buy
                  the sun of dawns to come.
                  Cast out of fear's coffers,
                  money will become a fraternal sword
                  with which to defend the right to sing
                  and celebrate the day that's come.

FINAL   The use of the word freedom is hereby
ARTICLE.   prohibited,
                  and will be struck from every dictionary
                  and from the deceptive mires of the
                      mouth.
                  Henceforth
                  freedom will be something living and
                      transparent
                  like a fire or a river,

a liberdade será algo vivo e transpar-
    ente
como um fogo ou um rio,
ou como a semente do trigo,
e a sua morada será sempre
o coração do homem.

like a grain of wheat,
and its home will always be
within the heart of man.

[Translated by Robert Márquez and Trudy Pax]

Canção do amor armado

Vinha a manhã no vento do verão,
e de repente aconteceu.
                    Melhor
é não contar quem foi nem como foi,
porque outra história vem, que vai ficar.
Foi hoje e foi aqui, no chão da pátria,
onde o voto, secreto como o beijo
no começo do amor, e universal
como o pássaro voando—sempre o voto
era um direito e era um dever sagrado.

De repente deixou de ser sagrado,
de repente deixou de ser direito,
de repente deixou de ser, o voto.
Deixou de ser completamente tudo.
Deixou de ser encontro e ser caminho,
deixou de ser dever e de ser cívico,
deixou de ser apaixonado e belo
e deixou de ser arma—de ser a arma,
porque o voto deixou de ser do povo.

Deixou de ser do povo e não sucede,
e não sucedeu nada, porém nada?

De repente não sucede.
Ninguém sabe nunca o tempo
que o povo tem de cantar.
Mas canta mesmo é no fim.

Só porque não tem mais voto,
o povo não e por isso
que vai deixar de cantar,
nem vai deixar de ser povo.

Song of Armed Love

The morning came in the summer wind,
and suddenly it happened.
                    Better not
to say who or how it was,
for another, lasting, history will come.
It happened today, here, in my country,
where the vote, secret as a kiss
at love's beginning, and universal
as a bird in flight—the vote
was always a right, a sacred duty.

Suddenly it ceased to be sacred,
suddenly it ceased to be a right,
suddenly it ceased to be—the vote.
It ceased to be anything at all.
It ceased to be a meeting and a way,
it ceased to be a duty, to be civic,
it ceased to be impassioned, to be beautiful,
it ceased to be an arm—to be a gun:
because the vote had ceased to be the people's.

It ceased to be the people's and nothing, nothing,
nothing at all happens?

Suddenly nothing happens.
No one ever knows when the people's
time for singing comes.
Yet they sing unendingly.

The people won't stop singing,
nor stop being the people,
just because they no longer have the vote.

They may have lost the vote

Pode ter perdido o voto,
que era sua arma e poder.
Mas não perdeu seu dever
nem seu direito de povo,
que é o de ter sempre sua arma,
sempre ao alcance da mão.

De canto e de paz é o povo,
quando tem arma que guarda
a alegria do seu pão.
Se não é mais a do voto,
que foi tirada a traição
outra há de ser, e qual seja
não custa o povo a saber,
ninguém nunca sabe o tempo
que o povo tem de chegar.

O povo sabe, eu não sei.
Sei sòmente que é um dever,
sòmente sei que é um direito.
Agora sim que é sagrado:
cada qual tenha sua arma
para quando a vez chegar
de defender, mais que a vida,
a canção dentro da vida,
para defender a chama
de liberdade acendida
no fundo do coração.

Cada qual que tenha a sua,
qualquer arma, nem que seja
algo assim leve e inocente
como êste poema em que canta
voz de povo—um simples canto
de amor.
                    Mas de amor armado.

that was their weapon and power,
but they didn't lose their duty,
their right as the people,
to have a gun
always within reach.

The people are a song and peace
when they have guns to guard
the joy of their own bread.
If it is no longer the joy of the vote,
so treasonously taken,
it will be another, one
the people will understand at once.
No one knows when the people's time has come.

I don't, only the people know.
I only know it is a duty.
I only know it is a right.
Now, truly, it is sacred:
everyone should have his weapon
so, when the time comes, he can defend,
more than life, life's song,
defend the flame
of liberty afire
deep in the heart.

Everyone should have his weapon,
any weapon, even a thing
as light and innocent as this
poem in which the people sing—
a simple song of love.
                    But of armed love.

Which is the same. Only now,
without the vote, love sings
the way it must whenever it defends
the right to love.

Que é o mesmo amor. Só que agora
que não tem voto, amor canta
no tom que seja preciso
sempre que fôr na defesa
do seu direito de amar.

O povo, não é por isso
que vai deixar de cantar.

For the people, this is no reason
to stop singing.

*[Translated by Robert Márquez and
David Arthur McMurray]*

Chile

A native of Santiago de Chile, **Enrique Lihn** (1929–) is one of the cultivators of the "new" anti-poetry typical of the younger Latin American poets. His is a poetry that aims at its own destruction as "poetry," but without the studied cynicism of, for instance, Nicanor Parra. "Lihn's poetry," the critic José Emilio Pacheco writes, "is characterized by its profound receptiveness to the real—a fondness for realism is in the nature of his creative imagination. If he oversteps the limits of verse, his deft rhythm saves him from falling into shortened narrative or expository prose, and even the most immediate references, least susceptible to being converted into poetic material, are filled with meaning and lyric sense."

In the only Latin American country to have produced two Nobel Prize poets—Gabriela Mistral and Pablo Neruda—Lihn is already established as a major new voice. In 1966 he was awarded the Casa de Las Américas prize for *Poesía de paso*. He has also published a collection of short stories and several other books of verse: *Nada se escurre* (1949), *Poemas de este tiempo y de otro* (1955), *La pieza oscura* (1963), *La musiquilla de las esferas* (1969), and *Escrito en Cuba* (1969).

Lihn went into voluntary exile after Eduardo Frei's defeat of the socialist Salvador Allende in 1964. He traveled in Europe and Latin America and then returned to Chile, where he was a supporter of the Unidad Popular government.

The poem included here appeared in the literary journal *Casa de Las Américas*.

Europeos

Esa gente se cree que somos transparentes
y para su tormento lejanamente salvajes
orientan hacia nosotros sus pequeñas narices despectivas
en las que brilla algo así como el sentido de una culpa
ante sus propios excesos de curiosidad intelectual
sudan pero lo hacen por tropicalizarse
bajo ese sol un huevo recocido
y se muestran espléndidas aunque se trate de exhibir sus
    propias vísceras en la célebre mesa de operaciones
cosa que hacen con una técnica envidiable

Una película de Godard es después de todo una película
    de Godard
"El estatus especialmente arbitrario de todo sistema
    lingüístico"
obliga a hablar con la boca cerrada
y no decir nunca nada que no nos hagan decir
Las palabras son cosas o no son más que mensajes
pero, claro, también la antinovela es una mierda
Esas narices se orientan hacia las regiones devastadas
con un desesperado sentido del humor
Paternalizarían pero se sienten huérfanas
No pueden evitar que la sangre les llegue mezclada al olor
    del cloroformo
Cloroformizan todo lo que huelen
reducen el dolor a la imagen del dolor
No es la realidad en su descripción la que aparece ante su
    vista
y eso cambia a cada nuevo enfoque
según la mayor o menor habilidad del que toma la película

A propósito de Godard me confieso equivocado
el canturreo de Pombo y el niño, debería gritar, dicién-
    dome a mí misma que saldré otra vez a la superficie

Europeans

Those people think we are transparent
and to their distress vaguely primitive
their small disapproving noses are turned to us
shining with something like a sense of guilt
faced with their own excesses of intellectual curiosity
they sweat but merely to be tropical
a baked egg beneath that sun
and splendidly put themselves on view even if it means
    displaying their own viscera on the celebrated operat-
    ing table
something they do with enviable technique

A picture by Godard is after all a picture by Godard
"The particularly arbitrary nature of every linguistic
    system"
forces one to speak with a closed mouth
and to never say anything one does not have to say
Words are things or they are no more than messages
but, of course, the antinovel is also a shit
Those noses turn to the devastated regions
with a desperate sense of humor
They would be paternal but feel they themselves are
    orphans
They cannot avoid the blood reaching them mingled with
    the smell of chloroform
They chloroform everything they smell
reduce pain to its image
It's not reality described which appears before their eyes
for that changes every time they focus
according to the greater or lesser skill of the one taking
    the picture

A propos Godard I confess myself mistaken
the monotonous humming of Pombo and the boy, I should

Cuánta habilidad y qué manera de echarle para adelante
sin concepciones a las profundidades por las que pasea un
ojo clínico
a poco preciosista pero rápido y tenebroso

Esa gente esa dama francesa esas narices como antenas
de dama y estiletes o radares
instrumentos de una extraordinaria precisión pero conde-
nados por ahora al juego al ocio a la indagación
hablo de ella que muy bien alimentada
apetecible como un jamón crudo de ojos azules
me confió en momento de cordialidad que Europa estaba
muerta
Todos estamos muertos—repetía—aunque sus grandes
piedras gritaran lo contrario
y su nariz aleteara extasiada de trópico
con una modestia ocasionalmente ejemplar entre sus
congéneres trasatlánticos
despojada de los excesos de la curiosidad intelectual
como ocurre por ley
cuando una mujer de cincuenta años viaja
sea francesa o no universalmente sola
Quiero decir qué destino histórico
y parecía avergonzada de su humanitarismo de izquierda
por el que, con una técnica impecable, habría podido
exhibir nobles sentimientos abstractos contra los
cuales se retorcía graciosamente las manos
como una imagen patética de la Sexta República indecisa
entre nacer o morir
Le dije a la Francia Eterna que no se diera por muerta
A la luz de las nuevas conquistas del marxismo
sus propios hijos, especialistas de fama internacional
etcétera, y tú—me dijo—qué me aconsejas
Bueno—le dije yo—usted sabe muy bien
el Tercer Mundo necesita de una publicidad adecuada
y en eso por qué no eres más modesta y te decides a
aportar tu granito de arena

108

shout, telling myself that I'll get to the top again
Such skill and what a way of moving on ahead
without preconceptions to the depths through which a
    clinical eye passes
not quite *precieux* but quick and gloomy

Those people that French dame those nostrils like a
    woman's antennae and stilettos or radar
instruments of an extraordinary precision condemned for
    now to gambling to leisure to searching
I speak of her who being quite well fed
as appetizing as a blue-eyed uncooked ham
confided to me in a moment of cordiality that Europe was
    dead
We are all dead—she went on—even if her large stones
    screamed otherwise
and her nose fluttered enraptured by the tropics
with an occasionally exemplary modesty among her
    transatlantic kinsmen
stripped of the excesses of intellectual curiosity as inevi-
    tably happens
when a woman of fifty travels
be she French or not universally alone
That is to say what a historic destiny
and she seemed ashamed of the leftist humanitarianism
that, with impeccable technique, would have allowed her
    to exhibit noble abstract sentiments against which
    she wrung her hands amusingly
like a pathetic image of the Sixth Republic unable to
    choose between being born or dying
I told Eternal France not to give herself up for dead
By the light of Marxism's newest conquests
her own sons, internationally famed experts
etc., and you—she asked—what do you suggest
Well—I said—you know very well
the Third World needs adequate publicity
why not be more modest and decide to add your little

Luego, como yo no era el elegido, la Dama de las Camelias
    se me escapó de las manos
como a un torpe el montón de manzanas en que apoya
    distraídamente el codo.

Esa gente se cree la muerte
Hasta para morir lo hace en el espejo ante las cámaras
Necesita ver necesita que la vean
No es la realidad la que tiene un sentido
sino quizá su imagen, los colores de su espectro sombrío
    su forma o su antiforma
Esas narices atraviesan un témpano con la mayor natural-
    idad
atraídas por el sol de los incomprensibles países
en que todavía existen los fotógrafos ambulantes y hasta
    se adora una vaca
o se lucha a muerte en la montaña recién desacralizada
un monumento crudo ni romántico ni gótico
Saben tanto nosotros como nosotros de ellos
pero aman la libertad y recuerdan la barbarie

grain of sand
Then, since I was not the chosen one, the Lady of the
Camelias slipped through my fingers
like a pile of apples from beneath the elbow of a clumsy
man absentmindedly leaning on them

Those people think they are something else
To die even they have to be before a mirror in front of the
cameras
They need to see they need to be seen
It's not reality that has any meaning
but possibly its image, the colors of their somber ghost
their form or anti-form
Those noses cross an ice-floe with the greatest ease
attracted by the sun of incomprehensible countries
where roving photographers still exist and they even pray
to a cow
or struggle to the death in the recently desanctified
mountain
a crude monument neither romantic nor gothic
They know of us as much as we of them
but they love freedom and remind one of barbarity

[*Translated by Robert Márquez*]

Anonymous. These proclamations are the work of a Chilean now in exile and active in the resistance movement against the Junta. They both reflect and mock the Junta mentality.

Bandos marciales
emitidos por la Junta Militar de Chile

Bando 35

Lamentamos informar que el extinto Presidente,
con quien cooperamos hasta un día antes de la gran
    decisión,
fue bastante grosero en sus últimos momentos.

Bando 103

Hemos encontrado la fórmula
para despolitizar las universidades:
expulsando la mitad del alumnado,
expulsando la mitad del profesorado
y acortando los estudios en la mitad.
Mens sana in corpore sano.

Bando 313

Nosotros no somos gorilas
como se ha dado en llamar a los hombres razonables.
Nos distinguimos del hermano Gobierno de Brazil
en una cosa muy importante: el clima.

Bando 403

Ordenamos presentarse con urgencia a los reservistas
de los años 70, 71 y 72.
No nos importa el grado que alcanzaron
en alguna rama de nuestras Fuerzas Armadas
ni la conducta que observaron después.

Proclamations
Issued by the Chilean Military Junta

No. 35

We regret to announce that the late President,
with whom we cooperated up to the day before the great
    decision,
was rather rude in his last moments.

No. 103

We have found the formula for depoliticizing the universi-
    ties:
expelling half the students,
expelling half the professors,
and cutting the curriculum in half.
Mens sana in corpore sano.

No. 313

We are not gorillas,
as people have fallen into calling reasonable men.
We distinguish ourselves from the brother government of
    Brazil
in one very important way: the climate.

No. 403

We hereby summon the reservists of '70, '71, and '72
to appear urgently.
We are not interested in the rank they achieved
in any of the branches of our armed forces,

Tampoco nos importa su curriculum
ni mucho menos su vitae.

Bando 288

Tobías Barros, militar, diplomático y poeta,
dirigirá nuestra propia revolución cultural.
Él mismo seleccionará, con ayuda nuestra,
los textos escolares y las obras literarias.
Sólo que no se publicará ningún libro de autor
desaparecido o de aquel que emplee palabras obscenas.
Nuestra consigna es: ni autores viejos ni modernos.

Bando 521

Hay una serie de organismos internationales
que están metiendo mucho ruido con algo tan abstracto
como los derechos humanos de gente que no conocen.

Bando 575

Es increíble la grosería de la población.
A nuestro Presidente Preventivo, general Pinochet,
se le llama "Pinocho" sin ningún respeto.
A nuestro almirante le dicen "Toribio el náufrago."
A nuestro general de aviación e integrante de la Junta
se le dice tranquilamente "El trapecista de la muerte."
Y así las cosas.
Es excesiva la promiscuidad de la democracia.

Bando 91

Para evitar la confusión de las informaciones
se han dejado circular sólo aquellos órganos de prensa

nor in the conduct they have observed since.
Neither are we interested in their *curriculum*
and much less in their *vitae.*

No. 288

Tobías Barros, officer, diplomat, and poet,
will direct our own cultural revolution.
He will select, with our help, schoolbooks and literary
    works.
However, no book by a deceased writer
or by one who uses obscenities will be published.
Our motto is: neither ancient nor modern authors.

No. 521

There are a number of international organizations
making a lot of noise about something as abstract
as the human rights of people they do not know.

No. 575

The rudeness of the population is incredible.
Showing no respect,
they call General Pinochet, our Preventive President,
    "Pinocchio."
They call our admiral "Toribio Shipwreck."
They calmly refer to our air commander
and member of the Junta as "Death's Flying Clown."
And so it goes.
The promiscuity of democracy is excessive.

de más larga trayectoria del país:
El Mercurio, La Segunda, Las Últimas Noticias, etc.,
cuyos directores exhiben una intachable hoja delictual
y han soportado la vida democrática con paciencia
y toda suerte de caprichos de los mandatarios constitu-
 cionales.
El único cambio que hemos introducido en estos diarios
es designar en ellos nuestros propios correctores de
 pruebas.

No. 91

To avoid confusion with regard to information
only those newspapers with the longest tradition
have been allowed to circulate:
El Mercurio, La Segunda, Las Últimas Noticias, etc.,
whose editors show an immaculate police record
and have patiently endured democratic life
as well as all the whims of constitutional presidents.
The only change we have introduced in these dailies
is to provide them with our own proofreaders.

Colombia

Anonymous

Colombia masacrada

8½ de la mañana
Domingo
      y los campesinos ya bajaron al mercado
las dos grandes ceibas ya mancharon de sombra la casita
    de adobe
               —blanquita—
Sólo se oye quietud en el aire y un panal
         el de la ceiba izquierda
hasta que llega el mayordomo con el sombrero sudado en
    la mano
jadeano como perro de presa me cuenta
¡QUE MATARON A DON JOSE!
¿Don José el de la casita de guadua junto a la quebrada?
¿El que baja a vender café y naranjas?
¿El que me regaló la flauta de bambú?
         ¡La Tropa!

La Tropa le disparó un Máuser en la espalda
estaba desayunando arepa y cacao
¡que ni se dio cuenta!
¿Y la familia?
En el pueblo que fueron de mañanita
a vender la marrana vieja la que crió los ocho marranitos
seguramente él se quedó arreglando alguna cosa o
    sanando algún
animal y ni se han enterado!

Tenía la cabeza hacia atrás sobre el espaldar del asiento
        con los brazos colgando como guamas
y sus piernas rígidas debajo de la mesa
la camisa kaki chorreando sangre
        —se le había formado un pozo sobre el
        cinturón—
los ojos para arriba

122

Colombia Massacred

8:30 A.M.
Sunday
        and the peasants had already gone to market
the two huge ceiba trees had bathed the small adobe
    house
                —that was so white—in shadow
All you could hear was stillness in the air and a hornets'
    nest
                in the ceiba to the left
until the overseer arrived his sweaty hat in hand
panting like a hunting dog he said
THEY'VE MURDERED DON JOSÉ!
The Don José with the little bamboo shack by the arroyo?
The one who sells coffee and oranges?
The one who gave me the bamboo flute?
                The troops!

The troops shot him in the back with a Mauser
he was eating a breakfast of corn cakes and chocolate
and never knew what hit him!
What about his family?
In the town
they left at sun-up
to sell the old sow that gave birth to eight little pigs
he must have been attending to something
or nursing some animal and his family hasn't even heard!

His head was flung back over his chair
                his arms hanging like a guama fruit
his legs stiff under the table
with blood running down his khaki shirt
                —a puddle formed just above his belt—
his eyes turned up
his mouth like an open oyster held

123

su boca como una ostra abierta
con un pedazo de arepa
apenas masticado
En el vientre por donde salió la bala .30 un agujero como
un plato sopero de grande

¡¡¡Bandolero!!!
Si tenía ocho hijos / el mayor de 12 años que me acompa-
ñaba a cazar borugos en el monte
y el único bandolerismo que le conocieron
los robos de manzanas en la finca de ricos
la de piscina
cuando era pequeño—me cuenta mi tío—
y las carreras detrás de las gallinas de doña Pepa
en la trocha que lleva al pueblo
Que su único partido fue la nobleza
nobleza campesina
Y la flauta
él mismo la había hecho con bambú y cabuya
todavía la tengo guardada
Lo enterramos con el pedazo de arepa en la boca

Y aquel día que bajamos al río
con las toallas al cuello por entre los cafetales
—al pozo tranquilo / el de los tachuelos—
y uno de mis primos señala: Miren ¡Arriba!
Un chulo venía en el río sobre algo que flotaba
y otros más revoloteaban
y uno bajaba y se paraba con el otro
y se les hundía el piso
y se tambaleaban y alzaban el vuelo
aquello flotaba como vástago de plátano
bajaban los animales y volvía a hundirse
¡Un Muerto! ¡Un muerto!
El vientre hinchado sobre el agua
donde se paraban los chulos

a half-chewed
                piece of corn cake
in his belly where the .30-caliber bullet had come out
    there was a hole as big as a huge soup bowl

Bandolero!!!
He had eight children
the oldest who was twelve used to come badger hunting
    with me in the woods
And the only stealing he'd ever had a hand in
was taking apples from the rich people's *finca*
                —the one with the swimming pool—
when he was a boy—my uncle tells me—
and running after Doña Pepa's hens
along the road to town
His only political party was nobility
                peasant nobility
and his flute
            one he himself made out of hemp and bamboo
I still have it tucked away
We buried him with the piece of corn cake still in his
    mouth

And when we went to the river through the coffee groves
    that day
—to the still pool near the balsams—
with towels around our necks
one of my cousins raised his arm and shouted: Look! Over
    there!
A buzzard was coming down the river perched on some
    floating thing
and there were others hovering about
one of them swooped down and came to rest beside the
    other
and their raft sank under them
                and they lost their balance and flew off

se hundía cuando eran dos
                    voraces lo picoteaban
Lentamente flotó dentro del pozo
el pelo como un helecho negro entre el agua
de los brazos le colgaba una camisa azul campesina
Los chulos hambrientos sobre los tachuelos dando
        vueltas
                    dio contra la orilla / allí se quedó
los tobillos amarrados con rejos y las manos a la espalda
Me acerqué un poco
parecía de natilla como la que hacía mi tía para Navidad
le habían arrancado el ombligo y seguramente los ojos
                dicen que los prefieren
La cara no la vi / no quise acercarme más
Ya venían el mayordomo y mi tío entre las matas de
        plátano
Se pusieron en cuclillas y lo miraban
a lo mejor lo conocían
Pero tan sólo reconocieron el escapulario del Carmen
¡Con Machete! dijo en voz baja el mayordomo
Hay que echarlo de aquí dijo mi tío
                ¡Asesinos!
y escupió en el agua
(un levantamiento de muerto era flotar uno mismo en el
        río)
Entre los dos lo empujaron con unas varas
                —me pareció que se le entraban—
Lo cogió la corriente y se fue / los animales arrancando
sus carnes
            cuando flotaba
            y se hundía otra vez

Ibamos de cacería y
allá arriba en el monte encontramos una trocha
Empezamos a subir
                cuando oímos en el suelo un

the thing floated like a banana stalk
the birds swooped down and it sank again
                    A corpse! A corpse!
On the river the swollen belly
where the buzzards were resting
sank whenever two stood on it
                    they pecked at it voraciously
it slowly drifted into the still pool
its hair like black ferns on the water
a blue peasant shirt hanging from the arms
The hungry buzzards circled over the balsams
            the corpse hit the river bank
            and stayed there
its ankles bound with rawhide its hands tied behind its
    back
I came a little closer
it looked like the custard my aunt used to make at
    Christmas
they'd torn out the navel and probably the eyes
            they say they like those best
I didn't see the face   I didn't want to come any closer
My uncle and the overseer were already coming through
    the clusters of bananas
They bent down and looked him over
likely as not they knew him
but all they recognized was the scapular of Nuestra
    Señora del Carmen
With a machete! the overseer said under his breath
We must get rid of him my uncle said
                    Murderers!
and he spat in the water
(to lift the dead was to float on the river yourself)
Between them they pushed the cadaver with some poles
                    —it looked to me like they were piercing
                    it—
It was caught by the current and floated away
            the buzzards tearing at its flesh

127

                    trum-trum-trum-trum-trum-trum
era la tropa que bajaba al trote
                    (si nos veían armados nos mataban)
nos tiramos a un matorral
vimos las botas de media caña
los pantalones entre las botas
las fundas de los machetes
                    y pasaron
Salimos y
el mismo trum-trum . . . caímos esta vez
junto a una piedra roja
          sentí los primeros picotazos en las piernas
trum-trum
los gritos del teniente
          el ruido del hormiguero
                    y pasaron

Y los bandoleros un día volaron una tiendita
de familia pobre al lado de la carretera
Al entrar un hombre decapitado
                    la cabeza entre unos matorrales
Todos habían muerto
no todos:
          La señora tenía 7 meses de embarazo
          la explosión le abrió el vientre y
los que llegaron primero sacaron del cadáver
                    una niña
la cortaron el cordón umbilical con una Gillette
dicen que vive (debe tener 8 años) huérfana
                    desde antes de nacer
Alguien se encontró un pedazo de cuero
                    con cabellos
y las niñas de la escuela
                    lo mostraban
Adentro todo salpicado de sangre
y olor a humo y tierra húmeda

128

as it bobbed
           and sank again

We were out hunting and
found a narrow trail up in the hills
We had started climbing
                when we heard
                    a thump thump thump thump thump
it was the troops coming down double time
                (if they saw us armed they'd kill us)
we threw ourselves into the underbrush
saw their three-quarter boots
the pants tucked in
the sheaths of their machetes
                and they were gone
We got up and left
and then the same thump thump . . . this time we fell
      next to
a reddish stone
          I felt the first itches on my legs
thump thump
the lieutenant's shouts
            the rumpus on the ant hill
                and they were gone

And once the bandits blew up a poor little
family store by the roadside
Beside the door was a decapitated man
                his head was in some bushes
They were all dead
no not all:
          The señora was seven months pregnant
            the explosion had torn her belly open
and those who arrived first pulled a girl out of her cadaver
cutting the umbilical cord with a Gillette

en el suelo
    la mujer destrozada
    los ojos llenos de barro
tres cajas de Coca-Cola
    en una esquina:
    del pico roto de una botella colgaba
un trozo de labio

Acababa de salir del Bar (no recuerdo cómo se llamaba
    "Las Dos Mirlas" o "El Mil Amores") ese que estaba
    enfrente de la Iglesia
Dejaba tras él un olor a cerveza Andina
se sentó en la banca de la esquina del parque debajo del
    tamarindo
miraba pasar la hilera de mulas cargadas de plátano
Mi tío y yo tomábamos tinto y Coca-Cola
En la radio la del bar una ranchera mexicana:
        El día en que a mí me maten . . .
Del cuartel salieron los soldados
    —uniforme kaki
    fusiles bayonetas machetes
        y todas esas vainas—
        Que sea de cinco balazos . . .
Se fueron regando entre los cafés y las tiendas
uno cargó su fusil junto a nosotros
    en el reloj de la Iglesia las 3¼
Nosotros aparentando tranquilidad fumábamos Pielroja
        Y estar cerquita de ti . . .
¡Aquél! dijo un soldado señalando al hombre
y el otro cruzó la calle
    el dedo en el gatillo
los demás en silencio mirando
        Para morir en tus brazos . . .
Entró en el parque
    recostó el fusil contra la ceiba
    se echó un poco hacia adelante

130

they say she's still alive (she must be eight by now) an
    orphan
                even before being born
Somebody found a piece of skin
                with hair on it
and the schoolgirls began
                showing it around
Inside the store there was blood spattered everywhere
and the smell of smoke and damp earth
on the floor
            the annihilated woman
            with mud-filled eyes
three cases of Coca-Cola
        in a corner:
        a piece of lip dangling
from the mouth of a broken bottle

He had just come out of the bar (I can't remember its
    name: "Two Blackbirds" or "A Thousand Loves") the
    one across from the church
He left behind a smell of Andina beer
He sat down on the corner bench in the park under the
    tamarind tree
and watched the line of mules loaded with bananas pass
    by
My uncle and I were drinking red wine and Coca-Cola
the radio in the bar was playing a Mexican *ranchera*:
            The day they shoot me down . . .
The soldiers came out of the barracks
        —khaki uniforms
        guns bayonets machetes
            and all the rest—
            Let it be with just five bullets . . .
They spread out around the stores and the cafés
one loaded his rifle right next to us
        the church clock read 3:15

y fijó la mira
en la cabeza del campesino
               Ay Ay Corazón por qué no amas . . .
Una mosca tábano volando sobre el casco de cazador de
    mi tío
¡Jeta di' oro! le gritó haciendo presión al gatillo / no me
    acuerdo del apodo del tipo pero tenía muchos dientes
    de oro
(le gritó el apodo) sonó el disparo del Máuser y
la bala de 7mm le pegó en la cara
               cuando volteaba a mirar
               y pareció levantarse
el mismo tiro hace como que lo levanta / el mismo tiro lo
    levanta sin que él quiera
               y volvió a caer dando vueltas
se quedó en el charco de un hielo derretido
el barro amarillo / salpicó de sangre
               Por caja quiero un sarape . . .
               Nadie se movió
Del café Tal (al fin no me acuerdo) un hombre salió
    corriendo
               el hermano:
en la esquina una bayoneta lo paró
               el metal entró en la izquierda del estómago
el soldado sonrió al sacar la bayoneta
               viendo como se doblaba.
               Por cruz mis dobles cananas . . .
caminó unos pasos
recostó la mano con el sombrero
a una pared blanca
               blanca como todas las del pueblo
               —todo era blanco—
apretando el sombrero
               de los pantalones le salía sangre y
               dejó las huellas rojas
               en el piso.
               Y escriban sobre mi tumba . . .

132

Pretending to be calm we smoked some Pielrojas
                    And close beside you . . .
That's him! a soldier yelled pointing to the man
and another one crossed the street
            his finger on the trigger
the rest looked on in silence
                    To die in your arms . . .
He went into the park
            braced his gun against the ceiba tree
            leaned forward a little
            and took aim
at the peasant's head
                    Ay, ay, why, love, don't you love me . . .
A horsefly buzzed around my uncle's hunting cap
Jeta di' oro! the soldier yelled pulling the trigger / I don't
    remember the guy's nickname but he had a lot of gold
    teeth
(he yelled out his nickname) the Mauser went off and the
    7mm. bullet
hit him in the face
            when he spun around to look
            and he seemed to be getting up
the shot itself seemed to lift him up / the shot itself made
    him leap involuntarily
            and then he fell again twisting and turning
he lay in a puddle of melting ice
the yellow mud / blood-spattered
                    For my coffin a sarape . . .
            No one moved
A man came running out of the whatever-you-call-it café
        (I still can't remember its name): it was his
        brother
a bayonet stopped him on the corner
            the blade went in the left side of his stomach
the soldier smiled as he pulled it out
            seeing how the man was doubling over
                    For a cross two bandoliers . . .

133

Me mataron
     dijo
            Me mataron
Lo rodearon / uno sacó el machete
Me matar . . . el machete sonó a coco cuando cayó en su
   cara
         que se abrió como una granada madura
         Otros machetazos en el suelo
            Mi último adiós con mil balas . . .
Varios mirando al otro muerto:
        Tras las axilas sudadas de los campesinos
         el cadáver
sin quijada
olor a sangre caliente y cerveza Andina
        sólo cuatro dientes delanteros / de oro
        un pedazo de lengua
le salía de la garganta
             Ay Ay Corazón por qué no amas . . .
       estaba desarmado
Con los dedos mojados en sangre alguien nos mostró un
   diente forrado en oro
Yo no sé si era bandolero
      a lo mejor era
¡Dos pájaros de un tiro! pasó diciendo un soldado con el
   machete rojo

Una noche como a las once
el murmullo de mucha gente en la portada
y me levanté
      Bandoleros . . .
       algunos heridos
y buscaban medicinas
      comida y
      aguardiente
Eran como 50
      les atendimos y se fueron

134

he walked a few steps
rested his hand with his hat
on a whitewashed wall
     white like every other wall in town
       —everything was white—
clutching his hat
     blood oozed out of his pants
     and left red splotches
     on the pavement
       And on my tombstone carve . . .
They've killed me
     he said
       they've killed me
They crowded around him / one pulled out his machete
they've kill . . . the machete sounded like a coconut when
    it hit his face
     and split it like a ripened pomegranate
     Other slashes hit the ground
       My last good-bye with a thousand
       rounds . . .
Several men stood looking at the other body:
     behind the peasants' sweaty armpits
     the corpse
without a jawbone
the smell of warm blood and Andina beer
     only four front teeth / gold teeth
     a shred of tongue
coming from the throat
       Ay, ay, why, love, don't you love me . . .
     he was unarmed
Someone with bloody fingers showed us a gold-capped
    tooth
I don't know if he was a bandit
     he might have been
Well two birds with one stone! the soldier with the red
    machete
said as he passed

135

Esa semana vimos muchos en el monte
ningún daño hicieron / sólo
se llevaron la burra que cargaba el agua y dos caballos
la tropa ya se había llevado los demás para bajar sus
    muertos
        De esa noche no recuerdo más ni
             nunca volvieron a entrar a la finca

Y nos contaba un sub-teniente:
        le pidieron
matar a un jefe bandolero
        amigo suyo
hacía tiempo se conocían y
le ofrecieron Cuatro Mil y un ascenso
        Aceptó
Con intermediarios se comunicó con el "Barbudo"
tenía una carta de su mamá / le mandó decir
y se encontraron en campo abierto
sin bandoleros el uno
sin soldados el otro (la tropa camuflada)
Le entregó la carta
el "Barbudo" no sabía leer / le pasó la carta a un mucha-
    chito que lo acompañaba
antes de que leyera la primer línea
        el sub-teniente les hizo una descarga de
          pistola
el "Barbudo" cayó herido / el muchacho muerto
el bandolero tendido en el pasto empezó a disparar
un tiro pegó en una de las granadas que el sub-teniente
    llevaba en las piernas
        hizo explosión
los dedos de la mano izquierda le quedaron deformados
la pierna se la tuvieron que cortar
        El bandolero murió
Y eso lo contaba con su muleta y sus $4,000 en el bolsillo
Después le pusieron una pierna de caucho y

136

One night about eleven
there was a group of people whispering in the doorway
and I got up
        Bandits . . .
        a few wounded
they were looking for medicine
        for food
        and brandy
There were about fifty
        we attended to them and they left
That week we saw a lot of them in the hills
they didn't harm anyone / they only
took the burro that carried the water and a couple of
    horses
the troops had already taken the rest to bring down their
    dead
            I don't remember anything else about that night
                and they never came back to the *finca*

A second lieutenant told us:
            they asked him
to kill a leader of the bandits
        a friend of his
they'd known each other for a long time
they offered him $4,000 along with a promotion
            He accepted
Through go-betweens he got in touch with "El Barbudo"
he had a letter from his mother / the message was passed
    on
and they met out in the open
the one without bandits
the other without soldiers (the troops were hidden)
He gave him the letter but
"El Barbudo" couldn't read / he passed the letter
            to a little boy who had come with him
before the boy had got as far as the first line

bailaba en el Club y contaba su historia

Y pasaban los soldados allá por la hondonada
                iban a pelear
Muchas veces los vi llegar de la ciudad
en los camiones canadienses del ejército
eran todos campesinitos
            de tierra fría con sus mejillas coloradas
y no conocían el terreno donde venían a morir
                inexpertos
            carne de bala "U"
Los veíamos pasar antes del desayuno
a paso rápido de dos en dos
            eran 50 o 100
                algunos a caballo o mula y
nos preguntábamos cuántos volverían
        y los mirábamos hasta que se perdían
                en el monte y
entonces íbamos a desayunar
Volvían por la tarde 20 o 30
bajaban en desorden
                mirando el suelo
algunos sin armas
los caballos y las mulas con los muertos amarrados
realmente nunca vi ningún herido / heridos nunca
y si nos veían nos apuntaban con el Máuser y
nos teníamos que echar al suelo
                lo hacían en silencio
sólo una vez nos gritaron
                ¡Hijueputas!
Y en la casa de mi tío Chucho pegada al cuartel
                contaban después:
"Si es que uno no sabe de donde le disparan
                si de arriba si del frente si de atrás
y uno no sabe donde meterse
                y no puede hacer nada."

the lieutenant fired his gun at both of
                them
"El Barbudo" fell wounded / the boy dead
lying in the grass the bandit began shooting
a bullet hit one of the grenades strapped to the
                lieutenant's legs
                it exploded
and left the fingers of his left hand crooked
they had to amputate his leg
                "El Barbudo" died
And the lieutenant told us this on crutches with the
    $4,000 in his pocket
Afterward they gave him a plastic leg and he
                danced at the Club and told his story

And soldiers passed down through the ravine
                they were going to fight
I often saw them coming from the city
in the Canadian trucks the army owned
all red-cheeked young peasants from the cold country
who didn't know the land they came to die in
                untrained
        meat for the "U" bullet
We used to see them going by just before breakfast
two by two in double time
                there were fifty or a hundred of them
                some on mules or horses and
we wondered how many would return
                and we looked at them until they disappeared
                into the hills and
then we went to breakfast
In the evening twenty or thirty returned
they came down in disorder
                staring at the ground
some without guns
the mules and horses with the dead slung on their backs

139

La bala "U" es pequeña
                     como medio dedo meñique
                     la mitad de ancho
Un buen rifle tiene hasta 500 metros de tiro fijo
                     nosotros tuvimos uno y
con mira telescópica como el de los bandoleros
"Cuando nos disparan desde los montes
                     con esos rifles" decían
"se oyen dos sonidos de diferentes partes
y al fin uno no sabe de donde sólo sabe uno
que le pueden meter un tiro entre ceja y ceja
                     a más de 300 metros
así que dos o tres en los churruscales acaban en una
sola emboscada con toda la tropa"
Y llegaban al cuartel camionadas y camionadas
                     y ni la mitad quedaron
Y ni saben pelear
                     Una cosa sí sabían: ODIAR
Y mataban a los campesinos bandoleros o no bandoleros
            los torturaban antes de degollarlos
                     o fusilarlos
y a los prisioneros
—nunca he creído que fueran bandoleros—
después de los calatazos
                     los planazos con el machete / los metían
                     entre
una especie de tienda de estacas y alambre de púas
medio acurrucados y sentados bajo el quemante sol
                     Mediodía   caliente: un campesino pide
                     agua
lo miro por entre
las rendijas de la cerca de guadua
            sin camisa
                     y la espalda con sangre seca
llevaba una semana en esa posición
y cuando les venía en gana le daban de beber
Saqué una totumada de agua de la alberca

I really never saw any wounded no wounded ever
and if they spotted us they aimed their Mausers at us and
we had to hit the dirt
                    they did it without a word
just once they shouted at us
                    Sons of bitches!
And in my uncle Chucho's house next to the barracks
                    they later explained:
"You can't tell where they're shooting from
                    above or ahead or behind
you don't know where to duck
                    and there's nothing you can do."
The "U" bullet is small
                    half as long as your little finger
                    and half as thick
A good rifle has a range of up to five hundred meters
                    we had one and
with a telescopic sight like the one the bandits have
"When they shoot at us from ambush
                    with those rifles," they said,
"you hear two sounds from different directions
and never know where the bullet's coming from—all you
    know
is it can hit you right between the eyes and
                    from more than three hundred meters
                        away
So two or three in a single ambush
can finish off the troops."
And truckload after truckload arrived at the barracks
                    and not even half remained
They didn't know the first thing about fighting
                    they knew one thing though: HOW TO
                        HATE
And they killed the peasants whether they were bandits
    or not
                    they tortured them before shooting them
                    or cutting off their heads

141

y se la lancé
desde el ciruelo cargado de jugosas ciruelas amarillas
                apenas lo salpicó
no podía mirarme no alzar la cabeza
                pero me lo agradeció / lo sé
                Dos días después sacaron
el cadáver
                olía a excusado

Y le teníamos más miedo a la tropa
Una noche todos los mayores habían bajado al pueblo
y llegó una muchacha de un caserío
                a dos horas de la finca
y llegó llorando
                El capitán / no recuerdo su nombre
pero más tarde lo vi con sus gafas negras en el Club
     Social
había sacado del caserío a todos los hombres y
                puestos en fila los fusilaron
Y quemaron los ranchitos sin dejar sacar nada
a otros ranchos más lejos les tiraron morteros
                andaba tras de una banda
El esposo y el hermano de la muchacha habían muerto y
     eso hacía cuatro horas apenas
Y vimos subir unas luces entre los matorrales
y se apagaban / y se encendían
si era la tropa estábamos muertos
Mi abuelita en su silla empezó el rosario
y una tía apagó las dos lámparas Coleman
Se oían los grillos en la oscuridad
                y el volar de los murciélagos
                y unas voces
acercándose
                pero no era la tropa
                eran mis tíos
se les fue la batería del Willys

142

and as for the prisoners
—I never thought they were bandits—
after hitting them with their rifle butts
                    and the flat end of their machetes / they
                            herded them into
a kind of tent made of barbed wire and stakes and
there they huddled and sat in the scorching sun
                    One hot noon: a peasant asked for water
I watched him through
the chinks in the bamboo fence
            he had no shirt
                        caked blood covered his back
he'd spent a week in that position
and when they felt like it they gave him a drink
I took a gourdful of water from the tank
and threw it to him
from the plum tree loaded with juicy yellow plums
                    it barely spattered him
he couldn't look at me or lift his head
                    but he thanked me / I know it
                    Two days later they took away
the corpse
                    it smelled of shit

And we were so afraid of the soldiers
One night all the adults had gone to the town
and a girl came from a little village
                    two hours from the *finca*
and she was crying
                The Captain—I don't remember his
                    name
but I saw him later with his dark glasses at the Social
    Club—
had taken all the men from the little village and
                lined them up and had them shot
And they burned down the shacks without allowing

143

y habían subido alumbrándose con fósforos
Pero apenas dormimos después:
        y en el silencio de la noche
        los sollozos . . .

Cinco años después nos contaba un capitán:
les habían cortado las provisiones
y bebían agua de los charcos llenos de larvas
la mayoría sufriendo de amebas y paludismo
Una tarde vio con sus binóculos 4 o 5 vacas pastando
era una emboscada y hasta las vacas murieron
Por la noche veían
de pronto una llamarada junto al campamento
y oían unos gritos—los prisioneros encendidos en gaso-
    lina—
los mismos compañeros los mataban
con sus ametralladoras
Una noche fue a unos matorrales a cazar y una linterna de
    mano
        lo alumbró en la cara
        y varios disparos desde un árbol
        escapó dando botes en le suelo
Era un muchacho de 17
años con una linterna
y una pistola
        lo cogieron vivo
El capitán trató de impedir que lo mataran
pero los bandoleros habían quemado a dos la noche
    anterior
"Capitán" le dijeron
        "le toca a usted
        a usted lo atacó"
Y lo metieron amarrado a una tolda / le dijeron que iba a
    comer y en la nuca
        le disparó el capitán
Otro día le informaron que la guardia de los bandoleros

anyone to get their things
and they fired mortar shells at the shacks farther away
                        he was after a group of bandits
They'd killed the girl's brother and husband
                    barely two hours before
Then we saw some lights in the underbrush
flickering on and off
if it was the troops we were as good as dead
My grandmother sitting in her chair started to say her
    rosary
and an aunt turned off the two Coleman lamps
You could hear the crickets chirping in the dark
                    and bats flying
                    and voices
approaching
                    but it wasn't the troops
                    it was my aunt and uncle
their Willys battery had quit
and they'd come lighting their way with matches
But later we hardly slept:
                    and there were the sobs
                    in the stillness of the night . . .

Five years later a captain told us:
their provisions had been cut
and they were drinking out of puddles full of larvae
and most of them were suffering from dysentery and
    malaria
One afternoon through his binoculars he saw four or five
    cows grazing
it was an ambush and even the cows were killed
At night they would suddenly see a burst of flame at the
    camp
and could hear some screaming—prisoners burning in
    gasoline—
their own comrades were killing them

145

estaba detrás del monte
y esa noche subieron a la colina y vieron
desde lejos unas antorchas
                entrando a una casa
                hicieron la descarga sobre la casa
A la otra noche subieron los morteros y los clavaron en
    tierra
y ya de día bajaron a ver los cadáveres:
                sólo mujeres y niños
          Una equivocación
"No sé cuántos eran" nos decía el capitán "¡eran muchos
    Dios mío!"
Todos vueltos pedazos
"Yo no tuve la culpa" nos decía golpeando sobre la mesa
"Nos dieron una información falsa
Yo no tuve la culpa
             ¿Verdad que no?"

Y esto es lo que yo he visto y oído y miles y miles y
millones de cosas más hay

Todo empezó en el 30
empezó un Domingo
con cuatro ametralladoras en las esquinas de una plaza
disparando contra los campesinos que salían de misa
           Los campesinos se subieron a los montes
           y se les llamó chusma
En otra parte
           campesinos arruinados por los capitalis-
           tas
           robaron fincas
           no peleaban por un partido
sino por comida
y se les llamó bandoleros en los periódicos
y los políticos brindaron con White Horse
patrocinaron guerrillas como Caucho-Sol

146

with their machine guns
One night he went hunting in the underbrush and a
    flashlight lit up his face
                    some shots came from a tree
                    and he escaped by leaping
                    and rolling on the ground
It was a boy of seventeen
with a flashlight and
a gun
              they brought him back alive
The captain tried to stop them from killing him
but the bandits had burned two men the night before
"Cap'n," they said
                    "now it's your turn
                    he attacked you"
And they tied him to a tentpost / told him he was going to
    eat
            and the captain
                  shot him in the back of the neck
Another time they told him the bandit guard was
                  just behind the mountain
and that night they climbed the mountain and saw
some torches in the distance
                  entering a house
                  they fired
The next night they took the mortars up and set them on
    the ground
and the next day went down to see the bodies:
                  nothing but women and children
      A mistake
"I don't know how many there were" the captain said
    "but, my god, there were a lot!"
All torn to pieces.
"It wasn't my fault" he said pounding the table
"They gave us the wrong information
It wasn't my fault
              was it?"

Cervecerías Bavaria
Coltejer y
Fabricaron la tela de los Hilos Perfectos
patrocinan LA VUELTA A COLOMBIA EN BICICLETA
y ya unos fueron liberales y otros conservadores
y se quemaron sus ranchos unos a otros
y se destruyeron sus siembras
los comunistas con sus cintitas rojas en la solapa
dijeron:
La Fruta Está Madura
y metieron armas de Checoeslovaquia
Y ahora ya no se pelea por comida ni por política sino
¡Porque sí!
Los hospitales se llenaron de niños macheteados
los campesinos que no peleaban huían a las ciudades
y quedaron abandonados los ranchitos y los platanares.
Y hubo también
Dictador de quijada larga y Cadillac Blindado
que también robó vacas
pero combatió a los bandoleros con sus helicópteros y
bombarderos
A su caída los bandoleros fueron peores en los llanos
y bajaron más cabezas por los ríos mientras en Bogotá
los jefes tomaban tinto con los políticos
1963:
y asaltan un bus y ametrallan a todos los ocupantes
mujeres y niños también y
Viernes 20 / Sept / 63
HEROICA E INTELIGENTE HA SIDO LA LABOR DEL
EJÉRCITO EN LOS CAMPOS
El Comité Nacional de
Cafeteros registra con
especial beneplácito
la importante labor que
vienen cumpliendo las
fuerzas armadas para

And this is what I've seen and heard and there are thousands and
thousands and millions of other things

It all started in the thirties
it all began on a Sunday
with four machine guns in a corner of the square
firing on peasants coming out of Mass
        The peasants went into the hills
        and they called them a mob
Somewhere else
        the peasants ruined by capitalists
        were robbing *fincas*
        they weren't fighting for a party
only for some food
and the newspapers called them bandits
and the politicians drank toasts with White Horse scotch
and sponsored guerrillas like Sun Rubber
        Bavarian Breweries
        Colonial Textiles and
        Super-thread Mills
sponsored COLOMBIA-ON-A-BICYCLE TOURS
and some were liberals and some conservatives
and they set fire to each other's homes
and destroyed each other's crops
the Communists with little red ribbons in their lapels
        said:
The Time Is Ripe
        and smuggled in arms from Czechoslo-
        vakia
And now they no longer fight for food or politics
        but just for the sake of fighting!
The hospitals filled with the victims of machetes
the peasants who weren't fighting would flee to the cities
and their little plots of ground and planted fields were left
    abandoned

149

alcanzar la pacificación
del país . . .
Domingo 22 / Sept / 63
MASACRADOS 19 CAMPESINOS
MIENTRAS EL PRESIDENTE CONDENABA
EL BANDIDAJE
Lunes 23 / Sept / 63
NUEVA MASACRE EN EL TOLIMA
ASESINADAS OTRAS NUEVE PERSONAS AYER
Nos hemos acostumbrado a ver
niñitos decapitados
y las quinceañeras leen los asesinatos / antes que la
Página Social
y nos seguimos matando por venganzas y odios políticos
y
odios odios odios odios odios odios odios
y se pide la pena de muerte en la TV
y odiamos . . .
Colombia está Macheteada

Señor perdónanos por nuestros crímenes nuestros
políticos nuestros periódicos radio TV
bandoleros liberales conservadores agiotistas
latifundistas Cámara de Representantes terroristas
contrabandistas
de armas jueces tropas abogados S.I.C. Sociedades
Anónimas / etc.
comunistas entrenadores compañías yanquis petroleras
madereras
mineras
bananeras / etc.
y el sacerdote en Mercedes Benz
el clero que incita a la política / el clero conformista
Bancos coroneles capitalistas Presidentes de la República
los que leen esto y les importa un carajo / etc. . . .

And there was too
a long-jawed dictator with a bullet-proof Cadillac
who also stole cows
but he fought the bandits with helicopters and with
    bombardiers
When he fell the bandits on the plains were even worse
and more heads floated down the river while in Bogotá
the leaders drank red wine with the politicians
            1963:
they stop a bus and machine gun all the occupants
even the women and children and
            Friday, September 20, 1963
WORK OF ARMY ON FARMS HEROIC AND INTELLI-
    GENT
            The National Committee of Coffee-
            Growers notes with particular
            pleasure the important work
            being carried out by the armed
            forces to bring peace to our country . . .
            Sunday, September 22, 1963
            19 PEASANTS MASSACRED
        AS PRESIDENT CONDEMNS BANDITRY
            Monday, September 23, 1963
        ANOTHER MASSACRE IN TOLIMA AREA
            9 MORE KILLED YESTERDAY
We've gotten used to seeing
                little children decapitated
and fifteen-year-olds read about the murders / before
    turning to the Society Page
and we keep killing each other for the sake of vengeance
    and
political feuds and hate hate hate hate hate hate hate
and on TV they ask for the death penalty
and we hate . . .
            Colombia is being massacred

Perdónanos por todos y por todo
Perdona a todos los colombianos Señor
que ya no haya más Violencia y
dános amor
    Amor
        AMOR

Forgive us Lord for our crimes our politicians
our newspapers radio TV our bandits liberals conserva-
    tives
moneylenders powerful landowners House of Representa-
    tives
terrorists gunrunners our judges soldiers lawyers *SIC*
    Corporations / etc.
                    our communists
                    athletic coaches
                    our yankee petroleum companies
                    lumber companies
                    banana companies
                    mining companies / etc.
and the priest in his Mercedes Benz
the clergy who encourage politics / the clergy who con-
    form
the banks the colonels capitalists Presidents of the Re-
    public
those who read this and who don't give a damn / etc.
Forgive us for everyone and everything
Forgive every Colombian Lord
and let the violence end
and give us love
            Love
                LOVE

[*Translated by Elinor Randall and Robert Márquez*]

Cuba

Nicolás Guillén (1902–   ) is the poet laureate of revolutionary Cuba and undoubtedly one of the great poets of the Spanish-speaking world. His poetry began to appear in journals and magazines in the early twenties and since the appearance of *Motivos de son* in 1930 he has been the major exponent of the "mulatto poem" in the Hispanic world. But his influence and his thematic scope are wider than that phrase might suggest. Though known primarily as a poet of folk rhythms, Black and popular themes, Guillén is no less admired for the artistic refinement of his art, for his humor, his love ballads, and for the compassionate poignancy of his political and revolutionary verse. His concern for Black people and Black culture is an inextricable part of his allegiance to Cuba and to the great mass of the world's disinherited. "All his work," as Ezequiel Martínez Estrada has pointed out, "is a battle against oppression, against the privileges and rivalries that separate human beings of whatever condition."

Winner of the Stalin Prize in 1953 and long a member of the Communist Party, Guillén was exiled from Batista's Cuba. He returned home in 1959 and has held various diplomatic posts in the revolutionary government. He was honored with the title "Poeta Nacional" in 1961 and has held the post of president of the Union of Cuban Artists and Writers (UNEAC) since its founding in 1962. He is also the editor of the journal *Gaceta de Cuba* and sits on the editorial board of the literary magazine *Unión*.

Guillén's most recent works move from elegy to celebration, exalting the achievements of the Cuban Revolution and expressing solidarity with liberation struggles throughout the world (including, of course, inside the United States). He continues to see the oppression of Blacks as the consequence not of one race living in close proximity to another but as the inevitable result of a racist, colonialist, and capitalistic socioeconomic and political structuring of society. Guillén's most recent works include *El diario que a diario* (1972), *El gran zoo* (1967), *La paloma de vuelo popular* (1958), *Tengo* (1964), and *La rueda dentada* (1972).

The poems reprinted here are taken from all but the first two of these volumes.

Crecen altas las flores

Si yo no fuera un hombre seguro; si no fuera
un hombre que ya sabe todo lo que le espera
        con Lynch en el timón, con Jim Crow en el mando
        y por nocturnos mares sangrientos navegando;
si yo no fuera un viejo caimán cuyo pellejo
es cada vez más duro por cada vez más viejo;
        si yo no fuera un negro de universal memoria
        y un blanco que conoce su pecado y su gloria;
si yo no fuera un chino libre del mandarín
mirando por los ojos de Shanghai y Pekín;
        si yo no fuera un indio de arrebatado cobre
        que hace ya cuatrocientos años que muere pobre;
si yo no fuera un hombre soviético, de mano
múltiple y conocida como mano de hermano:
        si yo no fuera todo lo que ya soy, te digo
        tal vez me pudiera engañar mi enemigo.

Murió McCarthy, dicen. (Yo mismo dije: "Es cierto,
murió McCarthy. . . .") Pero lo cierto es que no ha
    muerto.
        Vive y no esconde el bárbaro sus tenazas de
            hierro
        y el verdugo y la silla, y el *g-man* y el encierro.
Monstruo de dos cabezas bien norteamericano,
una mitad demócrata, otra republicano;
        monstruo de dos cabezas, mas ninguna con seso,
        no importa que nos hable de alianza y de pro-
            greso.
Y tal vez porque habla, pues nadie en nuestra América
(india pálida y virgen, pero no es histérica),
        librado ya del férreo dogal de las Españas
        va a creer a los yanquis sus tontas musarañas.
Alianza de Rockefeller con Mr. Ford: lo creo
y el progreso de entrambos no lo creo, lo veo.

The Flowers Grow High

If I were not a man secure, if I were not
a man, now wise, who knows the ghastly plot
  of awful helmsman Lynch, with Jim Crow in
    command,
   whose course through nights and seas of blood is
    planned;
if I were not an ancient alligator bold
whose hide grows tougher as he grows more old;
   if I were not a Black with memories of great
    length,
   or a White who knows his weakness and his
    strength;
if I were not Chinese, from mandarins set free,
with Shanghai and Peking now mine to keep;
   if I were not an Indian robbed of copper ore,
   for centuries dying hungry, dying poor;
if I were not a Soviet citizen whose hand
is known for helpfulness in every land;
   if I were not all that I am, all I will be . . .
   it's likely I'd be tricked by my enemy!

"McCarthy died," they say; I said with them, "That's
 right."
But it's a lie; he's with us day and night.
   Barbarian, he lives; we know his iron nails,
   his hangmen, torture, agents, and his jails.
A very North American monster of two heads,
this Democrat-Republican quadruped.
   A monster of two heads, and neither one with
    brains;
   his Progress and Alliance are our chains.
So even when he speaks, America down here
(native, pale and chaste, but free from fear,
   and free forevermore from Spain's oppressive ties)

157

Alianza de la Standard con la United . . . Pues
claro,
así no es el progreso de las dos nada raro.
Alianza del Chase Bank con el World Bank. Compañero
la alianza de dos "banks" es progreso y dinero.
Pero que no me vengan con cuentos de camino,
pues yo no sólo pienso, sino además opino
en alta voz y soy antes que nada un hombre
a quien gusta llamar las cosas por su nombre.
Y pregunto y respondo y me alzo y exijo
y sé cuándo la mona cargar no quiere al hijo.
Para el yanqui no somos más que escoria barata,
tribus de compra fácil con vidrio y hojalata;
generales imbéciles sin ciencia y sin escuela,
ante el jamón colgado cada uno en duermevela;
compadres argentinos, sátrapas peruanos,
betancures, peraltas, muñoces . . . Cuadrúmanos
a saltos en la selva; gente menuda y floja
que en curare mortífero sus agrias puntas moja.
Pero como tenemos bosques y cafetales,
hierro, carbón, petróleo, cobre, cañaverales,
(lo que en dólares quiere decir muchos millones)
no importa que seamos quéchuas o motilones.
Vienen pues a ayudarnos para que progresemos
y en pago de su ayuda nuestra sangre les demos.
Si en Paraguay tumultos contra Washington hay,
que vaya luego Stroessner y ayude al Paraguay.
Que quien gobierno y patria cifró en una botella,
ceda no al pueblo el mando sino a la ruda estrella
del espadón estulto cuya estulticia vende
el hogar a un extraño, y encarcela y ofende.
Que un macaco las nalgas ponga sobre el asiento
de Bolívar y ayude con terror y tormento
a que no rompa yugo si sacuda tutela
el alto guerrillero que ruge en Venezuela.

will see the Yankee promises as lies.
Alliance of Rockefeller with Mr. Ford, I see:
the two make Progress; I fall to my knees.
A great Alliance of Standard and United is arranged;
the Progress of those two is nothing strange.
Alliance of Chase with World Bank, very funny;
alliances of banks means Progress for their money.
So don't recite to me excuses of great length.
These aren't ideas, but facts; I have the strength
to back them up with words and deeds. I'm not afraid
to stand and fight, to call a spade a spade.
I ask and I respond, I speak and I reveal
what many times the nun's black cloth conceals.
The Yankee takes us for a filthy, worthless mass;
we're tribes he buys with toys and beads of glass.
We're untrained generals, pompous, dressed like fools
who stand before the slaughtered pig and drool.
We're Argentine *compadres,* satraps from Peru,
Muñozes, Peraltas, and Betancourts too.
We're apes who bound through jungles, small, weak quadrupeds;
mortiferous curare drips from our arrowheads.
But since we're rich in iron, coffee, cane and rum,
in forests, copper, coal, petroleum
(in dollars that means billions, at the very least),
who cares if we are Quechuas or beasts?
They come, enlighten us, and raise us from the mud,
to take in payment for this help our blood.
From Paraguay comes news of hate for Washington,
so Stroessner puts an end to this with guns.
And he who rules a country from the depths of cocktail glasses
hears not the peoples' voices, but those of desexed asses

159

Cada día en Colombia los soldados apuntan
contra los campesinos y obreros que se juntan.
　　　Ayuda para el cobre de Chile es lo primero.
　　　(El cobre de la "mining," no el cobre del minero.)
En la montaña pura suena triste la quena.
Habla con duras sílabas de estaño cuando suena.
　　　En Brasil, hacia el lado nordeste de su angustia,
　　　sangre y sudor revueltos riegan la tierra mustia
donde gringos de kepis se ayudan cada día . . .
Dígalo usted, Recife. ¿No es la verdad, Bahía?
　　　Centroamérica es una gran finca que progresa.
　　　Va el plátano en aumento, crece el café y no cesa.
(A veces silba el látigo, se oye una bofetada,
desplómase un peón . . . En fin, eso no es nada.)
　　　Ayudador deglute su inglés y se pasea
　　　orondo el sometido criado de vil librea
que en Puerto Rico manda, es decir obedece,
mientras que la vasta frente de Albizu resplandece.
　　　Junto al barroso Plata Buenos Aires rutila,
　　　pero le empaña el brillo la sombra del gorila
de venenosa lengua y ojo de fija hiel,
a cuya voz se aprontan la cárcel y el cuartel.

Adelante, Jim Crow; no te detengas; lanza
tu grito de victoria. Un ¡hurra! por la Alianza.
　　　Lynch, adelante, corre, busca tus fuetes. Eso,
　　　eso es lo que nos urge . . . ¡Hurra por el
　　　Progreso!
Así de día en día (aliados progresando
bajo la voz de Washington, que es una voz de mando)
　　　hacer de nuestras tierras el naziparaíso:
　　　ni un indio, ni un mal blanco, ni un negro, ni un
　　　mestizo;
y alcanzar la superba cumbre de la cultura
donde el genio mecánico de una gran raza pura
　　　nos muestra la profunda técnica que proclama
　　　en Jacksonville, Arkansas, Mississippi, Alabama
el Sur expeditivo cuyos torpes problemas

whose existence is an insult, whose cruelty never
    fails
to sell our homes to foreigners, to put us in their
    jails.
So let the rump of a buffoon fill Bolívar's fine gold throne
and with a militant terror, unyielding, cold as stone,
    let paternalism and the horrible yoke of slavery
    be smashed in Venezuela by *guerrillero* bravery!

Each day in Colombia armed soldiers take pains
to kill farmers and workers who are breaking their
    chains.
    So buy Chilean copper; now what could be finer?
    Since it's owned by the company, not by the
    miner.
High in pure mountains an Indian flute sings,
but hard is the voice of the tin as it rings.
    In northeast Brazil a hot anguish boils
    as blood mixed with sweat irrigates that fine soil
where gringo advisors are nothing so new . . .
Recife, Bahía: is it not true?
    And there's Central America, the best ranch
    around,
    where banana gets better and coffee abounds.
If at times there's a whiplash or a peasant who falls,
or a rifle shot . . . why, that's nothing at all.
    Flashy and pompous in vile traitor's clothes,
    he swaggers and chokes out what English he
    knows
(the leader in P.R. who merely obeys)
while Albizu's countenance glows with bright rays.
    Close by the muddy Plata, Buenos Aires lies
    in a brilliance clouded by a man whose eyes
are gall, whose tongue of venom, strong but smooth,
can send you to prison for one wrong move.

So, forward Jim Crow, with your voice of defiance;
don't stop till there's victory for the Alliance!

161

arregla con azotes, con perros y con quemas.
    Sólo que en nuestra América crecen altas las
        flores.
    Engarza el pueblo y pule sus más preciadas
        gemas.
De las guerrillas parten bazukas y poemas.
Con vengativa furia truenan los ruiseñores . . .

> March onward, Lynch, don't let your whip fall.
> That's what we need: your Progress for all!
Thus day after day (allied and progressing)
Washington's voice, a voice so distressing,
> urges us on toward the culture we lack
> while bad Whites, Mestizos, Indians and Blacks
are lost as we soar toward fascism's heights.
The mechanical genius of a race pure and bright
> shows us techniques by which they win out
> in Jacksonville, Arkansas, both North and South:
expeditious, they see to their problems, of course,
with whippings, police dogs, fires and force.
> But in our America the flowers grow high
> to embellish a people and sweeten the homes
of guerrillas who carry bazookas and poems . . .
with furious vengeance a nightingale cries!

[*Translated by David Arthur McMurray*]

Tengo

Cuando me veo y toco
yo, Juan sin Nada no más ayer,
y hoy Juan con Todo,
y hoy con todo,
vuelvo los ojos, miro,
me veo y toco
y me pregunto cómo ha podido ser.

Tengo, vamos a ver,
tengo el gusto de andar por mi país,
dueño de cuanto hay en él,
mirando bien de cerca lo que antes
no tuve ni podía tener.
Zafra puedo decir,
monte puedo decir,
ciudad puedo decir,
ejército decir,
ya míos para siempre y tuyos, nuestros,
y un ancho resplandor
de rayo, estrella, flor.

Tengo, vamos a ver,
tengo el gusto de ir
yo, campesino, obrero, gente simple,
tengo el gusto de ir
(es un ejemplo)
a un banco y hablar con el administrador,
no en inglés,
no en señor,
sino decirle compañero como se dice en español.

Tengo, vamos a ver,
que siendo un negro
nadie me puede detener

I Have

When I look at and touch myself,
I, John-only-yesterday-with-Nothing
and John-with-Everything-today,
with everything today,
I glance around, I look and see
and touch myself and wonder
how it could have happened.

I have, let's see:
I have the pleasure of walking my country,
the owner of all there is in it,
examining at very close range what
I could not and did not have before.
I can say cane,
I can say mountain,
I can say city,
I can say army,
army say,
now mine forever and yours, ours,
and the vast splendor of
the sunbeam, the star, the flower.

I have, let's see:
I have the pleasure of going,
me, a peasant, a worker, a simple man,
I have the pleasure of going
(just an example)
to a bank and speaking to the manager,
not in English,
not in "Sir,"
but in *compañero* as we say in Spanish.

I have, let's see:
that being Black

a la puerta de un dancing o de un bar.
O bien en la carpeta de un hotel
gritarme que no hay pieza,
una mínima pieza y no una pieza colosal,
una pequeña pieza donde yo pueda descansar.

Tengo, vamos a ver,
que no hay guardia rural
que me agarre y me encierre en un cuartel,
ni me arranque y me arroje de mi tierra
al medio del camino real.

Tengo que como tengo la tierra tengo el mar,
no country, no jailáif,
no tennis y no yacht,
sino de playa en playa y ola en ola,
gigante azul abierto democrático:
en fin, el mar.

Tengo, vamos a ver,
que ya aprendí a leer,
a contar,
tengo que ya aprendí a escribir
y a pensar
y a reir.
Tengo que ya tengo
donde trabajar
y ganar
lo que me tengo que comer.
Tengo, vamos a ver,
tengo lo que tenía que tener.

I can be stopped by no one at
the door of a dancing hall or bar.
Or even at the desk of a hotel
have someone yell at me there are no rooms,
a small room and not one that's immense,
a tiny room where I might rest.

I have, let's see:
that there are no rural police
to seize me and lock me in a precinct jail,
or tear me from my land and cast me
in the middle of the highway.

I have that having the land I have the sea,
no country clubs,
no high life,
no tennis and no yachts,
but, from beach to beach and wave on wave,
gigantic blue open democratic:
in short, the sea.

I have, let's see:
that I have learned to read,
to count,
I have that I have learned to write,
and to think
and to laugh.
I have that now I have
a place to work
and earn
what I have to eat.
I have, let's see:
I have what was coming to me.

[*Translated by Robert Márquez*]

Ángela Davis

Yo no he venido aquí a decirte que eres bella.
Creo que sí, que eres bella,
mas no se trata de eso.
Se trata de que quieren que estés muerta.
Necesitan tu cráneo
para adornar la tienda del Gran Jefe,
junto a las calaveras de Jackson y Lumumba.

Angela, y nosotros
necesitamos tu sonrisa.

Vamos a cambiarte los muros que alzó el odio,
por claros muros de aire,
y el techo de tu angustia,
por un techo de nubes y de pájaros,
y el guardián que te oculta,
por un arcángel con su espada.

¡Cómo se engañan tus verdugos! Estás hecha
de un material ardiente y áspero,
ímpetu inoxidable,
apto para permanecer por soles y por lluvias,
por vientos y por lunas
a la intemperie.
                    Perteneces
a esa clase de sueños en que el tiempo
siempre ha fundido sus estatuas
y escrito sus canciones.

Angela, no estoy frente a tu nombre
para hablarte de amor como un adolescente,
ni para desearte como un sátiro.
Ah, no se trata de eso.
Lo que yo digo es que eres fuerte y plástica

Angela Davis

I have not come to tell you you are beautiful.
I believe you are beautiful,
but that is not the issue.
The issue is they want you dead.
They need your skull
to decorate the tent of the Great Chief,
beside the skulls of Jackson and Lumumba.

And, Angela,
we need your smile.

We are going to change the walls hate has constructed,
for the transparent walls of air,
and the roof of your anguish,
for a roof of clouds and birds,
and the guard who conceals you,
for an archangel with his sword.

How your executioners mislead themselves!
You are made of rough and glowing stuff,
a rustproof impulse,
capable of lasting through suns and rains,
through winds and moons
in the unsheltered air.
                    You belong to
that class of dreams in which time
has always forged its statues
and written its songs.

Angela, I am not before your name
to speak to you of love like an adolescent,
or to desire you like a satyr.
That, alas, is not the issue.
I merely say that you are strong, resilient

169

para saltar al cuello (fracturándolo)
de quienes han querido y quieren todavía, querrán
    siempre
verte arder viva atada al sur de tu país,
atada a un poste calcinado,
atada a un roble sin follaje,
atada en cruz ardiendo viva atada al Sur.

El enemigo es torpe.
Quiere callar tu voz con la voz suya,
pero todos sabemos
que es tu voz la única que resuena,
la única que se enciende
alta en la noche como una columna fulminante,
un detenido rayo,
un vertical incendio abrasador,
repetido relámpago a cuya luz resaltan
negros de ardientes uñas,
pueblos desvencijados y coléricos.

Bajo el logrado sueño donde habito
junto a los milicianos decisivos,
al agrio borde de este mar terrible pero amigo,
viendo furiosas olas romperse en la rompiente,
grito, y hago viajar mi voz sobre los hombros
del gran viento que pasa
viento mío padre nuestro Caribe.

Digo tu nombre, Angela, vocifero. Junto mis manos
no en ruegos, preces, súplicas, plegarias
para que tus carceleros te perdonen,
sino en acción de aplauso mano y mano
duro y fuerte bien fuerte
mano y mano ¡para que sepas que soy tuyo!

enough to leap at (and fracture) the neck
of those who have wanted, still want, and will always
    want
to see you burned alive bound to the south of your
    country,
bound to a cindered post,
bound to a leafless oak,
bound to a burning cross alive bound to the South.

The enemy is clumsy.
He wants to silence your voice with his own,
but we all know
your voice alone resounds,
that it alone ignites
high in the night like an exploding column,
an arrested lightning flash,
a vertical consuming fire,
a recurring thunderbolt beneath whose light we glimpse
Blacks with fiery nails,
weakened and angry peoples.

Beneath the dream accomplished where I live
beside the decisive militia,
by the bitter edge of this terrible but friendly sea,
watching furious waves collapse on the breakers,
I yell, and make my voice travel on the shoulders
of the great passing wind
my wind our father the Caribbean.

Angela, I say your name, vociferate. I join my hands
not in pleas, entreaties, supplications, prayers
to your jailers for your pardon
but in applauding action, hand meeting hand,
hard and strong, very strong,
hand meeting hand so you will know I'm yours!

[*Translated by Robert Márquez*]

Lectura de domingo

He leído acostado
todo un blando domingo.
Yo en mi lecho tranquilo,
mi suave cabezal,
mi cobertor bien limpio,
tocando piedra, lodo, sangre,
garrapata, sed,
orines, asma:
indios callados que no entienden,
soldados que no entienden,
señores teorizantes que no entienden,
obreros, campesinos que no entienden.

Terminas de leer,
quedan tus ojos fijos
¿en qué sitio del viento?
El libro ardió en mis manos,
lo he puesto luego abierto,
como una brasa pura,
sobre mi pecho.
Siento
las últimas palabras
subir desde un gran hoyo negro.

Inti, Pablito, el Chino y Aniceto.
El cinturón del cerco.
La radio del ejército
mintiendo.
Aquella luna pequeñita
colgando suspendida
a una legua de Higueras
y dos de Pucará.
Después silencio.
No hay más páginas

Sunday Reading

I have spent a whole Sunday
just lying down, reading.
I in my peaceful bed,
on my fluffy pillow,
under my spotless quilt.
Feeling rock, mud, blood,
ticks, thirst, piss and asthma:
silent Indians who do not understand,
soldiers who do not understand,
theorizing gentlemen who do not understand,
workers, peasants, who do not understand.

You finish reading
your eyes fixed
on what spot in the wind?
The book burned in my hands.
I then lay it open,
like pure coal,
on my chest.
I feel
the last words rise
from a deep black hole.

Inti, Pablito, el Chino and Aniceto.
The circle closing in.
The army radio
lying.
That tiny little moon
hanging suspended
one league from Higueras
and two from Pucará.
Then silence.
No more pages.
This is getting serious.

173

Esto se pone serio.
Esto se acaba pronto.
Termina.
            Va a endenderse.
Se apaga.
            Va a nacer.

It will end soon.
It is ending.
            Bursting into flames.
Becoming ashes.
            Being born.

[*Translated by Robert Márquez*]

Roberto Fernández Retamar (1930–   ) belongs to that middle generation of Cuban poets who, in his own words, "are witnesses to yesterday, to today, and to tomorrow. But the major part of our lives will be found in the former, and to the latter we bring what was learned then, including, of course, the pain"—a generation of "transitional men" for whom the triumph of the Revolution meant passing from "the darkness . . . to the clearing; from nostalgia to hope; from estrangement to certainty."

Retamar turned first to the study of art and architecture but decided finally on literature and studied at the universities of Havana, Paris, and London. His first book of verse, *Elegía como un himno*, appeared in 1950 when he was just twenty. A short time later he was awarded the National Prize for Poetry for his second book, *Patrias*. With the advent of Batista, Retamar turned to writing for the underground press. He eventually exiled himself to the United States where he taught at Yale University before his return to Cuba in 1959.

Since the triumph of the Revolution, Retamar, a tireless and prolific writer, has taken his place among the most important and original voices of the new revolutionary culture and has become one of the most articulate spokesmen for Latin America's—indeed the whole of the Third World's—historical and cultural unity and for the need for a concerted effort in the face of the threat posed by the cultural presumptions of European and United States imperialism. In this regard his recent analysis of Latin American culture, "Calibán," is of seminal importance. As well as being a poet, essayist, critic, and editor of the *Casa de Las Américas*, Retamar is Coordinating Secretary of the Union of Cuban Artists and Writers (UNEAC) and is on the editorial board of its journal *Unión*.

Retamar's poetry has an unassuming elegance and a tone of conversational intimacy that makes it immediately accessible and simultaneously reflects the broad cultural resources of the critic and scholar. His themes, like so much of the poetry written by his generation immediately after 1959, are those of a poet responding positively to the new reality; they demonstrate, too, the complexities of his predicament as a "transitional man" and a synthesis of the subjective (love theme) and the objective (unfolding of the revolution). His very recent collection, *Cuaderno paralelo*, written during a two-month stay in the Democratic Republic of Vietnam in 1970, documents his experience of that daily struggle.

Retamar's published works include several books of essays and critiques and the following books of verse: *Vuelta a la antigua esperanza* (1959), *Con las mismas manos* (1962), *Buena suerte viviendo* (1967), *Poesía reunida* (1966), *Algo semejante a los monstruos antediluvianos* (1970), and the more recent anthology *A quien pueda interesar* (1970), which includes the *Cuaderno paralelo* and from which these poems are taken.

Epitafio de un invasor

Tu bisabuelo cabalgó por Texas,
Violó mexicanas trigueñas y robó caballos
Hasta que se casó con Mary Stonehill y fundó un hogar
De muebles de roble y *God Bless Our Home.*
Tu abuelo desembarcó en Santiago de Cuba,
Vio hundirse la Escuadra española, y llevó al hogar
El vaho del ron y una oscura nostalgia de mulatas.
Tu padre, hombre de paz,
Sólo pagó el sueldo de doce muchachos en Guatemala.
Fiel a los tuyos,
Te dispusiste a invadir a Cuba, en el otoño de 1962.

Hoy sirves de abono a las ceibas.

Epitaph for an Invader

Your great grandfather rode through Texas,
Raped dark Mexican women and stole horses
Until he married Mary Stonehill and built a house
With oak-wood furniture and *God Bless Our Home*.
Your grandfather landed in Santiago de Cuba,
Saw the Spanish fleet sink, and took home
The smell of rum, a dark nostalgia for mulatto women.
Your father, a man of peace,
Merely paid the salary of twelve boys in Guatemala.
Faithful to your own,
You prepared to invade Cuba, in the autumn of 1962.

Today you fertilize the ceiba tree.

[*Translated by Robert Márquez*]

Es bueno recordar

Cuando los nazis hicieron algo así,
En algún sitio de París, con sus negros y sus grises,
Picasso pintó Guernica, y luego dijo a un general nazi:
"Fueron ustedes quienes lo hicieron."
Luego, a algunos de esos nazis
Los sentaron en el banquillo de los acusados
Y los juzgaron y los condenaron
Y los ahorcaron.
"Fueron ustedes quienes lo hicieron."
Es bueno recordar.

We Do Well to Remember

When the Nazis did something like this,
Somewhere in Paris, with its blacks and grays,
Picasso painted *Guernica*, and told a Nazi general:
"You were the ones who did it."
Then, they sat some of those Nazis
On the defendant's bench
Judged them and condemned them
And they hanged them.
"You were the ones who did it."
We do well to remember.

[*Translated by Robert Márquez*]

Es mejor encender un cirio que maldecir la oscuridad

Como el soldado de la anécdota,
No desconocimos el miedo,
Pero estábamos en nuestro sitio.
Nuestro modesto sitio, era
Revelar destrucciones, crímenes;
Pero sobre todo revelar la combatiente grandeza de este
    pueblo,
Su decisión de victoria
Más allá de ciudades arrasadas a fuego,
De armas de geometría implacable;
Revelar que estas criaturas están más cerca de los
    números, del aire
Transparente del pensamiento, que los laboratorios
De donde salen aullando cifras, monstruos, espantos.
Y los hombres renovados cada minuto
Que en estas tierras resisten y vencen,
Garantizan que la historia, que la vida
Tiene sentido, y ese sentido se descubre
Entre estos rostros que pasan, rostros de ayer y de
    mañana
Donde el tiempo arde con la serena confianza
De un cirio en medio de la oscuridad.

It's Better to Light a Candle than to Curse the Darkness

Like the soldier in the anecdote,
Fear was not unknown to us,
But we were in our place.
Our modest place, to
Expose destruction, crime;
But above all to reveal the combative grandeur of this
    people,
Their victorious decision
Beyond cities leveled by fire,
By implacable geometric arms.
To reveal that these beings are closer to numbers, to air,
Transparent with thought, than the laboratories
From which the howling statistics, monsters, horrors
    come.
And the new men who
Resist and win in this land, without letup,
Guarantee that history, that life
Has meaning, and we discover this meaning
On the faces that pass, faces of yesterday and tomorrow
Where time burns with the serene confidence
Of a candle in the darkness.

[*Translated by Margaret Randall and Robert Cohen*]

Seria bueno merecer este epitafio

Puso a disposición de los hombres lo que tenía de
   inteligencia
(Poco o mucho, pues no es de eso de lo que se trata),
Y quedan por ahí algunos papeles y algunas ídeas y
   algunos amigos
(Y quizás hasta algunos alumnos, aunque esto es más
   dudoso)
Que podrán dar fe de ello.
Les entregó lo que tenía de coraje
(Poco o mucho, pues tampoco es de eso de lo que se
   trata).
No faltará algo o alguien
Que pueda verificarlo.
Se sabe que deploró de veras no haber estado la madru-
   gada de aquel 26 entre los atacantes al cuartel,
No haber venido en aquel yate,
No haberse alzado en la montaña.
No haber sido, en fin, de los elegidos.
Pero, como se ve
(Espero que el epitafio pueda llevar esta oración sin
   forzar la realidad),
Hizo su parte, llegado el momento.
Se sabe también que lamentó no haber escrito
"Nuestra América," *Trilce, El 18 Brumario*
(¿Para qué hablar del *Capital?*)
Aunque tú, lector, recuerdas
Probablemente
(Sobre este adverbio no debe insistirse mucho)
Aquella página.
Se equivocó más de una vez, y quiso sinceramente
   hacerlo mejor.
Acertó, y vio que acertar tampoco era gran cosa.
De todas maneras, llegado al final, declaró que volvería a
   empezar si lo dejaran.

It Would Be Nice to Deserve This Epitaph

He put at mankind's disposal what intelligence he had
(Whether a little or a lot is not the issue),
And there are, here and there, a few papers, a few ideas
    and a few friends
(And perhaps even a few disciples, though this is more
    doubtful)
Who can testify to it.
He gave them what courage he had
(Whether a little or a lot, again, is not the issue).
There will not be lacking something or someone
That can verify it.
We know that he truly regretted not having been among
    those who assaulted
The barracks on the morning of that 26th,
Not having come aboard that yacht,
Not having taken to the mountains in revolt.
Not having been, in short, among the chosen.
But, as you can see
(I hope this can go on the epitaph without forcing reality),
He did his part, when the time came.
We also know that he lamented not having written
"Our America," *Trilce, The 18th Brumaire*
(Why even mention *Kapital*?),
Though you, reader, probably
(One should not insist too much on this adverb)
Remember some page.
He was wrong more than once, and wanted sincerely to
    do better.
He was right, and saw that being right was no grand thing
    either.
In any case, when the end came, he said he would begin
    again if they would let him.
Good and bad was said of him while he lived, and with the
    years,

De él en vida se dijo bien y mal, y con los años, esos en los
    que
Todo se va borrando y confundiendo,
No faltará quien lo mencione de modo que lo hubiera
    complacido,
Mezclando su nombre con otros nombres, bajo el epígrafe
    revolución.

(Se ruega a los obituaristas vocativos de siempre
Simplificar lo más posible estas sugerencias.
Y, por favor, no precipitarse.)

Those which erase and confuse everything,
There will not be lacking someone who will mention him
    as he would have liked,
Mixing his name with other names, under the epigraph
    revolution.

(I beg the invocatory obituary writers of all times
To simplify these suggestions as much as possible.
And, please, don't be in a hurry.)

[*Translated by Robert Márquez*]

David Fernández Chericián (1940–) whose first few books of verse appeared under the name David Fernández, started out as a child actor on radio and T.V. and later turned to scriptwriting and directing. After the Revolution he was for a time director of the Cuban Radio Institute. He is a journalist and is currently on the staff of the *Gaceta de Cuba*. He is also a very talented translator whose work includes a translation of *Macbird!*, a small anthology of contemporary African poetry, and selections from the work of the United States' "Third World" poets.

Just eighteen when the *barbudos* arrived in Havana, Chericián belongs to that group of poets who came to maturity with the Revolution and whose work over the last fourteen years reflects the changes its generation of artists have gone through in creating with, from within, and as part of, the Revolution. They have moved from the unequivocal transparency of theme and language called forth by the enthusiasms, tensions, and uncertainties of the first few years to the unself-conscious serenity of an absolute conviction that, though no less expressive or committed, tends to be more meditative, aesthetically critical, and self-demanding. Referring specifically to the work of Cherician, Nicolás Guillén writes: "One reads David and one knows that one is before a solid, thought out, calculated poem; a poem that belongs equally to poetry and to architecture . . . [he] creates his lines and with them his poems so that they will remain beautifully intact." Cherician has tried his hand at any number of different forms, including verse for children, and his thematic concerns range from the bittersweet recollections of *Árbol y luego bosque* (1965) and *Árbol de la memoria* (1971), to the satirical humor and anti-imperialism of *La onda de David* (1967), from which these poems are taken. His other works include *Diecisiete anos* (1958), *Días y hombres* (1966), *Queriéndolos, nombrándolos* (1971), and a series of completed but as yet unpublished books.

Sección de anuncios clasificados

Se solicita un mundo
sin monopolios
ni policía.
Preguntar por cualquiera
en Asia, en Africa, en América
Latina.

Classified Section

Wanted: a world
without monopolies,
without police.
Inquire of anyone
in Asia, Africa, Latin America.

[*Translated by Robert Márquez*]

Respecto del Tercer Mundo

. . . somos intransigentes
porque llamamos pan a la necesidad
más esencial del hombre,
y fusil al tareco
más útil para conseguirlo.

On the Third World

. . . we are intransigent
because we call bread
man's most essential need,
and "gun" the most appropriate means
for getting it.

[*Translated by Robert Márquez*]

Una canción de paz

A: F.P.R.

Redwood City, California, Nov. 17 (A.P.) Sólo cuatro días después de leer una carta en que su hijo les decía que su suerte se estaba extinguiendo, Mr. y Mrs. Silvio Carnevale recibieron un telegrama anunciando su muerte en Viet Nam. "Estoy enfermo, enfermo por lo que he hecho y por lo que les ha pasado a mis amigos," decía la carta. "Me siento como si tuviera 100 años . . . Mi suerte se está extinguiendo. Por favor, hagan lo que puedan por mí . . . Papá, yo no quiero morir. Por favor, sáquenme de aquí . . ."

Quizás alguna vez
al pie de los naranjos de la rosada California,
robada por tu abuelo a otros abuelos,
soñaste con llegar a presidente
de tu nación, o sólo
llegar a ser un ciudadano honesto.
Tal vez ese fue el sueño
tras el que huyó tu bisabuelo
de la lejana Italia
y estableció por ello familia y casa y esperanza nuevas
en la reciente tierra de promisión del norte americano.

A Song of Peace

For F.P.R.

Redwood City, California,
Nov. 17 (A.P.) Only four days
after reading a letter in which
their son said that his luck
was running out, Mr. and
Mrs. Silvio Carnevale re-
ceived a telegram announcing
his death in Vietnam. "I am
sick, sickened by what I have
done and by what has hap-
pened to my friends," the let-
ter said. "I feel as if I were a
hundred years old . . . My
luck is running out. Please, do
what you can for me . . . Dad,
I don't want to die. Please, get
me out of here . . ."

Perhaps once
at the foot of the orange trees of rosy California,
robbed by your grandfather from other grandfathers,
you dreamt of becoming president
of your nation, or only of
becoming an honest citizen.
Perhaps that was the dream
with which your great-grandfather ran away
from far-off Italy
and thus established family and house and new hopes
in the new land of promise of the North American.

(I am only guessing, I am only
turning the pages of your possible history,

(Yo no hago más que suponer, no hago
más que pasar las hojas de tu posible historia,
más que inventar, aproximadamente,
lo que ya no serás porque la tierra
de promisión cavó tu tumba lejos,
muy lejos del naranjo)

Quizá tampoco
supiste nunca de ese lugar del mundo
que se llama Viet Nam,
donde ahora estás muriendo cada día,
donde pierde tu infancia interrumpida
todo sentido lógico, donde
—yo sé por qué y tú no—
empuñas un fusil que ya no es de juguete
y contra ti combaten las sombras y los árboles
y el viento y los caminos y las piedras y el humo
de tus propias hogueras y el silencio
de un monte que no es tuyo ni lo será y el agua
y el calor y la lluvia y—claro está—las balas
que tú mismo llevaste y ahora se vuelven contra ti.

Quizá nunca pensaste que pudiera ocurrir
esto que no es un sueño,
esto que rompe
algo dentro de ti, esto que arrasa
con los naranjos que plantó el abuelo
lejos, allá
donde tal vez quisieras
estar con los amigos a la sombra
de una canción de paz,
interrumpida aquí
por el paso de otros como tú, que vinieron
a destruir las casas, las familias, las esperanzas nuevas de
        este pueblo
que se llama Viet Nam,
del que tal vez nunca escuchaste hablar hasta ese día

only inventing, approximately,
what you will never be because the land
of promise dug your tomb far,
very far from the orange groves.)

Perhaps you never
knew of the place in the world
that is called Vietnam,
where now you are dying daily,
where your interrupted infancy loses
every logical sense, where
—I know why and you don't—
you grip a rifle that is no longer a toy,
and against you the shadows and the trees are fighting
and the winds and the roads and the stones and the
     smoke
from your own blazes and the silence
of a forest that is not yours nor will it be and the water
and the heat and the rain and—of course—the bullets
that you yourself brought, now turned against you.

Perhaps you never thought it could happen
this that is not a dream,
this that breaks
something inside you, this that devastates
the orange trees that grandfather planted
far away, there
where perhaps you would want
to be with friends in the shade
of a song of peace,
because this is already too much for you who know
why this song of peace
was interrupted here
by the passing of others like you, who came
to destroy the houses, the families, the new hopes of this
     nation
that is called Vietnam,

triste en que te mandaron junto con tus amigos,
sin decirte por qué,
hasta estas tierras donde ahora,
bajo las mismas armas que trajiste,
mueres, mueres, diaria, irremediablemente, mueres.

Noviembre 23/65

of which perhaps you never heard until that sad day
when they sent you, together with your friends,
without telling you why,
to these lands where now,
under the same weapons that you brought,
you die, you die, daily, irrevocably, you die.

November 23, 1965

Nancy Morejón (1944–   ) belongs to "the first generation of the Revolution," and brings to her immersion in the everyday reality of life in the Revolution, to its struggle to create the "new man" and the "new woman" an unobtrusive affirmation of her own, and Cuba's, Black cultural heritage.

Born in Havana, Morejón holds a Master of Arts degree in French Language and Literature. She has also served as a simultaneous translator at a number of international conferences held in Cuba, including the 1968 Havana Cultural Congress. She is a journalist and is currently on the staff of the *Gaceta de Cuba*. Her poems and articles have appeared in all the major Cuban journals and magazines—*Unión, Casa de Las Américas, El caimán barbudo,* and the *Gaceta,* among others. In 1966 she was awarded an honorable mention in the Union of Cuban Artists and Writers (UNEAC) poetry contest for her collection *Richard trajo su flauta y otros argumentos,* from which the following poems are taken.

Morejón's other published works include two collections of verse—*Mutismos* (1962) and *Amor, ciudad atribuida*—and, in collaboration with Carmen Gonce, an ethnohistorical monograph on the nickel-producing town of Nícaro. She is currently preparing a critical collection of articles and essays on the work of Nicolás Guillén for the *Valoración múltiple* series published by Casa de Las Américas.

Los Aqueos

A Mirta Aguirre

relata el asombrado y magnánimo Calcas:
"marchaban los aqueos
      la cicuta a su lado
seguían la línea de los dioses
envolvían incienso y tripas de Patroclo
      entre los velos
y los cráteres del mar azul"

Térsites Hermes Afrodita

"marchaban los aqueos"
—prosigue el asombrado anciano Calcas—
"y junto a la cicuta
junto a la lira esplendorosa
el poeta loco la parra
el pez de oro los laureles"

trajeron el mundo de las trabas

alguien nacía a los pies de Tebas
para llegar posteriormente a
      América
a este otro mundo

"pasen señores pasen
a esta última fase del hemisferio
aquí estamos
con la gangrena con la lanza
y una túnica de pútridas manzanas
pasen señores pasen"

después conquistaron el Hades los aqueos

The Achaeans

To Mirta Aguirre

Calchas the magnanimous and wonderstruck relates:
"the Achaeans marched
            the hemlock at their side
following in the footsteps of the gods
they wrapped incense and Patroclus' entrails
            between the veils
and craters of the azure sea"

Thersites Hermes Aphrodite

"the Achaeans marched"
—the wonderstruck sage continues—
"and next to the hemlock
next to the splendid lyre
the mad poet and the climbing vine
the golden fish of glory"

they brought the world of shackles

someone was being born at the feet of Thebes
to come later to
            America
to this other world

"come in gentlemen come in
to this hemisphere's last phase
here we are
with the gangrene and the lance
and a tunic of decaying apples
come in gentlemen come in"

then they conquered Hades the Achaeans

los romanos agonizaron en Dios Cristo
España grabó su nombre en nuestras tierras

por ahora
        nosotros nos cagamos en Dios

the Romans died in Jesus Christ Our Lord
Spain carved her name upon our lands

but now
         we say fuck God

[*Translated by Robert Márquez*]

Freedom Now

A la lucha de los negros en los Estados Unidos,
al SNCC

en el sur de los Estados Unidos
se fabrican ferrocarriles ganchos lámparas
ganchos pintura de uña para señoritas
cremas y helados de chocolate
tinte plateado autos edificios de propiedad horizontal
     televisores escuelas *democráticas*

se celebra Halloween en Estados Unidos
hay también Alabama Mississippi
     Texas
    la gran Texas rubita y pedigüeña
Birmingham Virginia
      New Orléans—gargajo de los *louis* con Mardí
      Gras y todo

es decir

ciudades misteriosas llenas de gente

que lincha negros y pisa cucarachas

cualquier vaca sureña exclamaría orgullosa:

"en estos tiempos de coca-cola
fuerza nuclear y conferencias internacionales
vale mucho más mi leche
que el semen de un estudiante negro"

Freedom Now

To the Black struggle in the United States,
to SNCC

in the southern part of the United States
they make trains hooks lamps
hooks fingernail polish for young women
facial creams and chocolate ice cream
silver dye cars horizontally owned buildings
     televisions *democratic* schools

they celebrate Halloween in the United States
they also have Alabama Mississippi
     Texas
   great Texas blond and importunate
Birmingham Virginia
     New Orleans—the spit of the *louis* with Mardi
        Gras and all

that is

mysterious cities full of people

who lynch Blacks and step on cockroaches

any southern cow would exclaim proudly:

"in these times of Coca-Cola
nuclear power and international conferences
my milk is worth much more
than the sperm of a Black student"

[Translated by Robert Márquez]

Dominican Republic

Despite his age, **Pedro Mir** (1913–) came late to the Latin American literary scene as a poet. He was virtually unknown outside his own country until very recently and his poetry is only now beginning to gain the international recognition it clearly deserves. In the introduction to the Mexican edition of his collection *Viaje a la muchedumbre* (1972), the poet Jaime Labastida, presenting Mir for the first time to that larger audience, wondered why his name had not appeared alongside that of the continent's great poets. Labastida wrote: "I do not vacillate in saying: we are before one of the most authentic and important poets of the present time. Perhaps in him and in a handful of American names we once again encounter the clear roots of the profoundly human and revolutionary political poetry that constitutes the most legitimate sign of Latin America's poetic present."

Mir, the son of a Puerto Rican mother and a Cuban father, was born in San Pedro de Macorís and is a Caribbean poet in the militant troubadour tradition of Guillén, Césaire, or Jacques Roumain; he is also a poet whose allegiance to the Dominican Republic and the archipelago encompasses a broader allegiance to Latin America and to all the wretched of the earth. Like the others, he is a popular poet of great complexity, technical skill, and intellectual power who, in opposition to the individualistic North American "I," defends the "furious *we*." His first books were published outside the Dominican Republic during his years of exile between 1949 and the late sixties. Of these works the most impressive are *Hay un país en el mundo* (1949), *Contracanto a Walt Whitman: Canto a nosotros mismos* (1953), and *Seis momentos de esperanza* (1953); these were followed by *Amén de mariposas* (1969) and *Viaje a la muchedumbre* (1972), both of which give particular emphasis to the last days of the bloody Trujillo regime and to the role of international gendarme played by the United States in the Caribbean and throughout the world. Mir has also written historical essays. He currently works as a journalist and writes a regular column for a leftist Dominican weekly. He has been a member of the Communist Party for several years.

Amén de mariposas

El autor
y bajo el título de

Amén de mariposas

A LA EMBAJADORA NORTEAMERICANA
EN MÉXICO, EL AÑO DE 1914

porque, durante la ocupación de Veracruz por tropas
de su propio país, exclamó:

"¡Ésta es la danza de la muerte
y creo que nosotros tocamos el violín!"

y por lo que en sus palabras suena de admonitorio,
de desgarrador y quién sabe si hasta de maternal,

dedica

este poema
cincuenta años después
cuando es más alegre el gatillo del violín,
cuando más tumultuoso el delirio de la danza.

Mariposa:
caricatura de aeroplano.
Pulso de abismo,
erudita de pétalos.
Antes que las manos
en la pared te mataron
. . . los ojos de los niños . . .
     PEDRO MA. CRUZ, *Raíces iluminadas*

Amen to Butterflies

The author
under the title

Amen to Butterflies

TO THE AMERICAN AMBASSADOR'S WIFE
IN MEXICO, 1914

because, during the occupation of Veracruz
by her country's troops, she said:

"This is the dance of death
and I believe we play the violin!"

and for the warning that those words contain,
for all they have of heartbreak and perhaps even of the
     maternal,

dedicates

this poem
fifty years later
when the trigger on the violin is gayer still,
much more tumultuous the frenzy of the dance.

Butterfly:
caricature of an airplane.
Pulse of the abyss,
scholar among blossoms.
Before those hands
smashed you on the wall
. . . the children's eyes . . .
     PEDRO MA. CRUZ, *Raíces iluminadas*

211

Primer tiempo

Cuando supe que habían caído las tres hermanas Mirabal
me dije:

la sociedad establecida ha muerto.
(Lapislázuli a cuento de todo emblema
      ruidoso
mentís en A referido a un imperio en
      agonía
y cuanto ha sido conocido desde enton-
      ces

me dije

y cuanto ha sido comprendido desde
      entonces

me dije

es que la sociedad establecida ha
      muerto)

Comprendí
que muchas unidades navales alrededor del mundo

inician su naufragio
en medio de la espuma
pensadora

y que grandes ejécitos reconocidos en el planeta

comienzan a derramarse
en el regazo de la duda
pesarosa

Es que
hay columnas de mármol impetuoso no rendidas al
      tiempo
y pirámides absolutas erigidas sobre las civilizaciones
que no pueden resistir la muerte de ciertas mariposas

Cuando supe que tres de los espejos de la sociedad
tres respetos del brazo y orgullo de los hombres
tres y entonces madres

y comienzo del día

habían caído
asesinadas

Act I

When I heard the three sisters Mirabal had fallen
I said to myself:
> society as it is is dead.
> (Lapis lazuli in place of pompous em-
> blems
> negation in A of a moribund empire
> and everything that has been known
> since
> > I said to myself
> and everything that has since been un-
> derstood
> > I said to myself
> society as it is is dead)

I understood
that several naval units around the world
> have started to sink
> within the thinking spume
and that huge armies famed throughout the globe
> have started to collapse
> in the lap of heavy doubts
Because
there are columns of impetuous marble that surrender not
> to time
and mighty pyramids built upon civilizations
that cannot but succumb to certain butterflies

When I heard that three pillars of society
three courtesies taken by the arm three times the pride of
> men
three and mothers then
> > and day's beginning
> > fell
> > murdered
> > O murdered

213

oh asesinadas
a pesar de sus telares en sonrisa
a pesar de sus abriles en riachuelo
a pesar de sus neblinas en reposo
(y todo el día lleno de grandes ojos abiertos)
roto el cráneo
despedazado el vientre
partida la plegaria
oh asesinadas
comprendí que el asesinato como bestia incendiada por la
cola
no se detendría ya
ante ninguna puerta de concordia
ante ninguna persiana de ternura
ante ningún dintel ni balaustrada
ni ante paredes
ni ante rendijas
ni ante el paroxismo
de los progenitores iniciales
Porque a partir de entonces el plomo perdió su rumbo
y el sentido su rango
y sólo quedaba en pie
la Humanidad
emplazada a durar sobre este punto
escandaloso
de la inmensidad
del Universo
Supe entonces que el asesinato ocupaba el lugar
del pensamiento
que en la luz de la casa
comenzaba a aclimatarse
el puerco cimarrón
y la araña peluda
que la lechuza se instalaba en la escuela
que en los parques infantiles
se aposentaba el hurón
y el tiburón en las fuentes

despite their smiling looms
despite the Aprils in a little spring
despite their mists in repose
(and the day filled with great wide-open eyes)
a fractured skull
a mangled womb
a prayer cut short
O murdered ones
I understood that murder like a beast whose tail is on fire
would no longer be stopped
by any door of peace
by any shade of tenderness
by any beam or any balustrade
or any walls
or any bars
or any spasms
of the first ancestors
for ever since the bullet lost its way
and reason lost its rank
and only Humanity was still
left standing
called to endure on this scandalous spot
in the immensity
of space
I knew then that murder held the place of thought
that the wild boar
and the black widow spider
were starting to make themselves
at home in the light of the house
that the owl had put itself in school
that now the ferret lodged
in children's playgrounds
the shark in water fountains
and gears and daggers
and stumps and crutches
in the corners of the crib
or that the crucial epoch was beginning

y engranaje y puñal
y muñón y muleta
en los copos de la cuna
o que empezaba entonces la época rotunda
del bien y del mal
desnudos
frente a frente
conminados a una sola
implacable definitiva
decidida victoria
muerte a muerte

Oh asesinadas
no era una vez
porque no puedo contar la historia de los hombres
que cayeron en Maimón
y Estero Hondo
a unos pocos disparos de Constanza
en el mismo corazón del año de 1959
puesto que todo el mundo sabe que somos el silencio
aún en horas de infortunio

No era una vez porque no puedo contar la historia
de este viejo país del que brotó la América Latina
puesto que todo el mundo sabe que brotó de sus vértebras
en una noche metálica denominada
silencio
de una vértebra llamada Esclavitud
de otra vértebra llamada Encomienda
de otra vértebra llamada Ingenio
y que de una gran vértebra dorsal le descendió completa
la Doctrina de Monroe

No contaré esta historia porque era una vez no la primera
que los hombres caían como caen los
hombres
con un gesto de fecundidad

of good and evil
stripped
face to face
menaced with a single
implacable final
decisive victory
death to death

O murdered ones
it did not happen once
because I cannot tell the story of the men
who fell at Maimón
and at Estero Hondo
a few shots from Constanza
in the very heart of 1959
because everybody knows that we are silence
even in our hours of misfortune

It did not happen once because I cannot tell the story
of this ancient country from which Latin America was
born
for everybody knows it came forth from her vertebrae
in a metallic night called
silence
from a vertebra called Slavery
from another vertebra called Encomienda
from another called Plantation
and that from a great spinal column there came down
intact
the Monroe Doctrine

I will not tell this story because it happened once and not
the first time
that men fell as men fall
with a fecund gesture
to endow with purest blood the muscles of the earth

para dotar de purísima sangre los músculos de la tierra

La espada tiene una espiga
la espiga tiene una espera
la espera tiene una sangre
que invade a la verdadera

que invade al cañaveral
litoral y cordillera
y a todos se nos parece
de perfil en la bandera

la espiga tiene una espada
la espada una calavera

Pero un día se supo que tres veces el crepúsculo
tres veces el equilibrio de la maternidad
tres la continuación de nuestro territorio
sobre la superficie de los niños adyacentes
reconocidas las tres en la movida fiebre
                de los regazos y los biberones
protegidas las tres por la andadura
                de su maternidad navegadora
                navegable
                por el espejo de su matrimonio
                por la certeza de su vecindario
                por la armonía de su crecimiento
                y su triple escuela de amparo
habían caído en un mismo silencio asesinadas
                y eran las tres hermanas Mirabal
                        oh asesinadas
entonces se supo que ya no quedaba más
                que dentro de los cañones había pavor
                que la pólvora tenía miedo
                que el estampido sudaba espanto
                y el plomo lividez

Each sword has a handle
each handle has a wait
each wait will have its blood
then true blood inundate

this blood that inundates
the canefield coast and crag
and to us all appears
in profile on the flag

each handle has a sword
each sword a skull its tag

But one day we heard that three times the dusk
three times the equilibrium of maternity
three times the extension of our territory
on the faces of children nearby
all three recognized in the feverish movement
                    of laps and feeding bottles
all three protected by the amble
                    of their navigating navigable maternity
                    by the mirror of their matrimony
                    by the self-assurance of their neighbor-
                        hood
                    by the harmony of their development
                    and by their triple school of charity
had fallen in an identical silence assassinated
                    and that they were the three sisters
                        Mirabal
                            O murdered ones
then we knew that there was nothing left
                    that terror lurked within the cannons
                    that the gunpowder was afraid
                    that the bombs sweat fear
                    and lead lividity
and that we were fully entering the death-throes of an age

y que entrábamos de lleno en la agonía de una edad
                que esto era el desenlace de la Era
                Cristiana

Oh dormidas
oh delicadas
qué injuria de meditar

El mes de noviembre descendía sobre los hombros
como los árboles aún debajo de la noche y aún
                        dando
                        sombra

Oh eternas

El péndulo palpitaba las horas del municipio
y el pequeño reloj destilaba en silencio gota a gota
veinticinco visiones de un día llamado de noviembre

Pero aún no era el fin
oh dormidas
aún no era el fin
                no era el fin

Segundo tiempo

Cuando supe que una pequeña inflamación del suelo
en el Cementerio de Arlington
se cubría de flores y manojos de lágrimas
con insistencia de pabellones y caballos nocturnos
alrededor de un toque de afligida trompeta
cuando todo periódico se abría en esas páginas
cuando se hicieron rojas todas las rosas amarillas
                en Dallas
                Texas

that this was the end of the Christian Era

O sleeping
O delicate ones
what a wrong to meditate upon

The month of November fell upon the shoulders
like trees still beneath the night and still
                                    giving shade

O immortal ones

The pendulum ticks out the hours of the municipality
and the small clock silently filters drop by drop
twenty-five visions of a day they say is of November

But still it was not the end
O sleeping ones
it was not yet the end
                        not yet the end

Act II

When I heard a small inflammation of the earth
in Arlington Cemetery
was being cloaked in flowers and clusters of tears
with the insistence of banners and black horses
by the moan of a grief-stricken trumpet
when every paper opened on those pages
when every yellow rose turned red
            in Dallas
            Texas
I said to myself
                    how presidential
                    the new month of November

221

me dije
                    como era presidencial
                    el nuevo mes de noviembre
            ya millones de seres tocaron lo imposible
ya millones de seres ya millones de estatuas ya millones
            de muros de columnas y de máquinas
            comprendieron de súbito
            que el asesinato
                    no ha sido
            ni un fragmento de minuto
calculado solamente para las cabezas semicoloniales
                    y sustantivas
            de las tres hermanas Mirabal
                    sino
que este inédito estilo de la muerte
producto de las manos de los hombres
            de manos de hermanos
            (por todo el siglo)
            muerte sana y artesana
            (por todo el mundo),
            provista de catálogo
            (por todo el tiempo)
de número de serie o serial number
y venida de fuera o made in usa
fría inalterable desdeñosa desde arriba desde entonces
esta muerte
            esta muerte
                    esta muerte
asume contenido universal
forzosamente adscrita a la condición
            del ser humano
en cuyo espectro solar figuran todas las fórmulas per-
    sonales
            y todas las instancias puras
            del individuo
            tal
            como va por la calle

now millions of people touched the impossible
now millions of people now millions of statues now
   millions
         of walls columns and machines
         understood suddenly
         that assassination
                  was not
         even a fragment of a minute
measured merely for the semi-colonial and prominent
   heads
         of the three sisters Mirabal
                  but that
this unexpected style of death
the product of men's hands
         of brothers' hands
         (throughout the century)
         a death clean and craftsman-like
         (throughout the world)
         provided with a catalogue
         (throughout all time)
a *número de serie* or serial number
and imported or made in U.S.A.
cold unalterable disdainful above us from
then on
         this death
                  this death
                           this death
assumes universal meaning
affixed by force to the condition
         of human beings
whose solar ghost includes every personal formula
         and every pristine state
         of the individual
         just as
         he moves through the street
a city dweller having every right
essential perpetuator of the population index

como habitante de la ciudad con todo su derecho como
continuador esencial del índice de población o séase
representante manufacturero indiferente agente de
seguros repartidor de leche asalariado guarda
campestre administrador o sabio o poeta o portador
de una botella de entusiasmo etílico donde están
convocadas todas las palabras
 ciclamen platabanda metempsícosis
 canícula claudia clavicémbalo
 cartulario venático vejiga
 trepa caterva mequetrefe
 primicia verdulero postulante
  palabras todas sustitutivas
  palabras pronunciables
  en lugar de presuntas actitudes
  y todas las maldiciones y protestas
  y las posiciones geométricas igual
  que la rotura del sentido igual
  que la rotura de una biela igual
  que el desgarrón de la barriga igual
  mente todo desquiciado y rom
  pido todo maligno y amargo
  todo reducido a sombra
   y nadidad y oscuridad
   y estadidad
  palabras mentirosas llenas
  de contenido impronunciable
  y desechos del organismo
  de cualquier muchacha igual
  que de cualquier cochero igual
  que el choque de la portezuela
  del catafalco igual
fue esta universal investidura de la que no está exento
  nadie nadie
  ni yo
  ni tú
  ni nosotros ni ellos ni nadie

224

or as a representative indifferent manufacturer insurance
     agent
milkman wage-earner rural guard administrator or
     scholar or poet or bearer
of a bottle of ethylic enthusiasm where all words come
     together
               cyclamen boundary metempsychosis
               canicule claudia clavichord
               spleen cartulary cranky
               cretin social-climber crowd
               first-fruits postulant provider
                    substitute words all
                    words one can say
                    in place of presumed attitudes
                    and every curse and protest
                    and geometrical positions just like
                    the rupture of a sense just like
                    the fracture of an axle just like
                    the belly's laceration and everything
                    identically become unhinged and bro-
                    ken and perverse and bitter and
                    reduced to shadow
                         and nothingness and darkness
                              and suspension
                    lying words full of
                    unspeakable meaning
                    and the remains of
                    any young girl's body
                    like to that of any coachman
                    like to the slamming of the door
                    of the funeral carriage like too
was this universal investiture from which no one is
     exempt
                    no one
                    not you
                    not me
                    not us not them no one

225

                    podridamente nadie
                    nadie
desde el mismo momento en que fueron golpeadas
            ciertamente
                    profesionalmente
                    maquinalmente
            tres de las hermanas Mirabal
                    hasta llegar
                    en punto
                    exactamente
                    al
                    fin fin fin
                    de la Era
                    Cristiana

(Oigamos
oigamos
esto retumba en el
más
absoluto silencio

muchas unidades navales en todos los océanos inician
                    su hundimiento después
                    de deglutir los archipiélagos
                    de miel envenenada
grandes ejércitos destacados en la entrada del mundo
                    comienzan a reintegrarse
                    a sus viejos orígenes
                    de sudor y clamor
                    en el seno de las masas
                    populares
en el más
en el más categórico y el más
absoluto
silencio)

              damning decay no one
                  no one
from the very moment the three sisters Mirabal
          were skillfully
                  professionally
                  mechanically
          struck down
                  to our arrival
                  exactly
                  on time
                  at the
                  end end end
                  of the Christian Era

(Listen
listen
it resounds
in the most
absolute silence

several naval units on every ocean are beginning
                  to sink after
                  swallowing archipelagos
                  of poisoned honey
huge armies stationed at the door to the world
                  are starting to return
                  to their ancient beginnings
                  of sweat and noise
                  in the heart of the popular
                  masses
in the most
in the most categorical and most
absolute
silence)

Because
there are columns of impetuous marble that surrender not
      to time

227

Porque
hay columnas de mármol impetuoso no rendidas al
     tiempo
y pirámides absolutas erigidas sobre las civilizaciones
que no pueden resistir la muerte de ciertas mariposas

y calles enteras de urbes imperiales llenas de transeúntes
sostenidas desde la base por tirantes y cuerdas de
     armonía
de padre a hija de joven a jovenzuela de escultor a modelo

y artilleros atormentados por la duda bajo el cráneo
cuyas miradas vuelan millares de leguas sobre el
     horizonte
para alcanzar un rostro flotante más allá de los mares

y camioneros rubios de grandes ojos azules obviamente
     veloces
que son los que dibujan o trazan las grandes carreteras
y transportan la grasa que engendra las bombas
     nucleares

y portaaviones nuevos de planchas adineradas
          invencibles
insospechablemente unidos al rumbo del acero y del
     petróleo
y gigantes de miedo y fronteras de radar y divisiones
     aéreas
y artefactos electrónicos y máquinas infernales dirigidas
de la tierra hacia el mar y del cielo a la tierra y viceversa
que no pueden
          resistir
               la muerte
                    de ciertas
                         mariposas

porque la vida entera se sostiene sobre un eje de sangre
y hay pirámides muertas sobre el suelo que humillaron

228

and mighty pyramids built upon civilizations
that cannot but succumb to certain butterflies

and whole streets of imperial cities full of passersby
supported at the base by suspenders and cords of har-
      mony
from father to daughter from young man to younger
      woman from sculpture to model

and gunners tormented by a doubt under the skull
whose glances fly thousands of miles beyond the horizon
to reach a floating face beyond the seas

and blond blue-eyed truckdrivers manifestly swift
who are the ones that outline or lay out the great
      highways
and carry the grease created by nuclear bombs

and new aircraft carriers with heavy armor-plate
            impregnable
unsuspectingly joined to the destiny of steel and oil
and giants of fear and frontiers of radar and aircraft
      divisions
electronic artifacts and infernal machines
            launched
from land to sea from the air to the ground
            and viceversa
which cannot
      avoid
            succumbing
                  to certain
                        butterflies

because all of life is sustained on an axis of blood
and there are pyramids dead on the ground that they
      humiliated
because murder must have respect to be respected

229

porque el asesinato tiene que respetar si quiere ser
   respetado

y los grandes imperios deben medir sus pasos respetuosos
porque lo necesariamente débil es lo necesariamente
   fuerte
cuando la sociedad establecida muere por los cuatro
   costados
cuando hay una hora en los relojes antiguos y los
   modernos
que anuncia que los más grandes imperios del planeta
no pueden resistir la muerte muerte
         de ciertas ciertas
                  debilidades amén
                        de mariposas

and the great empires must measure their steps with
    some respect
because the necessarily weak are the necessarily strong
when society as it is is dying on all sides
when there is one hour on the old and modern clocks
that says the world's great empires
cannot avoid succumbing succumbing
        to certain certain
                weaknesses amen
                    to butterflies

[Translated by Robert Márquez]

Ecuador

Jorge Enrique Adoum (1926–), a native of Quito, Ecuador, studied philosophy, law, and economics at the Central University of Ecuador and the University of Santiago de Chile. He has served as director of the publishing house of the Casa de la Cultura Ecuatoriana, as National Director of Culture attached to the Ministry of Education, and as secretary to the Institute of Theater and Folklore. He brings to his plays the same militancy evident in his verse. His recent play *El sol bajo las patas de los caballos* identifies the aims and techniques of the Spanish conquistadores with those of contemporary U.S. imperialism.

Adoum was Pablo Neruda's private secretary for a short time during the forties and, not surprisingly, came under his influence. But, forsaking neither his interest in the Ecuadorian landscape and its inhabitants nor his militant convictions, he went on to find a voice wholly his own. He has created a poetry whose language, set against a muted elegiac tone, has become steadily more rigorous, incisive, austere, and at the same time more playful, witty, and inventive. His recent *Prepoemas en postespa-*

ñol is the best example of this particular evolution of his style: with its abundance of neologisms, word plays, and double entendres it nearly defies translation.

Adoum, whose work has won him various prizes (including the Casa de las Américas poetry prize and the National Prize for Poetry in Ecuador), is very probably the most popular and influential poet among his country's younger writers. When Ecuador was taken over by a military dictatorship, Adoum became one of its severest critics and his poems had to be circulated clandestinely; he eventually went into exile. A much traveled writer, he has lived in Africa, India, Japan, and China. He now lives in Paris, where he works for UNESCO.

His works to date include *Ecuador amargo* (1949), *Los cuadernos de la tierra* (1951–1962), *Yo me fuí con tu nombre por la tierra* (1964), the only partly published *Curriculum mortis*, and the above-mentioned *Prepoemas*. Selections from all of these appear in *Informe personal sobre la situación*, published in 1973, from which the following are taken.

Condecoración y ascenso

Homenaje a Newton Moreno

¿Has preguntado, di, te has preguntado,
cuando el fácil cuchillo metió su lámina
abusiva en el costado, hurgándole su hueso
de agonía, dónde está el centinela, dónde
la guardia?

¿No preguntaste nunca, nunca
supiste dónde estaba cuando la pisada
de torpes poderosas suelas vino a espantar
la iguana de las islas mayúsculas, vino
a orinar en nuestros pedestales, vino
a pegar su chicle en nuestro idioma?

Estaba firme donde toda la vida
ha estado, disparándonos, templando
la red del tiro contra el pez del hombre,
puntería sin fecha fija contra el desocupado, Alto
Mando contra los panaderos para hacerlos
leña a la salida de la harina, matándonos de octubre
a julio y de mayo a enero cuando aprendíamos
a combatir con piedrecillas, ramas
de álamo, poemas: chatarra contra los cuadernos
de filosofía, chatarra contra el alba
de otro día.

Ahora está también
donde toda la vida, agonizando indios
en la cárcel y el surco, abriéndoles la voz
a puñetazos. Si no han hablado en cuatrocientos
años de golpes prehistóricos, terrestres, si no
han dicho nada ni de sus otras muertes.

Medals and Promotion

In homage to Newton Moreno

Have you asked, tell me, have you wondered
when the facile knife inserted its abusive blade
into his side, gnawing his anguished bone,
where is the sentry, where the guard?

Haven't you ever asked, ever known
where he was when the tramp of boots,
powerful and clumsy, came to frighten
the iguanas from the larger islands,
came to piss on our pedestals,
to stick their chewing gum on our language?

He was where he's been all his life,
shooting at us, softening
the casting net against the fish of man,
aiming with no set date against the idle,
the High Command against the bakers, knocking them
to smithereens as they left their flour, killing us
from October to July, from May to January,
as we learned to fight with pebbles, poplar
branches, poems: scrap iron against notebooks of philos-
    ophy,
scrap iron against the dawning
of another day.

    Now he is also
where he's been all his life, dying
with Indians in jail, in the ditch,
making way for their voices with his fists.
Because they haven't spoken in four hundred years
of terrestrial, prehistoric blows, because
they haven't said anything even of their other deaths.

Desde lo inmemorial de esta fotografía
están dándole coces entre todos, dándoles
Dios, Patria y Libertad para que aprendan.
¿Nuevos amos con estrellas en el páramo
del hombro? No, nuevos mayordomos, generales,
nuevos aciales para la antiguedad del odio, como
si se tratara de un remordimiento en su espejo
tenebroso, vengándose del padre o más bien
del ovario, por suprimir su piel color
de América, su pelo pensativo, su cornada,
para que nadie grite Traidor con todo
el cuerpo.

　　No lo creíais, madres, entre tanta
leche y cacerolas, pero las camisetas del hijo
ensangrentadas, sus tambores, pero los dientes
que os devuelven de la celda, pero el cadáver.
Me han matado así entre otros al amigo
con quien cuando muchachos disputábamos
el único Lautréamont que llegó al pueblo.
Era tan miope que debió acercarse mucho
para verme y cuando me di cuenta había entrado
en mi alma. Así entró en la ley, lleno de lentes,
buscándole un rincón, un banco donde pueda
sentarse a no morir el campesino y su gallina.
Lo han matado por eso, me lo han muerto
a golpes, a frío y golpes de oficial, dejándole
migas de sol cada tres días, pateándole por dentro
a Maldoror antiburgués y justo, golpeándolo
como una puerta contra las paredes de cuarteles,
hospitales, tumbas.
　　　　　　　　Su borbotón de bueno, el triste
pie, sus anteojos que no fueron a su entierro.

Están matando, todavía, donde toda la vida
pagamos por su oficio eficaz, profesional.

Pero, carajo, también se resucita por capricho.

236

Since time immemorial when this photograph was taken
they have been getting kicked, been given God,
Fatherland, and Liberty that they might learn.
New masters with stars on barren shoulders?
No, new overseers, generals, new whips
for the antiquity of hate, as if it were
a question of some guilt in their dark mirror,
of taking revenge on the father, or rather
on the ovary, for suppressing their America-colored skin,
their pensive hair, the thrust of their horn,
so no one would cry Traitor with his
whole body.

    In the midst of so much milk and so many pots,
mothers, you didn't believe it,
but what about your sons' bloody shirts,
their drums, the teeth returned to you
from the cell, what about the corpse?
That's how, among others, they have killed my friend,
the one with whom as boys I used to fight over
the only Lautréamont to reach the town.
He was so myopic he had to move quite close
to see me, and before I realized it he had moved
into my soul. So he went into law, all spectacles,
searching for a corner, a bench to sit on,
to keep the peasant and his hen alive.
That's why they murdered him, beat him to death,
with cold-blooded, officer blows, leaving him
crumbs of sun every three days, kicking the innards
of his Maldoror, the just and anti-bourgeois,
slamming him like a door against the walls
of barracks, hospitals, tombs.
              His good man's stammerings,
the melancholy foot, the spectacles that never made the
    burial.

They're still murdering, where all our lives
we pay for their calling's professional efficiency.

But, shit, one can also revive on a whim.

[*Translated by Elinor Randall and Robert Márquez*]

Pasadología

a contrapelo a contramano
contra la corriente
a contralluvia
a contracorazón y contraolvido
a contragolpe de lo sido
sobreviviendo a contracónyuge
a contradestino y contra los gobiernos
que son todo lo absurdo del destino
a contralucidez y contralógica
a contrageografía (porque era
contra pasaportes dictadores continentes
y contra la costumbre
que es más peor que nuestros dictadores)
contra tú y tus tengo miedo
contra yo y mi certeza al revés
contra nosotros mismos
o sea contratodo

y todo para qué

Pastology

against the grain against the current
and against the mainstream
uprain
against the heart and counter to oblivion
in counteraction to everything that's ever been
surviving against the conjugal
counter to destiny and against governments
that are all that is absurd in destiny
against lucidity and against logic
against geography (because it was
against passports dictators continents
and against custom
the worst of all our dictators)
against you and your I'm afraid
against me and my reverse certainty
against our very selves
or rather against everything

and everything for what

[*Translated by Robert Márquez*]

El Salvador

Roque Dalton (1933–   ) is one of the group of Salvadorian writers and poets whose work began to appear around 1956. He studied law and anthropology at the universities of El Salvador, Chile, and Mexico. In 1955 he became a member of the Communist Party of El Salvador and he has been continuously active in the revolutionary movement there. He has gone underground and been imprisoned several times, and periods of exile have taken him to Guatemala, Mexico, and Czechoslovakia. While under sentence of death several years ago, an earthquake destroyed the walls of his cell and gave him an unexpected opportunity for escape. He went into exile in Cuba, where he now lives and works, remaining in close contact with the movement in his own country.

Dalton's work reflects his long dedication to the revolution and is based on the premise that "anguish does exist." To give voice to that anguish, to concrete reality, he tells us in a poem of the same name, the poet must rescue "the ugly words" which "poetry once despised." Already recognized as one of El Salvador's major younger poets, the skill, consistency, and vigor with which he has created poetry under this mandate won him an honorable mention from the international jury of the Casa de Las Américas poetry contest in 1963 for the collection *El turno del ofendido*. In 1969 he won first prize for *Taberna y otros lugares*. Dalton's poems and essays have appeared in journals, magazines, and anthologies throughout the continent. His other published works include *La ventana en el rostro* (1961), *El mar* (1962), *Los testimonios* (1964), *Poemas* (1967), and a monograph on the life and work of César Vallejo (1963).

The poems that are reprinted here are taken from *El turno del ofendido* and *Taberna y otros lugares*.

Sobre dolores de cabeza

Es bello ser comunista,
aunque cause muchos dolores de cabeza.

Y es que el dolor de cabeza de los comunistas
se supone histórico, es decir
que no cede ante las tabletas analgésicas
sino sólo ante la realización del Paraíso en la tierra.
Así es la cosa.

Bajo el capitalismo nos duele la cabeza
y nos arrancan la cabeza.
En la lucha por la Revolución la cabeza es una bomba de
    retardo.

En la construcción socialista
planificamos el dolor de cabeza
lo cual no lo hace escasear, sino todo lo contrario.

El comunismo será, entre otras cosas,
una aspirina del tamaño del sol.

On Headaches

To be a communist is a beautiful thing,
though it causes many headaches.

And the problem is the communist headache
is, we assume, historical:
it will not cede to analgesic tablets
but only to the realization of Paradise on earth.
That's the way it is.

Under capitalism our head aches
and is torn from us.
In the struggle for the Revolution
the head is a delayed action bomb.

Under socialist construction
we plan the headache
which does not minimize it, quite the contrary.

Communism, among other things, will be
an aspirin the size of the sun.

[*Translated by Robert Márquez*]

OEA

El Presidente de mi país
se llama hoy por hoy Coronel Fidel Sánchez
    Hernández.
Pero el General Somoza, Presidente de Nicaragua,
también es Presidente de mi país.
Y el General Stroessner, Presidente del Paraguay,
es también un poquito Presidente de mi país, aunque
    menos
que el Presidente de Honduras o sea
el General López Arellano, y más que el Presidente
    de Haití,
Monsieur Duvalier.
Y el Presidente de los Estados Unidos es más
    Presidente de mi país
que el Presidente de mi país,
ese que, como dije, hoy por hoy,
se llama Coronel Fidel Sánchez Hernández.

OAS

The President of my country
is for the moment called Colonel Fidel Sánchez
    Hernández.
But General Somoza, the President of Nicaragua,
is also the President of my country.
And General Stroessner, the President of Paraguay,
is also a little the President of my country, although
    less
than the President of Honduras or rather
General López Arellano, and more than the President
    of Haiti,
Monsieur Duvalier.
And the President of the United States is more
    the President of my country
than the President of my country,
the one who, as I said, is for the moment
called Colonel Fidel Sánchez Hernández.

[*Translated by Robert Márquez*]

Karl Marx

Desde los ojos nobles de león brillando al fondo de tus
    barbas
desde la humedad polvorienta en las bibliotecas mal
    alumbradas
desde los lácteos brazos de Jenny de Westfalia
desde el remolino de la miseria en los exilios lentos y fríos
desde las cóleras en aquellas redacciones renanas llenas
    de humo
desde la fiebre como un pequeño mundo de luz en las
    noches sin fin
le corregiste la renca labor de Dios
tú oh gran culpable de la esperanza
oh responsable entre los responsables
de la felicidad que sigue caminando

Karl Marx

From the noble eyes of the lion shining deep in your beard
from dank and dusty libraries dimly lit
from the milky arms of Jenny of Westphalia
from the vortex of misery in cold slow exiles
from the anger in those smoke-filled Rhenish pressrooms
from fevers like a little world of light in the endless nights
you righted the crippled work of God
yes great guilty man of hope
responsible among the responsible
O man of happiness still walking

[Translated by Elinor Randall]

Dos guerrilleros griegos:
un viejo y un traidor

A la memoria de Nikos Kazantzakis,
que dio los personajes

Panayotaros nunca le puso rosas al fusil.

A sus primeras víctimas en las emboscadas
se negó a enterrar como era la costumbre:
las dejó para siempre huérfanas de la cruz
mientras el duro sol reía afilando sus garras.

Entonces había harto vino ácido y queso sustancial
y por las noches Demetrio el panadero
tocaba para bailes grotescos
su pequeña guitarra.

Panayotaros se fue cuando nos vino el hambre
y hasta las culebras llegaban a morir cerca de nuestros
    pies.
Ahora será ministro o algo así
a juzgar por el respeto con que pronuncian su nombre
todos los médicos en este hospital horrible de olvida-
dos . . .

Two Greek Guerrillas:
An Old Man and a Traitor

> *To the memory of Nikos Kazantzakis,*
> *whose characters they are*

Panayotaros never put roses in his gun.

He denied burial to his early victims
in the ambushes as was the custom:
left them forever orphans of the cross
while the cruel sun laughed sharpening its claws.

There was plenty of sour wine and real cheese in those
    days
and at night Demetrios the baker
would strum his small guitar
for grotesque dances.

Panayotaros went away when hunger came
and even the snakes began dying at our feet.
Now he'll be a minister or some such thing
judging by how much respect the doctors
in this vile hospital for the forgotten are giving to his
    name . . .

[Translated by Elinor Randall]

Guatemala

Otto René Castillo (1936–1967) was born in Quezalten-
ango, Guatemala. A student activist and organizer since
his high school days, he was exiled for the first time in
1954, at the age of seventeen, shortly after the CIA-engi-
neered coup that deposed Jacobo Arbenz. He was impris-
oned and exiled several times during the next decade but
managed to continue his studies, to found an experimen-
tal theater group, to organize and edit radical student
newspapers, and to become one of his country's—and
Latin America's—most important younger poets, al-
though he published only two books of verse during his
brief and heroic life. His influence, as poet and as
revolutionary, remains significant throughout Central
America.

After studying law at the University of Guatemala,
Castillo went on to study literature and cinematography
at the University of Leipzig. In 1955 he shared the Central
American Prize for Poetry with Roque Dalton. A year
later, returning from his first exile, he won the "Auto-
nomía" Prize in Guatemala City, and he was again
honored for his verse by the World Festival of Youth in
1957. It was not until 1964, however, that he finally

published his first book, *Tecún Uman*. By the time *Vámonos patria a caminar* appeared in 1965, Castillo was already recognized as one of the most promising of the new young poets.

In 1966 Castillo was imprisoned and exiled once again by the government of President Peralta Azurdia. He returned to Guatemala shortly afterward and immediately joined the Revolutionary Armed Forces (FAR), serving as a Director of Propaganda. In March 1967 his guerrilla group was ambushed. Castillo and one of his comrades were captured, brutally tortured for four days, and finally burned alive.

The poetry of Otto René Castillo is an unequivocal testimony to his profound and sensitive humanity, to his deep affection for his native Guatemala, and to the struggle for its liberation to which he was dedicated and to which he gave his life. The poems that follow, most of which appeared originally in *Vámonos patria a caminar*, are taken from the more recent edition of his collected work, published in Havana in 1971 in recognition of his caliber as a poet and revolutionary.

Informe de una justicia

Tal vez no lo imagines,
pero aquí,
delante de mis ojos,
una anciana,
Damiana Murcia, v. de García,
de 77 años de ceniza,
debajo de la lluvia,
junto a sus muebles
rotos, sucios, viejos,
recibe
sobre la curva de su espalda
toda la injusticia
maldita
del sistema de lo mío y lo tuyo.

Por ser pobre,
los juzgados de los ricos
ordenaron desahucio.
Quizá ya no conozcas
más esta palabra.
Así de noble
es el mundo donde vives.
Poco a poco
van perdiendo ahí
su crueldad
las amargas palabras.
Y cada día,
como el amanecer,
surgen nuevos vocablos,
todos llenos de amor
y de ternura para el hombre.

Desahucio.
¿Cómo aclararte?

Report of an Injustice

Perhaps you won't believe it,
but here,
before my eyes,
an old woman,
Damiana Murcia, widow of García,
77 years of ashes,
under the rain,
beside her furniture,
broken, dirty, old,
receives
all the monstrous injustice
of the system of "yours" and "mine"
on the curve of her back.

For being poor
the courts of the rich
ordered eviction.
Perhaps you no longer
know the meaning of that word.
That's how noble the world
you live in is.
Little by little
bitter words
lose their cruelty there.
And each day,
like the dawn,
new words emerge,
all full of love
and tenderness for man.

Eviction.
How can I explain?
You know,
here when you can't pay the rent,

Sabes, aquí,
cuando
no puedes pagar el alquiler,
las autoridades de los ricos
vienen y te lanzan
con todas tus cosas
a la calle.
Y te quedas sin techo
para la altura de tus sueños.
Eso significa la palabra
desahucio: soledad
abierta al cielo, al ojo juzgor
y miserable.

Este es el mundo libre, dicen.
¡Qué bien que tú
ya no conozcas
estas horrendas libertades!

Damiana Murcia, v. de García,
es muy pequeña,
sabes,
y ha de tener tantísimo frío.
¡Qué grande ha de ser su soledad!

No te imaginas
lo que duelen estas injusticias.
Normales son entre nostros.
Lo anormal es la ternura
y el odio que se tiene a la pobreza.
Por eso hoy más que siempre
amo tu mundo.
Lo entiendo,
lo glorifico
atronado de cósmicos orgullos.
Y me pregunto:
¿Por qué, entre nosotros,

the authorities of the rich
come and throw you and all you own
into the street.
And you're left without a roof
for the height of your dreams.
That's what the word eviction means:
loneliness open to the sky,
to the judging and merciless eye.

This is the free world, they say.
How lucky that you
no longer know
these terrible freedoms!

Damiana Murcia, widow of García
is very small,
you know,
and must be very cold.
How great her loneliness must be!

You can't imagine
how these injustices hurt.
Among us they are normal.
What's abnormal is tenderness
and the hate one has of poverty.
And so today more than ever
I love your world.
Understand
and glorify it
shot through with cosmic pride.
And I ask myself:
Why do the old
suffer among us so,
if age comes to us all
one day?
But the worst of all is the habit.
Man loses his humanity

sufren tanto los ancianos,
si todos se harán viejos algún día?
Pero lo peor de todo
es la costumbre.
El hombre pierde su humanidad
y ya no tiene importancia para él
lo enorme del dolor ajeno,
y come,
y ríe
y se olvida de todo.
Yo no quiero
para mi patria
estas cosas.
Yo no quiero
para ninguno
estas cosas.
Yo no quiero
para nadie en el mundo
estas cosas.
Y digo yo,
por qué el dolor
debe llevar
claramente establecida su aureola.
Este es el mundo libre, dicen.

      Ahora compárame en el tiempo.
Y dile a tus amigos
que la risa mía
se ha vuelto una mueca
grotesca
en medio de la cara.
Y que digo amén a su mundo.
Y ló construyan bello.
Y que me alegro mucho
de que ya no conozcan
injusticias
tan hondas y abundantes.

and is no longer concerned
with the huge pain of another,
and he eats,
he laughs,
he forgets everything.
I don't want these things
for my country.
I don't want these things
for anyone.
I don't want these things
for anyone in the world.
And I say I
because pain
ought to have
its unmistakable identity.
This is the free world, they say.

     Look at me now.
And tell your friends
my laughter
has turned into a grotesque
smirk
in the middle of my face.
That I say amen to their world.
Build it beautifully.
And that I am so glad
they no longer know
injustices
so deep and so abundant.

[*Translated by Margaret Randall and Robert Márquez*]

Revolución

Los que no ven
nos dicen ciegos,
pero tú nos has enseñado
a ver el color
del tiempo que viene.

Los que no oyen
nos dicen sordos,
pero tú nos has enseñado
a escuchar en todas partes
el ágil sonido
de la ternura humana.

Los cobardes nos dicen cobardes,
pero contigo nos enfrentamos
a las sombras
y les cambiamos el rostro.
Los criminales nos dicen criminales,
pero contigo revivimos la esperanza,
le marcamos el alto al crimen,
a la prostitución,
al hambre.
Y le ponemos ojos,
voz,
oídos,
alma,
al corazón del hombre.
Los racistas nos dicen antihumanos,
pero contigo le damos al odio
su tumba mundial
en la ciudad de los abrazos.

Nos dicen tantas cosas.

Revolution

Those who can't see
call us blind,
but you have shown us
how to see the color
of the time to come.

Those who can't hear
call us deaf,
but you have shown us
how to hear everywhere
the supple sound
of human tenderness.

The cowards call us cowards,
but with you we face
the darkness,
change its face.
The criminals call us criminals,
but with you we revive hope,
put an end to crime,
to prostitution,
hunger.
And we give eyes,
a voice,
ears,
a soul,
to the heart of man.
The racists call us anti-human,
but with you we give hate
its universal tomb
in the city of embraces.

They call us so many things.

Y los que las pronuncian
olvidan,
estúpidos que son,
que sus nietos
amarán mañana
jubilosamente
la palabra estrellada
de tu nombre:
    revolución.

And those who say them
forget,
they are so stupid,
that tomorrow
their grandchildren
will joyously
fall in love with
the star-filled letters
of your name:
                    revolution.

[*Translated by Robert Márquez*]

Intelectuales apolíticos

I

Un día,
los intelectuales apolíticos
de mi país
serán interrogados
por el hombre
sencillo
de nuestro pueblo.

Se les preguntará
sobre lo que hicieron
cuando
la patria se apagaba
lentamente,
como una hoguera dulce,
pequeña y sola.

No serán interrogados
sobre sus trajes,
ni sobre sus largas
siestas
después de la merienda,
tampoco sobre sus estériles
combates con la nada,
ni sobre su ontológica
manera
de llegar a las monedas.
No se les interrogará
sobre la mitología griega,
ni sobre el asco
que sintieron de sí
cuando alguien, en su fondo,
se disponía a morir cobardemente.

Apolitical Intellectuals

I

One day
the apolitical
intellectuals
of my country
will be interrogated
by the simplest
of our people.

They will be asked
what they did
when their nation died out
slowly,
like a sweet fire,
small and alone.

No one will ask them
about their dress,
their long siestas
after lunch,
no one will want to know
about their sterile struggles
with "the idea
of the void"
no one will care about the way
they ontologically acquired their funds.
They won't be questioned
on Greek mythology,
or about the self-disgust they felt
when someone within them
began to die
the coward's death.

Nada se les preguntará
sobre sus justificaciones
absurdas
crecidas a la sombra
de una mentira rotunda.

II

    Ese día vendrán
los hombres sencillos,
los que nunca cupieron
en los libros y versos
de los intelectuales apolíticos
pero que llegaban todos los días
a dejarles la leche y el pan,
los huevos y las tortillas,
los que les cosían la ropa,
los que les manejaban los carros,
les cuidaban sus perros y jardines,
y trabajaban para ellos,
y preguntarán:
"¿Qué hicisteis cuando los pobres
sufrían y se quemaban en ellos,
gravemente, la ternura y la vida?"

III

    Intelectuales apolíticos
de mi dulce país,
no podréis responder nada.

    Os devorará un buitre de silencio
las entrañas.
Os roerá el alma

They'll be asked nothing
about their absurd
justifications
born in the shadow
of the total lie.

II

On that day
the simple men will come,
those who had no place
in the books and poems
of the apolitical intellectuals
but daily delivered
their bread and milk,
their tortillas and eggs,
those who mended their clothes,
those who drove their cars,
who cared for their dogs and gardens,
and worked for them,
and they'll ask:
"What did you do when the poor
suffered, when tenderness
and life
burned out in them?"

III

Apolitical intellectuals
of my sweet country,
you will not be able to answer.

A vulture of silence
will eat your guts.

267

vuestra propia miseria,
y callaréis,
avergonzados de vosotros.

Your own misery
will gnaw at your souls.
And you will be mute
in your own shame.

[*Translated by Margaret Randall*]

Viudo del mundo

Compañeros míos
yo cumplo mi papel
luchando
con lo mejor que tengo.
Qué lástima que tuviera
vida tan pequeña,
para tragedia tan grande
y para tanto trabajo.

No me apena dejaros.
Con vosotros queda mi esperanza.

Sabéis,
me hubiera gustado
llegar hasta el final
de todos estos ajetreos
con vosotros
en medio de júbilo
tan alto. Lo imagino
y no quisiera marcharme.
Pero lo sé, oscuramente
me lo dice la sangre
con su tímida voz,
que muy pronto
quedaré viudo de mundo.

Widowed of the World

Compañeros
I do my job
fighting
as best I can.
A shame to have a life
so short,
with the tragedy so great
and so much to be done.

It doesn't hurt me to leave you.
My hopes remain with you.

Listen,
I would have liked
to come to the end
of all these confusions
with you
sharing a so intense
jubilation. I imagine that
and hate to leave.
But I know, darkly
my blood tells me
in its timid voice
that soon I shall be
widowed of the world.

[*Translated by Tim Reynolds*]

Marco Antonio Flores (1937–) studied medicine and psychology at the University of San Carlos. He later traveled to Cuba to study cinematography for a year and, in addition to being a poet, is also a film director. He has traveled extensively throughout Europe and Latin America and was for a time a correspondent for *El corno emplumado*, the bilingual literary journal published in Mexico until 1968.

A close friend of Otto René Castillo—the poet referred to in his poem "On Jail"—Flores shares that poet's directness of expression, combativeness, and fierce tenderness. He has been the recipient of various prizes and awards, including first prize in the Floral Games of Chiquimula, Guatemala (1961) and the Central American Poetry Prize sponsored by El Salvador (1962). He has published anthologies of Czech and Cuban poetry as well as his own works. To date these include *La voz acumulada* (1964) and *Muros de luz* (1968), from which the following are taken.

De la cárcel

Alejandra
hoy ya tienes un mes
Cuando las fiestas pascuas
se alejaban
tú naciste
Yo estoy preso
guardado
de la luz
Pero te juro niña
que por este balbuceo
que me roban
de tu primera edad
habrán de padecer
hambre de amor
Los condeno
con toda mi violencia
a quedarse sin lágrimas
sin agonía corta
sin mamá
Mi lengua
mis manos
mis ojeras
encadenaron a sus pies
los cerdos
En la noche
            llevando entre la piel
los alfileres
del susto
del silencio
marchamos con mi amigo
a la cárcel
Mi amigo es un poeta
muy pálido
muy serio

On Jail

Alejandra
today you're already a month old
You were born
when the Christmas holidays
were coming to an end
I am a prisoner
being kept
from the light
But I swear to you my child
that for the babble
of your first years
that they now take from me
they will suffer
the hunger of love
I condemn them
with my every ounce of violence
to be left without tears
with no quick painless death
without a mother
My tongue
my hands
the rings under my eyes
enchained their feet
the pigs
At night
            the needle-points of fear
of silence
on our skin
we marched off to jail
with my friend
My friend is a poet
very pale
very serious
always smiling

275

muy sonriente
Marchamos con el miedo
sujeto
en las almenas del estómago
                        muy hondo
y nuestras caras
de santones lúgubres
reían
Nuestras manos
                temblaban de traidoras que son
pero no las mirábamos
Estaba muy lejana la mañana
con su baño de luz
El mundo está partido
                        niña mía
De un lado están
los ángeles y dios
y del otro
                nosotros
De un lado está la sombra
y las sotanas
y al frente
los hombres con su bandera roja
De un lado
los birretes y los bancos
y aguantando
tu padre y sus amigos

No te confundas hija
tu madre está conmigo
desde esta madrugada
que voy preso
y juntos
aunque faltemos
de tu lado
habremos de mostrarte
el lado de la paz

We went off with our fear
tied
to the merlons deep down
                    in our stomachs
and our gloomy-saint faces
laughed
Our hands trembled
                    traitors that they are
but we didn't look at them
Morning was very far away
with its bath of light
The world is split in two
                    my child
On one side god and the angels
and on the other
            us
On one side the darkness
and cassocks
and facing them
the men with their red flag
On one side
the birettas and the banks
and hanging on
your father and his friends

Don't worry child
your mother has been with me
since this morning
when I was arrested
and together
even if we're not
by your side
we will show you
the side of peace
and its flag
The rotted apple
of its eyes

277

con su bandera
La manzana podrida
de sus ojos
hurgó entre
mi paciencia
¿Tienes hijos
quizá?
me preguntó
Y nació tu estatura
en su fichero:
                    "Ya tiene treinta días
                    y me alegro
                    Me alegro por sus ojos
                    por su crecimiento
                    por su risa
                    que no ha nacido aún
                    y por sus manos
                    que serán buenas"
Así le contesté
Me contempló extrañado
Tal vez
se figure que estoy loco

Con todas las luciérnagas
del mundo
haré un muro de luz
para alumbrar
la sombra de las cárceles
Tomad mis manos
—que después de mil años
de gritar sus fusiles—
clamarán todavía
por ser mazos
que destruyan sus rejas
Tomad mis ojos
que se han acostumbrado
a retener en su color

278

gnawed at
my patience
Have you any
children?
he asked
And your small frame was born
within his files:
                    "She's already thirty days old
                    and I am happy
                    I am happy because of her eyes
                    the way she grows
                    her smile
                    which hasn't yet been born
                    and because of her hands
                    those hands will be good hands"
That's how I answered him
He stared at me strangely
Maybe
he thought I was crazy

I am going to build a wall of light
with all the fireflies
in the world
and light the darkness
of its jails
Take my hands
—which after a thousand years
with their screaming guns—
they will still
cry out to be hammers
that will destroy the bars
Take my eyes
which have become accustomed
to retaining the screams
of tortured men
in their dark color
and pour them like a salve

oscuro
los gritos
de los hombres torturados
y volcadlos como bálsamo
en su espalda
Tomad al fin
mi miedo
el que me atenazó
la piel
las manos
la alegría
y hacedlo
mil palomas
que salgan
de algún
grito
que agonice
en las horribles cárceles
del mundo

on their backs
Take finally
my fear
the one that attacked
my skin
my hands
my happiness
and turn it
into a thousand doves
coming from
some scream
of agony
in the world's
horrible jails

[*Translated by Robert Márquez*]

De la madre

Está bien
        me digo
que al llegar
a los treinta
tenga ya encima de mis dedos
viajes
encima del dolor muchos
recuerdos
encima de la frente
una esperanza
en los ojos dos hijas una esposa
y en la ausencia
ya no vivir contigo
Está bien
        Me repito
que ahora me dé cuenta
que tú fuiste
una madre como pocas

Voy
    camino
        alrededor de mi silueta
platico
con la gente
escucho sus problemas
(soy el hombre maduro
que tú hiciste)
me cuentan
tantas cosas de su vida
y recién hoy
descubro
que todos (los amigos de ahora)
no tienen una
madre

Mother

It's alright
          I tell myself
that on reaching
                thirty
I should already have trips on my
fingers
many memories
upon my pain
upon my brow
a hope
two daughters and a wife within my eyes
and in this absence
no longer live with you
It's alright
          I tell myself again
that now I know
that you were
like very few mothers

I go
    I walk
              around my silhouette
I talk
with people
listen to their problems
(I'm the mature man
that you made)
they tell me
so many things about their lives
and I just now
discover
that not all (my friends of today)
have a mother
like you: my daughters' grandmother

como tú: abuela de mis hijas
Está bien también
agradecértelo
porque de aquel
salvaje
que te hacía
llorar todas las noches
ha nacido
un soldado de los pobres
uno que canta
por lo que vendrá
uno a quien no comprendes
y con tu amor
lo hiciste
Está bien
        yo me digo
que no me entiendas
porque tú eres
amor
y yo soy
lucha

It's alright too
to thank you for it
because that little savage
that used to make you cry
every night
has been born
a soldier of the poor
someone who sings
for what is yet to come
someone you don't understand
and with your love
you made
It's alright
        I tell myself
that you don't understand me
for you are
love
and I am
struggle

[*Translated by Robert Márquez*]

Habana 59

De tanto hablar
quedáronse sin voces las cadenas
se sometió la noche
a la alborada
fuese la muerte
con su doble rabo
huyó la peste
con su sable al hombro
los relojes quedáronse
sin ojos
sin orejas
sin orillas de piel
sin botas negras
quedóse el hambre
sin sus mil testigos
el dueño de la vid sin sus
calzones
y el amo sin su sombra:
$\qquad$ sin su esclavo

Havana 59

From so much talk
the chains had lost their voice
night surrendered
to the dawn
death ran away
with its double tail
pestilence fled
its sword on its shoulder
clocks were left
without their eyes
their ears
fur linings
or black boots
hunger no longer had
its thousand witnesses
the owner of the vineyard
was left without his pants
and the master no longer had his shadow:
                no longer had his slave

[*Translated by Robert Márquez*]

Haiti

René Depestre (1926–   ) is Haiti's most important living
poet, heir to the mantle of Jacques Roumain. He is also
one of the major figures of the group of *négritude* poets
that came immediately after Léopold Senghor, León
Damas, and Aimé Césaire. A Marxist in the tradition of
Roumain and Frantz Fanon, he recognizes the *négritude*
movement's importance in fomenting a cultural *prise de
conscience* on the part of Black intellectuals but is at the
same time one of the severest critics of the lyrical
mysticism to which it has fallen victim and which has
permitted its manipulation by native elites in the Third
World—particularly in Senegal, by Senghor himself, and
in Haiti under the Duvaliers. Depestre defends a more
broadly encompassing *négritude* that is conscious of the
crucial importance of both class and race to what he
refers to as the "zombification of man" under capitalism
and colonialism. "The new Black Orpheus," he points out,
"will be a revolutionary because he is a contemporary
and an ally of Ho Chi Minh, of Fidel Castro, and of
Ernesto Che Guevara."

Depestre published his first book of poems, *Étincelles*,
in 1945. Later he helped to found *La Ruche*, a journal of

288

the radical Haitian left, and, though now banned in his own country, his poems and essays have appeared in journals and magazines in Europe—particularly France—and throughout Latin America. An active revolutionary from the age of nineteen, he was exiled during the late forties and again in 1958; he has now been declared *persona non grata* by the reactionary regime of the Duvaliers.

Widely traveled in Eastern and Western Europe, Depestre has lived in Cuba since 1959, where he is on the staff of Radio La Habana. He frequently contributes to *Casa de Las Américas*, and is a member of its editorial board. His several books include a collection of essays, *Por la revolución, por la poesía* (1969), and the following books of verse: *Journal d'un animal marin* (1964), *Traduit du grand large* (1952), *Végétations de clarté* (1951), *Minerai noir* (1957), *Cantata de octubre a la vida y a la muerte del comandante Ernesto Che Guevara* (1969), and *Un arc-en-ciel pour l'occident chrétien* (1967). The poems that follow were originally published in *Étincelles* and *Minerai noir*.

Minerai noir

Quand la sueur de l'indien se trouva brusquement tarié
    par le soleil
Quand la frénesie de l'or draina au marché la dernière
    goutte de sang indien
De sorte qu'il ne resta plus un seul indien aux alentours
    des mines d'or
On se tourna vers le fleuve musculaire de l'Afrique
Pour assurer la relève du désespoir
Alors commença la ruée vers l'inépuisable
Trésorerie de la chair noire
Alors commença la bousculade échevelée
Vers le rayonnant midi du corps noir
Et toute la terre retentit du vacarme des pioches
Dans l'épaisseur du minerai noir
Et tout juste si des chimistes ne pensèrent
Aux moyens d'obtenir quelque alliage précieux
Avec le métal noir tout juste si des dames ne
Rêvèrent d'une batterie de cuisine
En nègre du Sénégal d'un service à thé
En massif négrillon des Antilles
Tout juste si quelque curé
Ne promit à sa paroisse
Une cloche coulée dans la sonorité du sang noir
Ou encore si un brave Père Noël ne songea
Pour sa visite annuelle
A des petits soldats de plomb noir
Ou si quelque vaillant capitaine
Ne tailla son épée dans l'ébène minéral
Toute la terre retentit de la secousse des foreuses
Dans les entrailles de ma race
Dans le gisement musculaire de l'homme noir
Voilà de nombreux siècles que dure l'extraction
Des merveilles de cette race
O couches métalliques de mon peuple

Black Ore

When all of a sudden the stream of Indian sweat was
    dried up by the sun
When the gold-fever drained out the final drop of Indian
    blood in the marketplace
And every last Indian vanished from around the mines
It was time to look to Africa's river of muscle
For a changing of the guard of misery
And so began the rush to that rich and limitless
Storehouse of black flesh
And so began the breathless dash
To the noonday splendor of the black-skinned body
Then all the earth rang out with the clatter of the picks
Digging deep in the thick black ore
How many a chemist all but turned his mind
To making some new precious alloy formed
With this black mineral how many a lady almost
Set her heart on finding pots and pans
Of black Senegalese or a fine tea-service
Of stocky Caribbean pickaninny
Who knows what parish padre somewhere
Almost gave his solemn word
To get a churchbell cast in the sonority of black blood
Or what nice Santa Claus almost dreamed
Of little black tin soldiers
For his yearly rounds
Or what valiant man at arms
Would have gladly hewn his blade from this ebony metal
The earth rang out with the shake and shatter of the drills
Deep in the entrails of my people
Deep in the black man's muscled mineral bed
For centuries now they have dug from the depths
The wonders of this race
O mines of ore that are my people
Limitless vein of human dew

Minerai inépuisable de rosée humaine
Combien de libustiers se sont frayés leur chemin
A travers la riche végétation de clartés de ton corps
Jonchant tes années de tiges mortes
Et de flaques de larmes
Peuple dévalisé peuple de fond en comble retourné
Comme une terre en labours
Peuple défriché pour l'enrichissement
Des grandes foires du monde
Mûris ton grisou dans le secret de ta nuit corporelle
Nul n'osera plus couler des canons et des pièces d'or
Dans le noir métal de ta colère en crues.

How many pirates have plunged their weapons deep
To probe the dark recesses of your flesh
How many plunderers have hacked themselves a path
Through the lush illumined vegetation of your body
Strewing over your passing days dead stalks
And pools of tears
O pillaged people dug up from top to bottom
Like land beneath the plough
People harrowed to enrich
The great markets of the world
Store up your firedamp deep in your body's secret dark of
    night
Then none will dare to cast more cannons and more
    golden coins
From that black metal of your fury's rising flood.

[*Translated by Norman R. Shapiro*]

Confession

À Gérard Gourgue

On a jalonné mon passé
de promesses stériles
on a sillonné ma tunique de coutures
le silence du résigné
comme un relent
coula dans le creux de ma peine.
On inventa la bible
on inventa les chaînes
on inventa mille façons
d'inoculer
la soumission dans toutes mes cellules
mais depuis j'ai su la vérité
plus de baumes pour ma plaie
plus d'accolades
plus d'oublis.
Mon espoir
sauvage
fumant
bouillonne
comme une lave aux flancs de l'histoire.
Promesses, baumes, accolades, oublis,
défroques
ombres avilies par la massue des faits
vaut mieux la conquête
vaut mieux la fonte
de mon angoisse
de ma confiance
de ma force
dans le creuset des chaudes rencontres
pour que ma vie
jeune
décidée
jaillisse, bondissante, sur un mode écroulé.

Confession

For Gérard Gourgue

They've staked out my past
with sterile promises
striped my jacket with stitch and patch
the silence of the unresisting
like a stale smell
flowed through the hollow of my pain.
They invented the Bible
they invented chains
they invented a thousand ways
of injecting
my every cell with self-surrender
but then I learned the truth
now no more salve to ease my wounds
no more caresses
no more forgetfulness.
My hope
savage
steaming
boils up
like lava along the flanks of history.
Promises, salves, caresses, forgetfulness,
cast-off rags
shadows discredited by hammerblows of fact
better to fight and win
better to smelt down
my anguish
my confidence
my strength
in the crucible of hot encounters
so that my life
young
resolute
may spout forth, leaping, over a world in ruins.

[*Translated by Norman R. Shapiro*]

295

Mexico

Juan Bañuelos (1932–   ) was born in Tuxtla Gutiérrez, Chiapas, Mexico. He was one of the founding members of the Ateneo of Chiapas. He went on to study philosophy and law at the University of Mexico, and currently works as a proofreader for a publishing house in Mexico City. A poet of refined sensibilities who has tried his hand at a variety of forms and styles, there is, even in his harshest denunciations, the understated, muted tone of a whisper, a carefully crafted verbal elegance.

Bañuelos' first book of poems, *Puertas del mundo*, appeared in the collective volume *La espiga amotinada* (1960). His poems have been published in a variety of Mexican and Latin American literary journals. His other books include *Escribo en las paredes* (1965), and *Espejo humeante* (1968). The following poems are taken from the latter.

En Vietnam las púas
gotean nubes de corderos

Gusanos de sesenta inviernos aspiran sangre y el fosfo-
   rescente silencio del napalm.
La ceniza amarilla de los niños silba una sed de flores de
   frutos, de pájaros y arroz,
mientras en un rancho de Texas se asa a la parrilla la res
   lazada en la mañana,
y huele igual que el cuerpo en llamas de una madre de
   Da-Nang.

La mueca torva del fusil se hunde en las cuevas de
   estómagos hendidos; las púas gotean nubes de cor-
   deros
y el esplendor del aire es un vellón sombrío.
   Todo. Todo será bajo las mangas de helicópteros
y del monzón que rueda como un tanque ciego. Todo será.
Y la muerte en cada bombardeo no detendrá al sol.

Decid en cada calle, en cada casa de todas las ciudades,
   que en cada fosa que se cierra un arrozal furioso se
   levanta.
(Yo no conozco, hermanos, vuestras tierras, pero veo las
   fotos, alguna rápida película, y lo sé todo:
Y en la estremecida quietud de cada rostro sorprendo el
   incendio deslumbrado de un pueblo,
para que el futuro comience allí donde se acaba la
   palabra.)

In Vietnam the Thorns Drip
Clouds of Lambs

Worms of sixty winters breathe blood and the phospho-
    rescent silence of napalm.
The yellow ash of children hisses a thirst of flowers
    and fruits, of birds and rice,
while on a Texas ranch they grill a calf butchered that
    morning,
and it smells exactly like the flaming corpse of a mother
    from Danang.

The severe grimace of the gun is buried in the caves
    of shattered stomachs; the thorns drip clouds of
    lambs;
the brilliance in the air is somber wool.
    All things. All things will be beneath the sleeves of
    helicopters
and the monsoon that rolls like a blind tank. All things
    will be.
And the death in every bombing will not detain the sun.

Tell them on every street, in every house of every city,
    that for every grave created a furious ricefield rises.
(Brothers, I do not know your lands, but see the photos,
    some quick film, and know it all:
And in the trembling silence of each face I catch
    a people's dazzling fire,
that the future may begin where the word ends.)

[*Translated by Robert Márquez*]

299

Perros

Birmingham, Alabama—
". . . y la policía lanzó contra
ellos bravos perros . . . una
niña de color fue despeda-
zada . . ."

United Press

SILENCIO que ahora llegan perros de barro
con sus mandíbulas buscando negros huesos
Sucumbe la hoja en el tubo
de plomo enrarecido
Rostros para los golpes servirán de ejemplo
Los dementes saludan al terror
      I'll never go back to Alabama
      That's not the place for me
      They killed ma brother and ma sister
Navajas de yeso degollaron las tupidas
cabezas nocturnas Kentucky Alabama
Puma roedor Ámbar de encina fría
y la magia nube de la niña muerta
hallada con una hoja de naranjo en la boca
Oh estruendo sin edad del cuerpo fulminado
Qué tristeza estar vivo sin tu sitio en la tierra
Es necesario llevarte en la mirada
es necesario Muerta sin rencor
La mejilla a la altura de la pena deja correr
su amor como un carrete de violetas
      If you miss me at the back of the bus
      You can't find me no where
      Look for me at the front of the bus
      I'll be sittin' right there
Aquel rostro llenaba la impostura el desafío
del musgo en la piedra del silencio
Alegría feroz cruzada por la muerte

Dogs

Birmingham, Alabama—
". . . and the police let wild
dogs loose on them . . . a
young black girl was mauled
to death . . ."

United Press

QUIET the dogs of clay are coming
with jaws in search of Negro bones
The leaf succumbs to the rarefied lead pipe
Faces for the blows will serve as an example
The demented give terror a salute
> *I'll never go back to Alabama*
> *That's not the place for me*
> *They killed ma brother and ma sister*

Plaster knives decapitate bushy
nocturnal heads Kentucky Alabama
Gnawing puma amber of cold evergreen
and the magic cloud of the dead child
found with the leaf of an orange blossom in her mouth
O ageless thunder of that body thunderstruck
It's so sad living with no place on the earth
One has to carry you within the eyes
one has to, O dead rancorless child
My cheek at the level of the pain lets its love
unwind like a spool of violets
> *If you miss me at the back of the bus*
> *You can't find me no where*
> *Look for me at the front of the bus*
> *I'll be sittin' right there*

That face took on the imposture the challenge
of the moss on the rock of silence
A furious gaiety cut down by death
lost like a stranger in the city

perdida como un extraño en la ciudad
Niños cuadriculados
viejos de esperanza viva
Chorros de agua dolorosa
Por asalto el planeta
por asalto

      Sun's a risin'
      This is gonna be ma song

Debajo de los arcos del olvido
hicieron que la sangre caminara con sandalias de oro y
    dólar
(qué tristeza estar vivo sin tu sitio en la tierra)
Ah el dolor se vuelve un hueso
que soporta la confesión de la vida
Pero el Amor vigila el agujero rojo
hecho en un flanco
cuando desova sombras
      Por ti
        Muerta
por asalto
el surgimiento se levanta
a través de las mareas
del corazón armado

Children squared up
Old men full of hope
Streams of painful water
The planet taken by storm
by storm
            Sun's a risin'
            This is gonna be ma song
They made the blood run beneath oblivion's arches
with sandals of gold and dollars
(it's so sad living with no place on the earth)
O the pain becomes a bone
that sustains life's confession
But love is watching the red hole
made in someone's side
when it spawns shadows
            For you
                        Taken
by storm
the upsurge rises
above the tide
of the armed heart

[*Translated by Robert Márquez*]

Fusil, hoja que conmueve
a todo el árbol

:Me dicen que escriba algo acerca de tu muerte. (Me han
tomado por quien no era y no los voy a desmentir.)
Yo no sé lo que pasa. Ya dije que no entiendo nada ni me
importa.
Sólo sé que tú no estás de paso (únicamente un poco
de fatiga, ¡claro! que hasta la piedra convalece del
tiempo).
¿Buscar la tinta en el fondo de los ojos? De ningún modo.
Por lo tanto pongámonos de acuerdo: esto no será un
poema. Bueno, al menos yo no quiero.
Apenas humano, me decido; miro a izquierda y a derecha
para pasar la calle y lo que cruzo es la realidad.
Todos ahora se aprestan a desembolsar una oda, o una
elegía, o un sollozo reprimido, después de haber
ayudado de alguna manera a tu muerte.
Yo no comparto ningún duelo. Hasta Barrientos, tu
asesino (esa mierda envuelta en lo mismo), siente
"tremendo dolor" por tu muerte, ha dicho.
No. Yo no voy a llorarte ahora que todos están infestados
de arrepentimiento. Un día de estos te escribiré un
poema, que será corto y más bien un diálogo. Hoy no.
Hoy tengo que salir a buscar *money* para la operación
de mi mujer (tú lo sabes: este México, esta patria).

Lo mejor que he leído acerca de ti es que eres un
personaje de historia-ficción, y que has decidido
abandonar el planeta para volver pronto. Ojalá así
sea. Espero que así sea.
Desapareciste, y yo dormido en la mañana me levanté
tarde, me afeité cuidadosamente, como lo hago
cuando se trata de una cita amorosa, y me senté a la
mesa silbando un viejo jazz seguro de que no debía
suicidarme.

A Gun, the Leaf That Moves
the Entire Tree

:I'm asked to write about your death. (They've taken me
  for someone I am not, and I won't disappoint them.)
I don't know what's happening. I've said already that I
  don't understand nor do I care.
    I only know you're not just passing through (just a
    little tired, naturally! even a stone recovers in time).
Search for ink in the recesses of your eyes? By no means.
  So let's agree: this won't be a poem. Well, at any rate,
  I don't want it to be.
Barely human, I decide; I look to left and right to cross the
  street, and I cross reality instead.
Now everyone is ready with an ode, an elegy, or a muffled
  sob, after having helped in some way to bring about
  your death.
I take part in no mourning. Even Barrientos, your assas-
  sin (that shit immersed in shit), feels "a great loss" at
  your death, he said.
No. I won't weep for you now that everyone reeks with
  remorse. One of these days I'll write you a poem—a
  short one, more likely a dialogue. But not today.
  Today I have to go out and find some money for my
  wife's operation (you know this Mexico, this land of
  ours).

The best of what I've read about you is that you're a
  character of fiction-history and have decided to for-
  sake the planet to return soon. I wish for that, and
  hope you will.
You disappeared, and I, sleeping away the morning, got
  up late, shaved carefully, as I do when I have a
  rendezvous, and sat down at the table whistling an
  old jazz tune, convinced I shouldn't kill myself.
I read the paper: its pages went by like proud flags

Leí el periódico: sus páginas pasaban como banderas
orgullosas flameando de hambre, de dinero, y de
todas esas cosas que nos endilgan como la misma
comida diariamente en mi viejo Comedor Público del
Carmen.

Y ahí estabas: tendido, obstinación de tierra entre los
dientes, asilo de ojos espoleados hacia la dura dulzura
de una boca florida, un saurio sobre el yermo de la
fotografía, una nube de piel hecha fetiche acidulando
la espuma barbuda del cercenado.

Ahí estás: no entre las bajas moderadas en Vietnam, ni
entre los condecorados, sino entre el advenimiento y
los leopardos límites del sueño. Lacónicamente dán-
dote por muerto, sin nuestro consentimiento y sin el
tuyo

¡como si pudiera morir mi Comandante Guevara!

La hoja que conmueve a todo el árbol no se desprende
nunca. Hay un horóscopo despierto, una oropéndola,
oh viajero, sobre la espalda de esa hoja. Viene la
gente y cambia. Lloran o ríen y se alejan, y no es
posible recordar: sólo una vez el mundo es nuestro.

Todas estas cosas son lo más humano posible.

Hombres vivos, hombres muertos, hombres en liber-
tad o condenados, mas en medio el desacuerdo y sus
humeantes togas son prerrogativas destazadas como
un ave en cuyas entrañas se lee el desastre.

No. No estoy enfermo ni desesperado. Apenas si percibo
una obscena sensación de estar desnudo, de estar
como una fruta pudriéndose en la sombra. Y bien, yo
te conozco más ahora que el día que no nos presenta-
ron, y cada vez que veo tu foto en los periódicos,
sospecho que te envidio como al muchacho que se
lleva a la chica más guapa del pueblo.

Hoy es distinto. Como si sólo un sonido tuviera la esquila
de la vida. Estás hechizado en tus nupcias verdaderas
bajo la sinagoga de los Andes.

blazing with hunger, money, and all those things that
lead us by the nose, like the same meal daily in my old
"Comedor Público del Carmen."

And there you were: stretched out, a stubbornness of
earth between your teeth, an asylum of eyes spurred
on to the hard gentleness of a graceful mouth, a
saurian on the arid spaces of the photograph, a cloud
of skin become a fetish turning the bearded foam
around it sour.

There you are: not among the moderate casualties in
Vietnam, nor among the decorated, but between
the advent and the leopard limits of the dream, la-
conically considered dead, without our consent or
yours,

as if Comandante Guevara could die!

The leaf that moves the entire tree never falls.

There's a clear-sighted horoscope, a golden oriole, O
voyager, on that leaf's back. People come and go.
They cry or laugh, move on, and one cannot remem-
ber: the world is ours but once.

These things are all that is humanly possible.

Men living, men dead, men free or condemned, but in
their midst discord and its fuming togas are preroga-
tives dismembered like a bird in whose entrails one
can read disaster.

No. I am neither sick nor desperate. I can barely feel an
obscene sensation of nakedness, of being like a fruit
rotting in the shade. And, well, I know you better now
than the day we were not introduced, and each time I
see your picture in the papers I suspect I envy you as
one envies the boy who carries off the prettiest girl in
town.

Today is different. As though the bell of life had only one
sound. You're spellbound in your true nuptials be-
neath the synagogue of the Andes.

Estás más joven, de pie sobre la cortadura de un cuchillo,
   estás la misma música de Bach, que ahora escucho,
   como una torre que se quema desde lejos.
Y llueve. Llueve fríamente. El día no es más que un dedo
   que ha perdido su anillo. Pero ¿qué diablos tenemos
   tú y yo que ver con la muerte? ¿Qué diablos?
Es que me refiero a esa manera congruente, acordonada
   tortuga de la sangre en donde la desgracia abufanda
   sus ayes. Es que me refiero a este desaforado equili-
   brio en el alambre, como aquél que suelta el asa de su
   cesta a la hora en que se oye un silbido entre las hojas
   y ve a dos sombras de caballos que se mueven con la
   noche.
No, yo no tengo paciencia para sufrir, no me puedo dar un
   baño sin figurarme que soy un animal tolerado en un
   hotel. Todo esto es cierto, y aún así quieren que
   escriba algo acerca de tu ausencia.
Sin aceptar la muerte sino sólo cuando bosteza entre los
   frutos quietos, amigo, yo apoyo mi mano en el
   silencio, en la pared, y la pared se queja.

No quiero quedarme aquí solo escribiendo este cuento
   largo. En este instante la multitud de mi persona
   desemboca en la avenida Juárez y empiezo a oír el
   dodecafónico tableteo de las armas entre las églogas
   del miedo.
Vaho del cordero,
embestida del ganado,
sello en todas las cartas,
tu nombre no se dice, *mas tu fuerza está en nosotros.*
   Porque no hay tregua, ni guarniciones, ni compás de
   espera, ¿vamos a seguir sembrando de héroes el
   suelo de América?
Tú sólo eres EL LIBERTADOR.
   Que se muera el que pierda su tiempo en homenajes,
   mientras el enemigo atiza el infierno de la caridad, y

You're younger, standing on a knife's cutting edge, you're
   the very music of Bach I'm now listening to, like a
   tower burning in the distance.
And it's raining. Coldly raining. The day is just a finger
   that has lost its ring. But what the hell do you and I
   have to do with death? What the hell?
I'm talking about that sensible way, that lean turtle of the
   blood in which misfortune muffles its pain. I'm talk-
   ing about this outrageous balancing on the wire, like
   someone who drops the handle to his basket when he
   hears a whistling in the leaves and sees the shadows
   of two horses that move with the night.
No, I don't have the patience for suffering; I can't take a
   bath without imagining myself an animal tolerated in
   a hotel. This is all true, and even so they want me to
   write about your absence.
Without accepting death save when it yawns among the
   quiet fruit, my friend, I rest my hand on the silence,
   on the wall, and the wall complains.

I don't want to stay here by myself writing this long story.
   At this very moment the multitudes of my person are
   spilling out onto the Avenida Juárez and I begin to
   hear the dodecaphonic staccato of guns amid the
   eclogues of fear.
Breath of the lamb,
the herd's attack,
a stamp on every letter,
your name is not spoken, *but your strength is in us.*
   Because there is no truce, no garrisons, no measure
   of waiting, will we continue to plant America's soil
   with heroes?
You are the only LIBERATOR.
   Let him die who wastes his time in homages while the
   enemy stirs up the hell of charity; underdevelopment
   is no more than a beacon blinding its own eyes.

el subdesarrollo no es más que un faro que se ciega a
sí mismo.

Tú solamente eres la Gran Molienda, o un payador
tropezando entre los astros. Salgo a la calle y desco-
nozco a todos. *Hypocrites citoyens.*

¿En dónde está Bolivia? ¿Por dónde la Quebrada del
Yuro? Y me da en toda la madre la fría lluvia del
último ciclón.

De pronto, al fin tengo el derecho de llegar a un pacto
contigo: que cambiemos las armas mientras vuelves.
¿Para qué poesía sin fusil, en una hora en que dormir
es como abotonarse la guerrera de los asesinos?

Bueno, viejo, te deseo selvas y sobre todo sol para los
tuyos, porque vos vas de la mano con las sierras, esa
tu juventud perpetua de violentar las cosas para abrir
todas las puertas del mundo.

Y si esto es un poema, que me lo perdone la Revolución o
la REBOLUSIÓN de los analfabetos y hambrientos de
este Continente, porque yo, porque yo sólo quería y
quiero, mi Comandante Guevara, tomar un fusil y
seguir tus pasos, por aquéllos.

You alone are the Great Grist Mill, or a troubadour
stumbling among the stars. I go into the street and
don't recognize a soul. *Citoyens hipocrites.*
Where is Bolivia? Where the Quebrada del Yuro?
And the cold rain of the last cyclone hits me in the
balls.
Suddenly, I finally have the right to make a pact with you:
that we exchange weapons until you return. Why
poetry without the gun, at a time when sleeping is
like buttoning the assassins' army jacket?

Well, old man, I wish you jungles and sun especially for
yours, because you walk hand in hand with sierras,
your perpetual youth forcing things so all the world's
doors open.
And if this is a poem, may the Revolution (or REBO-
LUSHUN of this continent's illiterate and hungry)
forgive me because all I wanted and want, Com-
andante Guevara, is to take a gun and follow in your
footsteps, for them.

[*Translated by Robert Márquez*]

Nicaragua

Ernesto Cardenal (1925–   ) is the revolutionary mystic of Latin American poetry. Born in Granada, Nicaragua, he was actively involved in the underground against Anastasio Somoza, and in 1954 took part in the abortive "Conspiración de abril," which attempted to capture the dictator in his own palace. In the years that followed Cardenal underwent a religious conversion and he entered the Trappist monastery of Our Lady of Gethsemani, Kentucky, in 1957 as a novitiate under the direct tutelage of the late Thomas Merton. He also spent some time in the Benedictine monastery of Santa María de la Resurrección in Cuernavaca, Mexico, and studied theology at the seminary in La Ceja, Antioquia, Colombia. He was ordained in 1965 and a year later founded a religious colony—Nuestra Señora de Solentiname—on the island of Solentiname in the Lake of Nicaragua. Save for an occasional trip to Cuba, Chile, and other Latin American countries, he has been there ever since.

Cardenal belongs to the Nicaraguan "Generation of 1940." His earliest poems combine love, a revolutionary and political theme, an *exteriorista* interest in the facts—statistics, chronicles, anecdotes, historical documents, etc.—and the prosaic realities of everyday life in Central America. All this was part of the poet's reaction against a too subjective and escapist literary tradition. "I have always," he says, "tried to write a poetry that is not hermetic, obscure, or difficult, that will reach the people."

An avid reader (and one-time translator) of United States poetry, he attributes this fondness for the direct and rhetorically unadorned poem to his reading of Ezra Pound, whose work he acknowledges as the greatest single influence on his technique.

Cardenal's turn to the religious life was a transmutation rather than an abandonment of his revolutionary convictions, but its effect on his poetry was decisive. The major themes remained—his repudiation of a world ruled by greed, institutionalized violence, and the concept of private property—but to these was added the mystic love of God. The poet's vision becomes at once more tender and more apocalyptic. In *Salmos* (Psalms), for example, "the poet wants to provoke the Biblical cataclysm, the destruction by love, the fire that will ignite true human fraternity." It is this combination of tone, content, and form that makes Cardenal one of the most popular poets of contemporary Latin America.

His works include the co-editorship of two anthologies, *Nueva poesía nicaragüense* (1949) and *Antología de la poesía norteamericana moderna* (1963); a book of vignettes, *En Cuba* (1972); and the following books of poetry: *Hora O* (1960), *Epigramas* (1961), *Gethsemani, Ky* (1964), *Salmos* (1964), *Oración por Marilyn Monroe y otros poemas* (1965), *El estrecho dudoso* (1966), and *Homenaje a los indios americanos* (1969). The poems appearing here are from *Hora O* and *Salmos*.

Salmo 48

Óiganme todos los pueblos
    Escuchad todos vosotros habitantes del mundo
plebeyos y nobles
los proletarios y los millonarios
                todas las clases sociales
Hablaré con proverbios
    y sabias palabras
        acompañado del arpa . . .

    "Por qué temeré yo las persecuciones
    de los que ponen su confianza en un Banco
    y su seguridad en una Póliza de Aseguros?"

La vida no se puede comprar con un cheque
sus Acciones son muy altas
no se pueden pagar con dinero

Vivir siempre y no ver jamás el sepulcro:
¡nadie puede comprar esa Póliza!

Pensaron que vivirían siempre y que siempre estarían en
    el poder
y les ponían sus nombres a sus tierras
a todas las propiedades que robaban
Les quitaron los nombres a las ciudades
para ponerles los suyos
Sus estatuas estaban en todas las plazas
¿Y ahora quién los mienta?

Fueron derribadas sus estatuas de bronce
las placas de bronce fueron arrancadas
Ahora su Palacio es un Mausoleo
No te impacientes pues si ves a uno enriquecerse
si tiene muchos millones

Psalm 48

Hear me peoples of the earth
      Give ear all ye inhabitants of the world
both noble and plebeian
the proletarians and the millionaires
              all the social classes
My mouth shall speak with proverbs
      and words of wisdom
            upon the harp . . .

      "Wherefore should I fear the persecutions
      of those who put their trust in a bank
      and their security in an insurance policy?"

Life is not bought with a check
its shares are too high
they cannot be paid with money

To live forever and never see the grave:
no one can buy that policy!

They thought they would live forever and would always
    be in power
and put their names on their lands
on all the property they stole
They removed the names of the cities
that they might be named after them
Their statues were in every square
and now who names them?

Their bronze statues were demolished
their bronze plaques were torn away
Now their palace is a mausoleum
Therefore be not impatient if one is made rich
if he has many millions

y se acrecienta la gloria de su casa
y es un Hombre Fuerte
Porque en la muerte ya no tendrá ningún gobierno
ni ningún Partido
Aunque en su vida la Prensa Oficial proclamase:
"Te alabarán porque has logrado tu felicidad"
tendrá que irse a la morada de sus padres
para no ver ya jamás la luz

Pero el hombre puesto en suma dignidad no entiende
el hombre que está en el poder
el gobernante gordo lleno de condecoraciones
y se ríe y cree que no morirá nunca
y no sabe que es como esos animales
sentenciados a morir el día de la Fiesta

and the glory of his house is increased
and he is a strong man
For in death he shall have no government
nor any party
Even if in life the official press proclaims:
"You shall be praised for you have won your happiness"
he shall have to go to the place wherein his fathers dwell
and never see the light again

But the man in high office understands not
the man in power
the fat ruler heavy with decorations
and laughs and thinks he shall never die
and does not know he is as those beasts
condemned to die on the day of the feast

[*Translated by Robert Márquez*]

Salmo 36

No te impacientes si los ves hacer muchos millones
Sus acciones comerciales
>   son como el heno de los campos
No envidies a los millonarios ni a las estrellas de cine
a los que figuran a ocho columnas en los diarios
a los que viven en hoteles lujosos
y comen en lujosos restaurantes
porque pronto sus nombres no estarán en ningún diario
y ni los eruditos conocerán sus nombres
>   Porque pronto serán segados como el
>   heno de los campos

No te impacienten sus inventos
>   y su progreso técnico
Al Líder que ves ahora pronto no lo verás
lo buscarás en su palacio
>   y no lo hallarás
Los hombres mansos serán los nuevos líderes
>   (los "pacifistas")

Están agrandando los campos de concentración
están inventando nuevas torturas
nuevos sistemas de "investigación"
En la noche no duermen haciendo planes
planeando como aplastarnos más
>   como explotarnos más
pero el Señor se ríe de ellos
porque ve que pronto caerán del poder

Las armas que ellos fabrican se volverán contra ellos
Sus sistemas políticos serán borrados de la tierra
y ya no existirán sus partidos políticos
De nada valdrán los planos de sus técnicos
Las grandes potencias
>   son como la flor de los prados

318

Psalm 36

Be not impatient if you see them make many millions
Their commercial transactions
                              are as the wheat of the fields
Be not envious of the millionaires or of the movie stars
of those who appear in eight column headlines
of those who live in plush hotels
and eat in plush restaurants
for their names soon shall not be in any newspaper
neither will the scholars know their names
                    For soon they shall be harvested as the
                    wheat of the fields

Be not made impatient by their inventions
                         and their technical progress
The Leader you see now soon shall not be
You will seek him in his palace
                              and will find him not
The meek shall be the new leaders
                         (the "pacifists")

They are enlarging the concentration camps
they are inventing new tortures
new systems of "investigation"
At night they sleep not making plans
plotting how to crush us further
                              how further to exploit us
but the Lord is laughing at them
for he sees that they soon shall fall from power

The arms they manufacture shall be turned against them
Their political systems shall be erased from the earth
and their political parties shall exist no longer
The plans of their technicians shall serve for nothing
The great powers
                    are as the flowers of the field

Los imperialismos
                    son como el humo

No espían todo el día
Tienen ya preparadas las sentencias
Pero el Señor no nos entregará a su Policía
No permitirá que seamos condenados en el Juicio
Yo vi el retrato del dictador en todas partes
                            —se extendía como un árbol
                                    vigoroso—
y volví a pasar
                y ya no estaba
Lo busqué y no lo hallé
Lo busqué y ya no había ningún retrato
y su nombre no se podía pronunciar

Imperialisms
                    are as smoke

All day long they spy upon us
Already they have the sentences prepared
Yet will the Lord not deliver us to their police
He will not allow us to be condemned at the Judgment
I saw the dictator's picture everywhere
                    —it spread itself like a green
                                bay tree—
and I turned to pass again
                    and it was no longer
I searched for it and found it not
I searched for it and now there was not any picture
and his name could not be spoken

[*Translated by Robert Márquez*]

Salmo 5

Escucha mis palabras oh Señor
Oye mis gemidos
Escucha mi protesta
Porque no eres tú un Dios amigo de los dictadores
ni partidario de su política
ni te influencia la propaganda
ni estás en sociedad con el gángster

No existe sinceridad en sus discursos
ni en sus declaraciones de prensa

Hablan de paz en sus discursos
mientras aumentan su producción de guerra
Hablan de paz en las Conferencias de Paz
y en secreto se preparan para la guerra
Sus radios mentirosos rugen toda la
noche
Sus escritorios están llenos de planes criminales y expe-
dientes siniestros
Pero tú me salvarás de sus planes
Hablan con la boca de las ametralladoras
Sus lenguas relucientes
son las bayonetas . . .

Castígalos oh Dios
malogra su política
confunde sus memorandums
impide sus programas
A la hora de la Sirena de Alarma
tú estarás conmigo
tú serás mi refugio el día de la Bomba
Al que no cree en la mentira de sus anuncios comerciales
ni en sus campañas publicitarias ni en sus campañas
políticas

322

Psalm 5

Give ear to my words, O Lord,
                              Harken unto my moaning
Pay heed to my protest
For you are not a God friendly to dictators
neither are you a partisan of their politics
nor are you influenced by their propaganda
neither are you in league with the gangster

There is no sincerity in their speeches
nor in their press releases

They speak of peace in their speeches
while they increase their war production
They speak of peace at Peace Conferences
and secretly prepare for war
                              Their lying radios roar into the
                                       night
Their desks are strewn with criminal intentions and
     sinister reports
But you will deliver me from their plans
They speak through the mouth of the submachine-gun
Their flashing tongues are bayonets . . .

Punish them, O Lord,
                         thwart them in their policies
confuse their memorandums
                              obstruct their programs
At the hour of Alarm
you shall be with me
you shall be my refuge on the day of the Bomb
To him who believes not in the lies of their commercial
     messages
nor in their publicity campaigns nor in their political
     campaigns

tú lo bendices

Lo rodeas con tu amor

como con tanques blindados

you will give your blessing

With love do you compass him

as with armor-plated tanks

[Translated by Robert Márquez]

La hora cero

¡Centinela! ¿Qué hora es de la noche?
¡Centinela! ¿Qué hora es de la noche?
Isaías, 21, 11

Noches Tropicales de Centroamérica,
con lagunas y volcanes bajo la luna
y luces de palacios presidenciales,
cuarteles y tristes toques de queda.
"Muchas veces fumando un cigarrillo
he decidido la muerte de un hombre,"
dice Ubico fumando un cigarrillo . . .
en su palacio como un queque rosado
Ubico está resfriado. Afuera el pueblo
fue dispersado con bombas de fósforo.
San Salvador bajo la noche y el espionaje
con cuchicheos en los hogares y pensiones
y gritos en las estaciones de policía.
El palacio de Carías apedreado por el pueblo.
Una ventana de su despacho ha sido quebrada,
y la policía ha disparado contra el pueblo.
Y Managua apuntada por las ametralladoras
desde el palacio de bizcocho de chocolate
y los cascos de acero patrullando las calles.

¡Centinela! ¿Qué hora es de la noche?
¡Centinela! ¿Qué hora es de la noche?

Los campesinos hondureños traían el dinero en el som-
    brero
cuando los campesinos sembraban sus siembras
y los hondureños eran dueños de su tierra.
Cuando había dinero.
Y no había empréstitos extranjeros
ni los impuestos eran para Pierpont Morgan & Cía.

Zero Hour

> Watchman, what of the night?
> Watchman, what of the night?
>   *Isaiah*, 21, 11

Tropical nights of Central America,
lagoons and volcanos under the moon
and lights in the palaces of presidents,
barrack-rooms and sad bugles at curfew.
"Often I have decided to send a man to death
while smoking a cigarette,"
Ubico says smoking a cigarette,
in his palace like a pink birthday cake
Ubico has caught a cold. Outside
they scattered the people with phosphorus bombs.
San Salvador under the night and spies
with whispers in living-rooms and boarding houses
and screams from the police stations.
The palace of Carías stoned by the people.
One of the windows of his office has been smashed
and the police have fired on the people.
And Managua a target for the machine-gunners
from the windows of the chocolate-cookie-colored palace
and steel helmets patrolling the streets.

Watchman, what of the night?
Watchman, what of the night?

The *campesinos* of Honduras kept their money in their
       sombreros
when the *campesinos* sowed their own crops
and the Hondureños were masters of their own land.
When they had money.
And when there were no foreign loans
before Pierpont Morgan & Co. took their taxes

y la compañía frutera no competía con el pequeño
cosechero.
Pero vino la United Fruit Company
con sus subsidiaria la Tela Railroad Company
y la Trujillo Railroad Company
aliada con la Cuyamel Fruit Company
y Vaccaro Brothers & Company
más tarde Standard Fruit & Steamship Company
de la Standard Fruit & Steamship Corporation:
        la United Fruit Company
con sus revoluciones para la obtención de concesiones
y exenciones de millones de impuestos en importaciones
y exportaciones, revisiones de viejas concesiones
y subvenciones para nuevas explotaciones,
violaciones de contrato, violaciones
de la Constitución . . .
Y todas las condiciones son dictadas por la Compañía
con las obligaciones en caso de confiscación
(obligaciones de la nación, no de la Compañía),
y las condiciones puestas por esta (la Compañía)
(dadas gratis por la nación a la Compañía)
a los 99 años . . .
"y todas las otras plantaciones pertenecientes
a cualquier otra persona o compañía o empresas
dependientes de los contratantes y en las cuales
esta última tiene o puede tener más adelante
interés de cualquier clase quedarán por lo tanto
incluidas en los anteriores términos y condiciones . . ."
(Porque la Compañía también corrompía la prosa.)
La condición era que la Compañía construyera el Ferro-
        carril,
pero la Compañía no lo construía,
porque las mulas en Honduras eran más baratas que el
        Ferrocarril,
Y "un Diputado más barato que una mula"
        —como decía Zemurray—
aunque seguía disfrutando de las exenciones de impuesto

328

and the fruit company competed with the small holder.
But the United Fruit Company came along
with its subsidiaries the Tela Railroad Company
and the Trujillo Railroad Company
allied to the Cuyamel Fruit Company
and Vaccaro Brothers and Company
later the Standard Fruit and Steamship Company
of the Standard Fruit and Steamship Corporation:
            the United Fruit Company
that stirred up revolutions to obtain concessions
and exemptions from millions of dollars of import
and export duties, revisions of old concessions
and subsidies for further exploitations,
violations of contracts, violations
of the Constitution . . .
And all the obligations in case of confiscation
(the nation's obligations, not the Company's)
and the conditions that it (the Company) imposed
for the return of the plantations to the nation
(leased for free by the nation to the Company)
for 99 years . . .
"and all the other plantations that pertain
to any other party, company or corporation whatsoever
that is dependent on the contracting parties and in whom
the latter holds or may hold later
interests of any category whatsoever will remain for that
        reason
included in the aforementioned clauses and condi-
        tions . . ."
(Because the Company also corrupted the language.)
The condition was that the Company should build the
        railroad,
but the Company didn't build it,
because in Honduras mules cost less than the railroad
and "a deputy less than a mule"
            —as Zemurray said—
though it continued to profit by the exemption from taxes

329

y los 175,000 acres de subvención para la Compañía,
con la obligación de pagar a la nación por cada milla
que no construyera, pero no pagaba nada a la nación
aunque no construía ninguna milla (Carías es el dictador
que más millas de línea férrea no construyó)
y después de todo el tal ferrocarril de mierda no era
de ningún beneficio para la nación
porque era un ferrocarril entre dos plantaciones
y no entre Trujillo y Tegucigalpa.

Corrompen la prosa y corrompen el Congreso.
El banano es dejado podrir en las plantaciones,
o podrir en los vagones a lo largo de la vía férrea,
o cortado maduro para poder ser rechazado
al llegar al muelle, o ser echado en el mar;
los racimos declarados golpeados, o delgados,
o marchitos, o verdes, o maduros, o enfermos:
para que no haya banano barato,
   o para comprar banano barato.
Hasta que haya hambre en la Costa Atlántica de Nica-
  ragua.
Y los campesinos son encarcelados por no vender a 30
  ctvs.
Y sus bananos son bayoneteados
y la Mexican Trader Steamship les hunde sus lanchones,
y los huelgistas dominados a tiros.
(Y los diputados nicaragüenses invitados a un garden
  party.)
Pero el negro tiene siete hijos.
Y uno qué va a hacer. Uno tiene que comer.
Y se tienen que aceptar sus condiciones de pago.
   24 ctvs. el racimo.
Mientras la subsidiaria Tropical Radio cablegrafía a Bos-
  ton:
"Esperamos que tendrá la aprobación de Boston
la erogación hecha en diputados nicaragüenses de la
  mayoría

and the 175,000 acres granted to the Company,
with the obligation to pay the nation for every mile
that it didn't build, it paid the nation nothing
although it didn't build any miles (Carías is the dictator
who holds the record for miles of railroad he didn't build)
and when all was concluded it was a shit of a railroad
and of no benefit to the nation
because it was a railroad between two plantations
and not between Trujillo and Tegucigalpa.

They corrupt the language and they corrupt Congress.
The bananas are left to rot on the plantations,
or rot in the freight cars by the railroad,
or are cut overripe so they are rejected
when they arrive at the dock, or are thrown into the sea;
they declare that the bunches are bruised, or too small,
or wormy, or underripe, or overripe, or rotten:
so there shall be no such thing as a cheap banana,
              or so bananas shall be bought cheaply.
Until there was starvation on the Atlantic coast of
        Nicaragua.
And the *campesinos* are put in jail for not selling at 30
        centavos.
And their bananas are bayoneted
and the Mexican Trader Steamship sinks their barges,
and the strikers are put down by shots.
(And the Nicaraguan deputies are invited to a garden
        party.)
But the Negro has seven kids to look after.
And you have to do something. You have to eat.
And you have to take what they pay you.
              24 centavos a bunch.
Meanwhile the subsidiary company Tropical Radio sends
        a cablegram to Boston:
"We hope that the distribution we have made
among the deputies of the majority party in Nicaragua
will have the approval of Boston

por los incalculables beneficios que para la Compañía
   representa."
Y de Boston a Galveston por telégrafo
y de Galveston por cable y teléfono a México
y de México por cable a San Juan del Sur
y de San Juan del Sur por telégrafo a Puerto Limón
y desde Puerto Limón en canoa hasta adentro en la
   montaña
llega la orden de la United Fruit Company:
"La Iunai no compra más banano."
Y hay despido de trabajadores en Puerto Limón.
Los pequeños talleres se cierran.
Nadie puede pagar una deuda.
Y los bananos pudriéndose en los vagones del ferrocarril.
         Para que no haya banano barato
         y para que haya banano barato.
               —19 ctvs. el racimo.
para la devolución de las plantaciones a la nación
Los trabajadores reciben vales en vez de jornales.
En vez de pago, deudas.
Y abandonadas las plantaciones, que ya no sirven para
   nada,
y dadas a colonias de desocupados.
Y la United Fruit Company en Costa Rica
con sus subsidiarias la Costa Rica Banana Company
y la Northern Railway Company y
la International Radio Telegraph Company
y la Costa Rica Supply Company
         pelean en los tribunales contra un huérfano.
El costo del descarrilamiento son 25 dólares de indemni-
   zación
(pero hubiera sido más caro componer la línea férrea).

Y los diputados más baratos que las mulas—decía Ze-
   murray.
Sam Zemurray, el turco vendedor de bananas al menudeo
en Mobile, Alabama, que un día hizo un viaje a Nueva

332

because of the incalculable benefits it represents for the
  Company."
And from Boston to Galveston by telegram
and from Galveston by cable and telegram to Mexico
and from Mexico by cable to San Juan del Sur
and from San Juan del Sur by telegram to Puerto Limón
and from Puerto Limón by canoe to the jungle
the order of the United Fruit Company arrives:
"The United is not buying any more bananas."
And they fire the workmen in Puerto Limón.
The small factories close down.
No one can pay their debts.
And the bananas are rotting in the freight cars by the
  railroad.
        So there shall be no such thing as a cheap banana
        and so bananas shall be bought cheaply.
              —19 centavos a bunch.
The workers get scrip instead of a day's wages.
Instead of a salary, debts.
And the plantations are abandoned as they are now no
  use for anything
and given over to colonies of the unemployed.
And the United Fruit Company in Costa Rica
with its subsidiaries the Costa Rica Banana Company,
and the Northern Railway Company and
the International Radio Telegraph Company
and the Costa Rica Supply Company
        litigate in the law courts against an orphan.
The cost of the derailment is twenty-five dollars compen-
  sation
(but it would have cost much more to repair the railroad).

And the deputies are cheaper than mules—Zemurray
  said.
Sam Zemurray, the Turkish retail dealer in bananas
in Mobile, Alabama, who made a journey one day to New
  Orleans

Orleáns
y vio en los muelles de la United echar los bananos al mar
y ofreció comprar toda la fruta para fabricar vinagre,
la compró, y la vendió allí mismo en Nueva Orleáns
y la United Tuvo que darle tierras en Honduras
con tal de que renunciara a su contrato en Nueva Orleáns,
y así fue como Sam Zemurray puso presidentes en
    Honduras.
Provocó disputas fronterizas entre Guatemala y Hondu-
    ras
(que eran la United Fruit Company y su compañía)
"una pulgada de tierra no sólo en la franja disputada,
sino también en cualquier otra zona hondureña
(de su compañía) no en disputa . . ."
(mientras la United defendía los derechos de Honduras
de la United de Honduras, en su litigio con Nicaragua
Lumber Company—no Nicaragua: Nicaragua Lumber
    Company
¡el tal "Territorio en Litigio"!) hasta que cesó la disputa
(la de Guatemala y Honduras) porque Sam se alió con la
    United
y después le vendió todas sus acciones a la United
y con el dinero de la venta compró acciones en la United
y con las acciones cogió por asalto la presidencia de
    Boston
(juntamente con sus empleados presidentes de Honduras)
y ya fue dueño igualmente de Honduras y Guatemala
y quedó abandonada la disputa de las tierras agotadas
que ya no le servían ni a Guatemala ni a Honduras.

Había un nicaragüense en el extranjero,
un "nica" de Niquinohomo,
trabajando en la Huasteca Petroleum Co., de Tampico.
Y tenía economizados cinco mil dólares.
Y no era ni militar ni político.
Y cogió tres mil dólares de los cinco mil
y se fue a Nicaragua a la revolución de Moncada.

334

and saw the bananas being thrown into the sea from the docks of the United
and offered to buy up all the fruit to make vinegar,
bought it and sold it there in New Orleans,
and so it was that Sam Zemurray made presidents in Honduras.
He provoked frontier disputes between Guatemala and Honduras
(that is, between the United Fruit Company and his company)
proclaiming that Honduras (by which he meant his company)
"wouldn't lose an inch of land either on the disputed frontier,
or for that matter in any other region of Honduras
(that belonged to his company) which was not under dispute . . ."
(while the United defended the rights of Honduras,
of the United Honduras, in its suit with the Nicaragua
Lumber Company—not Nicaragua: the Nicaragua Lumber Company,
the so-called "Territory under Dispute"!) until the dispute ended
(the one between Guatemala and Honduras) because Sam came to terms with the United
and then sold all his shares to the United
and with the money from the sale bought shares in the United
and with the shares he had bought took over the presidency in Boston
(together with its employees, the presidents of Honduras)
and so he became master both of Honduras and Guatemala
and the dispute was abandoned between the exhausted lands
which were now no use to either Guatemala or Honduras.

Pero cuando llegó, Moncada estaba entregando las armas.
Pasó tres días, triste, en el Cerro del Común.
Triste, sin saber qué hacer.
Y no era ni político ni militar.
Pensó, y pensó, y se dijo por fin:
Alguien tiene que ser.
          Y entonces escribió su primer manifiesto.

El Gral. Moncada telegrafía a los americanos:
TODOS MIS HOMBRES ACEPTAN LA RENDICION
    MENOS UNO.
Mr. Stimpson le pone un ultimátum.
        "El pueblo no agradece nada . . ."
        le manda a decir Moncada.
El reúne a sus hombres en el Chipote:
29 hombres (y con él 30) contra EE. UU.
        MENOS UNO.
        ("Uno de Niquinohomo . . .")
—Y con él 30!
"El que se mete a redentor muere crucificado,"
le manda otra vez a decir Moncada.
Porque Moncada y Sandino eran vecinos;
Moncada de Masatepe y Sandino de Niquinohomo.
Y Sandino le contesta a Moncada:
"La muerte no tiene la menor importancia."
Y a Stimpson: "Confío en el valor de mis hombres . . ."
Y a Stimpson, después de la primera derrota:
"El que cree que estamos vencidos
        no conoce a mis hombres."
Y no era ni militar ni político.
Y sus hombres:
        muchos eran muchachos,
con sombreros de palma y con caites
o descalzos, con machetes, ancianos
de barba blanca, niños de doce años con sus rifles,
blancos, indios impenetrables, y rubios, y negros murru-
    cos,

There was a Nicaraguan living abroad,
a "Nica" of Niquinihomo,
working with the Huasteca Petroleum Co., in Tampico.
And he had saved up five thousand dollars.
And went to Nicaragua to enlist in Moncada's revolution.
But when he arrived Moncada was surrendering his arms.
He spent three sad days on Común Mountain.
Sad because he didn't know what to do.
And he was neither a military man nor a politician.
He thought and thought and finally made up his mind:
Somebody has to do something.
     And then he scribbled out his first manifesto.

General Moncada sends a telegram to the Americans:
ALL MY MEN ACCEPT THE SURRENDER EXCEPT
    ONE.
Mr. Stimpson imposes an ultimatum on him.
      "The people will not thank you . . ."
      Moncada informs him.
He assembles his men in el Chipote:
29 men (and with him 30) against the U.S.A.
      EXCEPT ONE.
      ("A man from Niquinihomo . . .")
—And with him 30!
Moncada wrote to him again
"If you set yourself up as savior they will crucify you."
For Moncada and Sandino were neighbors;
Moncada from Masatepe and Sandino from Niquini-
    homo.
And Sandino answered Moncada:
"My death is not of the least importance."
And to Stimpson: "I have confidence in the courage of my
    men . . ."
And to Stimpson after the first defeat:
"If you think we are beaten
      you don't know my men."
And he was neither a military man nor a politician.

con los pantalones despedazados y sin provisiones,
los pantalones hechos jirones,
desfilando en fila india con la bandera adelante
—un harapo levantado en un palo de la montaña—
callados debajo de la lluvia, y cansados,
chapoteando las caites en los charcos del pueblo
       ¡Viva Sandino!
y de la montaña venían, y a la montaña volvían,
marchando, chapoteando, con la bandera adelante.
Un ejército descalzo o con caites y casi sin armas
que no tenía ni disciplina ni desorden
y donde ni los jefes ni la tropa ganaban paga
pero no se obligaba a pelear a nadie:
y tenían jerarquía militar pero todos eran iguales
sin distinción en la repartición de la comida
y el vestido, con la misma ración para todos.
Y los jefes no tenían ayudantes:
más bien como una comunidad que como un ejército
y más unidos por amor que por disciplina militar
aunque nunca ha habido mayor unidad en un ejército.
Un ejército alegre, con guitarras y con abrazos.
Una canción de amor era su himno de guerra:
       Si Adelita se fuera con otro
       La seguiría por tierra y por mar
       Si por mar en un buque de guerra
       Y si por tierra en un tren militar
"El abrazo es el saludo de todos nosotros,"
decía Sandino—y nadie ha abrazado como él.
Y siempre que hablaban de ellos decían *todos:*
"Todos nosotros . . ." "Todos somos iguales."
"Aquí todos somos hermanos," decía Umanzor.
Y todos estuvieron unidos hasta que los mataron a todos.
Peleando contra aeroplanos con tropas de zacate,
sin más paga que la comida y el vestido y las armas,
y economizando cada bala como si fuera de oro;
con morteros hechos con tubos
y con bombas hechas con piedras y pedazos de vidrios,

And as for his men:
        many of them were kids
wearing sombreros of palm leaves and sandals,
or they went barefoot and carried machetes, old men
with white beards, twelve-year-old boys with rifles,
Spanish, impenetrable Indians, blonds, curly-headed Ne-
        groes,
with their trousers in tatters, with no provisions,
with pennants they made from the rags of their trousers,
marching in Indian file with their banner in front
—a rag tied to a pole they had cut from the jungle—
marching silently under torrents of rain, worn-out,
their sandals splashing through the puddles in the villages
        Viva Sandino!
and they came from the jungle and went back to the
        jungle,
splashing through puddles with the banner in front.
An army in sandals or barefoot with hardly any weapons
which had neither discipline nor disorder
and neither the leaders nor the troops had any pay
but no one was compelled to fight;
and though they had a military hierarchy they were all
        equal
with no distinction of rank when they shared their food
and their clothes; they all had the same rations.
And the leaders had no adjutants:
it was more like a community than an army
and it was not military discipline that united them but
        love,
though never was there so much unity in an army.
An army of happy men who embraced each other and
        strummed guitars.
Their battle-hymn was a love-song:
        Si Adelita se fuera con otro
        La seguiría por tierra y por mar
        Si por mar en un buque de guerra
        Y si por tierra en un tren militar.

rellenas con dinamita de las minas y envueltas en cueros;
con granadas fabricadas con latas de sardinas.

"He is a *bandido*," decía Somoza, "a *bandolero*."
Y Sandino nunca tuvo propiedades.
Que traducido al español quiere decir:
Somoza le llamaba a Sandino bandolero.
Y Sandino nunca tuvo propiedades.
Y Moncada le llamaba bandido en los banquetes
y Sandino en las montañas no tenía sal
y sus hombres tiritando de frío en las montañas,
y la casa de su suegro la tenía hipotecada
para libertar a Nicaragua, mientras en la Casa Presiden-
cial
Moncada tenía hipotecada a Nicaragua.
"Claro que no es"—dice el Ministro Americano
riendo—"pero le llamamos bandolero en sentido técnico."
¿Qué es aquella luz allá lejos? ¿Es una estrella?
Es la luz de Sandino en la montaña negra.
Allá están él y sus hombres junto a la fogata roja
con sus rifles al hombro y envueltos en sus colchas,
fumando o cantando canciones tristes del Norte,
los hombres sin moverse y moviéndose sus sombras.

Su cara era vaga como la de un espíritu,
lejana por las meditaciones y los pensamientos
y seria por las campañas y la intemperie.
Y Sandino no tenía cara de soldado,
sino de poeta convertido en soldado por necesidad,
y de un hombre nervioso dominado por la serenidad.
Había dos rostros superpuestos en su rostro:
una fisonomía sombría y a la vez iluminada;
triste como un atardecer en la montaña.
y alegre como la mañana en la montaña.
En la luz su rostro se le rejuvenecía,
y en la sombra se le llenaba de cansancio.
Y Sandino no era inteligente ni era culto,

340

"All of us embrace each other instead of saluting,"
Sandino said, and no one could embrace a man as he did.
And whenever they spoke of themselves they said *all:*
"All of us . . ." "We are all equals."
"We are all brothers here," Umanzor said.
And they were all united until all of them were killed.
They decoyed airplanes with soldiers made of straw,
and food and clothes and arms was all their pay;
they hoarded every bullet as though it were gold;
their mortars were made of lead-piping,
their bombs of stones and broken glass
which they loaded with dynamite from the mines and
    wrapped in leather;
their grenades were made of sardine cans.

"He is a *bandido,*" Somoza said, "a *bandolero.*"
And Sandino never sold anyone's property.
Which, being translated, means
that Somoza called Sandino a gangster.
And Sandino never stole anyone's property.
And Moncada called Sandino a bandit at public banquets
and in the mountains Sandino didn't have any salt,
and his men were shivering with cold in the mountains,
and he had mortgaged his father-in-law's house
to set Nicaragua free while in the Presidential palace
Moncada had mortgaged the whole of Nicaragua.
"It's obvious that he isn't"—the American Minister said
    laughing
—"but it's in a technical sense that we call him *bando-
    lero.*"
What is that light in the distance? Is it a star?
It's Sandino's light as he moves through the dark of the
    forest.
That's where he is with his men around their red bonfire
wrapped in their blankets with rifles on their shoulders
smoking or singing sad songs from the north,
none of them stirring, only their shadows stirring.

341

pero salió inteligente de la montaña.
"En la montaña todo enseña" decía Sandino
(soñando con las Segovias llenas de escuelas)
y recibía menajes de todas las montañas
y parecía que cada cabaña espiaba para él
(donde los extranjeros fueran como hermanos
todos los extranjeros hasta los "americanos")
　　　—"hasta los yanquis . . ."
Y: "Dios hablará por los segovianos . . ." decía.
"Nunca creí que saldría vivo de esta guerra
pero siempre he creído que era necessaria . . ."
Y: "¿Creen que yo voy a ser latifundista?"

Es medianoche en las montañas de las Segovias.
¡Y aquella luz es Sandino! Una luz con un canto . . .
　　　Si Adelita se fuera con otro
Pero las naciones tienen su sino.
Y Sandino no fue nunca presidente
sino que el asesino de Sandino fue el presidente
¡y 20 años presidente!
　　　Si Adelita se fuera con otro
　　　La seguiría por tierra y por mar
Se firmó el desarme. Cargaron las armas en carretas.
Guatuceros amarrados con cabuyas, rifles sarrosos
y unas cuantas ametralladoras viejas.
Y las carretas van bajando por la sierra.
　　　Si por mar en un buque de guerra
　　　Y si por tierra en un tren militar
Telegrama del Ministro Americano (Mr. Lane)
al Secretario de Estado—depositado en Managua
el 14 de febrero de 1934 a las 6:05 P.M.
y recibido en Washington a las 8:50 P.M.:
　　　"Informado por fuente official
　　　que el avión no pudo aterrizar en Wiwilí
　　　y por tanto la venida de Sandino se re-
　　　　　trasa"

342

His features were indistinct like those of a ghost,
deeply abstracted by meditation
and preoccupied by the difficulties of a guerrilla campaign
with its life of continual exposure to torrential rain and
    sun.
And Sandino's face wasn't the face of a soldier,
but of a poet turned soldier by necessity,
and of a highly strung man dominated by serenity.
He had two faces superimposed on each other:
a dark physiognomy which was at the same time lit up;
sad as the sunset over the jungle
and cheerful as morning over the jungle.
In the light his face was youthful
and in the shadows it seemed overwhelmed by exhaus-
    tion.
And Sandino was not intelligent or well read
but became intelligent in the mountains.
"In the mountains everything teaches you," Sandino said
(dreaming of Las Segovias full of schools)
and he received messages from all parts of the mountains
and it seemed as though every cabin was spying for him
(where foreigners would be regarded as brothers,
all kinds of foreigners even the "Americans")
        —"even the yanquis . . ."
And: "God will speak through the people of Las Sego-
    vias . . ." he said
"I have never expected to come out of this alive
but I have always believed it was necessary . . ."
And: "Do you think I will become a landowner?"

It is the middle of the night in the mountains of Las
    Segovias.
And that light is Sandino! A light and a song . . .
        Si Adelita se fuera con otro
But the nations are following their destiny.
And Sandino never became president
but Sandino's assassin was the president

343

El telegrama del Ministro Americano (Mr. Lane)
al Secretario de Estado el 16 de febrero
anunciando la llegada de Sandino a Managua
Not Printed
no fue publicado en la memoria del Depto. de Estado.
Como la guardatinaja que salió del matorral
a la carretera y es acorralada por los perros
y se queda parada delante de los tiradores
porque sabe que no tiene para donde correr . . .
"I talked with Sandino for half an hour"
—dijo Somoza al Ministro Americano—
"but I can't tell you what he talked about
because I don't know what he talked about
because I don't know what he talked about."

"Y ya verán que yo nunca tendré propiedades . . ."
Y: "Es in-cons-ti-tu-cio-nal," decía Sandino.
"La Guardia Nacional es inconstitucional."
"An insult!" dijo Somoza al Ministro Americano
el VEINTIUNO DE FEBRERO a las 6 de la tarde.
"An insult! I want to stop Sandino."

Cuatro presos están cavando un hoyo.
"¿Quién ha muerto?" dijo un preso.
"Nadie," dijo el guardia.
"¿Entonces para qué es el hoyo?"

"Qué perdés," dijo el guardia, "seguí cavando."

El Ministro Americano está almorzando con Moncada.
"Will you have coffee, sir?
It's very good coffee, sir."
"What?" Moncada aparta la mirada de la ventana
y mira al criado: "Oh, yes, I'll have coffee."
Y se ríe. "Certainly."

En un cuartel cinco hombres están en un cuarto cerrado
con centinelas en las puertas y en las ventanas.

344

and president for twenty years!
>*Si Adelita se fuera con otro*
>*La seguiría por tierra y por mar*

The ceasefire was signed. The weapons were loaded on
carts.
Guns lashed together with cords, rusty rifles
and half a dozen old machine-guns
and the carts wind slowly down the mountainside.
>*Si por mar en un buque de guerra*
>*Y si por tierra en un tren militar*

Telegram from the American Minister (Mr. Lane)
to the Secretary of State—sent from Managua
February 14, 1934, at 6:05 P.M.
and received in Washington at 8:50 P.M.:
>"Informed by official sources
>that the airplane was unable to land at Wiwilí
>and Sandino's arrival is delayed . . ."

The telegram from the American Minister (Mr. Lane)
to the Secretary of State on February 16
announcing Sandino's arrival in Managua
Not Printed
was not published in the records of the State Department.
Like the *guardatiniaje* that runs out of the bushes
onto the highway and is surrounded by dogs
and remains motionless before the hunters
because he knows there is nowhere he can go . . .
"I talked to Sandino for half an hour"
—Somoza told the American Minister—
"but I can't tell you what he talked about
because I don't know what he talked about
because I don't know what he talked about."

"And you will see that I won't own any property . . ."
And: "It is UNCONSTITUTIONAL," Sandino said.
"The Guardia Nacional is unconstitutional."
"An insult!" Somoza told the American Minister

A uno de los hombres le falta un brazo.
Entra el jefe gordo con condecoraciones y les dice: "Yes."

Otro hombre va a cenar esta noche con el Presidente
(el hombre para el que estuvieron cavando el hoyo)
y les dice a sus amigos: "Vámonos. Ya es hora."
Y suben a cenar con el Presidente de Nicaragua.
A las 10 de la noche bajan en automóvil a Managua.
En la mitad de la bajada los detienen los guardias.
A los dos más viejos se los llevan en un auto
y a los otros tres en otro auto para otro lado.
A donde cuatro presos estuvieron cavando un hoyo.
"¿Adónde vamos?"
preguntó el hombre para el que hicieron el hoyo.
      Y nadie le contestó.
Después el auto se paró y un guardia les dijo:
"Salgan." Los tres salieron,
y un hombre al que le faltaba un brazo gritó "¡Fuego!"

"I was in a Concierto," dijo Somoza.
Y era cierto había estado en un concierto
o en un banquete viendo bailar a una bailarina o
quién sabe qué mierda sería.
Y a las 10 de la noche, Somoza tuvo miedo.
De pronto afuera repicó el teléfono.
"¡Sandino lo llama por teléfono!"
Y tuvo miedo. Uno de sus amigos le dijo:
"¡No seas pendejo, jodido!"
Somoza mandó no contestar al teléfono.
La bailarina seguía bailando para el asesino.
Y afuera en la oscuridad siguió repicando y repicando el
    teléfono.

A la luz de una lámpara tubular
cuatro guardias están cerrando un hoyo.
Y a la luz de una luna de febrero.

346

on the TWENTY-FIRST OF FEBRUARY at six in the
    evening.
"An insult! I want to stop Sandino."

Four convicts were digging a pit.
"Who've they done in?" one of the convicts asked.
"No one," said the guard.
"Then who's the pit for?"

"Quit bellyaching and dig," said the guard.

The American Minister is having lunch with Moncada.
"Will you have coffee, sir?
It's very good coffee, sir."
"What?" Moncada turns away from the window
and stares at the servant: "Oh, yes, I'll have coffee."
And he laughed. "Certainly."

There are five men in a locked room in the barracks
with guards posted at the doors and windows.
One of the men has only one arm.
The fat bemedalled officer comes in and says: "Yes."

Another man is going to have dinner with the President
    tonight
(the man for whom they were digging the pit)
and he says to his friends: "Let's go. It's time now."
And they go to have dinner with the President of Nica-
    ragua.
At ten o'clock they get into the car to go, down to
    Managua.
In the middle of the journey they are stopped by the
    guards.
They take the two older men off in one car
and the other three in another car in another direction.
To the place where four convicts were digging a pit.
"Where are we going?"

Es hora en que el lucero nistoyolero de Chontales
levanta a las inditas a hacer nistoyol,
y salen el chiclero, el maderero y el reicillero
con los platanales todavía plateados por la luna,
con el grito del coyotesolo y el perico melero
y el chiflido de la lechuza a la luz de la luna.
La guardatinaja y la guatuza salen de sus hoyos
y los pocoyos y cadejos se esconden en los suyos.
La Llorona va llorando a la orilla de los ríos:
"¿Lo hallaste?" "¡No!" "¿Lo hallaste?" "¡No!"
Un pájaro se queja como el crujido de un palo,
después la cañada se calla como oyendo algo,
y de pronto un grito . . . El pájaro pronuncia
la misma palabra triste, la misma palabra triste.
Los campistos empiezan a totear sus vacas:
Tóooo-tó-tó-tó; Tóoo-tó-tó-tó, Tóoo-tó-tó-tó;
los lancheros levantan las velas de sus lanchas;
el telegrafista de San Rafael del Norte telegrafía:
BUENOS DÍAS SIN NOVEDAD EN SAN RAFAEL DEL
    NORTE
y el telegrafista de Juigalpa: SIN NOVEDAD EN JUI-
    GALPA.
Y las tucas van bajando por el Río Escondido
con los patos gritando cuá-cuá-cuá, y los ecos,
los ecos, mientras el remolcador va con las tucas
resbalando sobre el verde río de vidrio
hacia el Atlántico . . .

Y mientras en los salones del Palacio Presidencial
y en los patios de las prisiones y en los cuarteles
y la Legación Americana y la Estación de Policía
los que velaron esa noche se ven en el alba lívida
con las manos y las caras como manchadas de sangre.

"I did it," dijo después Somoza.
"I did it, for the good of Nicaragua."

348

the man for whom they were digging the pit asked them.
      And no one answered him.
Then the car stopped and a guard said to them:
"Get out." The three of them got out,
and a man who had only one arm shouted "Fire!"

"I was in a *concierto*," Somoza said.
And it was true, he had been at a concert
or at a banquet or watching a ballerina dance or
whatever the shit it was he was doing.
And at ten o'clock Somoza began to be afraid.
Suddenly the telephone rang outside.
"Sandino is calling him on the telephone!"
And he began to be afraid. One of his friends told him:
"Don't be chicken-shit, man!"
Somoza ordered them not to answer the phone.
The ballerina went on dancing for the assassin.
And in the dark outside the telephone went on ringing and
      ringing.

By the light of a moon in February
four guards were shoveling earth in a pit.
By the light of a moon in February.

It is the hour when the morning star of the Indian of
      Chontales
wakens the Indian girls to grind the corn,
and the gatherer of chicle goes out, and the woodcutter
      and the gatherer of raicilla
with the plantain trees turned silver by the moon,
with the cry of the coyote and the wildcat
and the owl hooting in the moonlight.
The *guardatinaja* and the *guatuza* come out of their holes
and the *pocoyos* and *cadejos* go back to theirs.
The Weeping Woman wanders weeping by the banks of
      the rivers:
"Did you find him?" "No!" "Did you find him?" "No!"

349

Y William Walker dijo cuando lo iban a matar:
"El Presidente de Nicaragua es nicaragüense."

En abril, en Nicaragua, los campos están secos.
Es el mes de las quemas de los campos,
del calor, y los potreros cubiertos de brasas,
y los cerros que son de color de carbón;
del viento caliente, y el aire que huele a quemado,
y de los campos que se ven azulados por el humo
y las polvaredas de los tractores destroncando;
de los cauces de los ríos secos como caminos
y las ramas de los palos peladas como raíces;
de los soles borrosos y rojos como sangre
y las lunas enormes y rojas como soles,
y las quemas lejanas, de noche, como estrellas.

En mayo llegan las primeras lluvias.
La hierba tierna renace de las cenizas.
Los lodosos tractores roturan la tierra.
Los caminos se llenan de mariposas y de charcos,
y las noches son frescas, y cargadas de insectos,
y llueve toda la noche. En mayo
florecen los malinches en las calles de Managua.
Pero abril en Nicaragua es el mes de la muerte.

En abril los mataron.
Yo estuve con ellos en la rebelión de abril
y aprendí a manejar una ametralladora Rising.
        Y Adolfo Báez Bone era mi amigo:
Lo persiguieron con aviones, con camiones,
con reflectores, con bombas lacrimógenas,
con radios, con perros, con guardias;
y yo recuerdo las nubes rojas sobre la Casa Presidencial
como algodones ensangrentados,
y la luna roja sobre la Casa Presidencial.
La radio clandestina decía que vivía.
El pueblo no creía que había muerto.

350

A bird laments like a pole creaking,
and then the ravine is silent as if listening to something,
and then another cry . . . The bird pronounces
the same sad word, the same sad word.
The herdsmen are beginning to call their cows:
Tooo-to-to-to; tooo-to-to-to;
the boatmen unfurl the sails on their boats;
the telegraph officer of San Rafael del Norte cables:
SAN RAFAEL DEL NORTE REPORTING ALL'S WELL
and the telegraph officer in Juigalpa: ALL'S WELL IN
    JUIGALPA.
And the logs are traveling down the Río Escondido
and the ducks cry quack quack, and the echoes,
the echoes, while the tugboat goes off with the logs
sliding along the glassy green surface of the river
toward the Atlantic . . .

While in the rooms of the Presidential Palace
and the courtyards of the prisons and in the barracks
and in the American Embassy and the Police Station
those who stayed awake this night look at their hands and
    faces
and in the light of dawn they seem stained with blood.

"I did it," Somoza said later.
"I did it, for the good of Nicaragua."

And William Walker said when they were going to kill
    him:
"El Presidente de Nicaragua es nicaragüense."

In April the fields are dry in Nicaragua.
It is the month when there are fires in the fields,
it is the hottest month and the pastures are covered with
    red-hot cinders,
and the hillsides are the color of coal;
the month of the hot wind when the air smells of smoke

351

(Y no ha muerto.)
Porque a veces nace un hombre en una tierra
    que es esa tierra.
Y la tierra en que es enterrado ese hombre
    es esa tierra.
Y los hombres que después nacen en esa tierra
    son ese hombre.
Y Adolfo Báez Bone era ese hombre.

"Si a mí me pusieran a escoger mi destino
(me había dicho Báez Bone tres días antes)
entre morir asesinado como Sandino
o ser Presidente como el asesino de Sandino
yo escogería el destino de Sandino."
        Y él escogió su destino.
La gloria no es la que enseñan los textos de historia:
es una zopilotera en un campo y un gran hedor.
Pero cuando muere un héroe
        no se muere:
sino que ese héroe renace
        en una Nación.

Después EE. UU. le mandó más armas a Somoza;
como media mañana estuvieron pasando las armas;
camiones y camiones cargados con cajones de armas;
todos marcados U.S.A., MADE IN U.S.A.,
armas para echar más presos, para perseguir libros,
para robarle a Juan Potosme cinco pesos.
Yo vi pasar esas armas por la Avenida Roosevelt.
Y la gente callada en las calles las veía pasar:
el flaco, el descalzo, el de la bicicleta,
el negro, el trompudo, aquella la de amarillo,
el alto, el chele, el pelón, el bigotudo,
el ñato, el chirizo, el murruco, el requeneto:
y la cara de toda esa gente
        era la de un ex teniente muerto.

352

and the fields turn blue under the smoke
and the tractors turn over the clods with clouds of dust;
the beds of rivers are as dry as roads
and the branches of the trees stripped bare as roots;
it is the month when the sun is blurred and red as blood
and when the moon is enormous and red as the sun,
and far off in the night the bonfires burn like stars.

In May the first rains begin to fall.
The young grass is reborn from the ashes.
The tractors plough through fields heavy with mud.
The paths are littered with butterflies and puddles,
and the nights are fresh and full of insects,
and it rains all night. In May
the malinche trees are in flower in the streets of Managua.
But April is the month of death in Nicaragua.

They killed them in April.
I was with them in the April rebellion
          And Adolfo Báez Bone was my friend:
They hunted him down with airplanes and armored cars,
with searchlights, with tear-gas bombs,
with radios, with cops, and with police dogs;
and I remember the red clouds over the Presidential
     Palace
like bloody balls of cotton wool,
and the moon red over the Presidential Palace.
The secret radio said he was alive.
The people didn't believe he had been killed.
Because there are times when a man is born in a country.
And the country in which that man is buried
          is that man.
And the men who are born after him in that land
          are that man.
And Adolfo Báez Bone was that man.

"If they gave me a choice between the destiny
(Báez Bone said to me three days earlier)

353

La música de los mambos bajaba hasta Managua.
Con sus ojos rojos y turbios como los de los tiburones
pero un tiburón con guardaespaldas y con armamentos
(*Eulamia nicaragüensis*)
Somoza estaba bailando mambo

mambo mambo
qué rico el mambo
cuando los estaban matando.
Y Tachito Somoza (el hijo) sube a la Casa Presidencial
a cambiarse una camisa manchada de sangre
por otra limpia.

Manchada de sangre con chile.
Los perros de la prisión aullaban de lástima.
Los vecinos de los cuarteles oían los gritos.
Primero era un grito solo en mitad de la noche,
y después más gritos y más gritos
y después un silencio . . . Después una descarga
y un tiro solo. Después otro silencio,

y una ambulancia.

¡Y en la cárcel otra vez están aullando los perros!
El ruido de la puerta de hierro que se cierra
detrás de vos y entonces empiezan las preguntas
y la acusación, la acusación de conspiración
y la confesión, y después las alucinaciones,
la foto de tu esposa relumbrando como un foco
delante de vos y las noches llenas de alaridos
y de ruidos y de silencio, un silencio sepulcral,
y otra vez la misma pregunta, la misma pregunta,
y el mismo ruido repetido y el foco en los ojos
y después los largos meses que siguieron.
¡Ah, poder acostarse uno esta noche en su cama
sin temor a ser levantado y sacado de su casa,
a los golpes en la puerta y al timbre de noche!

Suenan tiros en la noche, o parecen tiros.
Pasan pesados camiones, y se paran,

of being assassinated like Sandino
or becoming President like Sandino's assassin
I would choose Sandino's destiny."
          And he chose his destiny.
Glory is not the way they teach it in the history textbooks:
it is a flock of vultures in a field and a bad smell.
But when a hero dies
          he is not dead
for the hero is reborn
          in a Nation.

Then the U.S. sent more arms to Somoza;
for fully half a day the arms rolled past;
truck after truck loaded with cases of arms;
all of them labelled U.S.A., MADE IN U.S.A.,
arms to take more prisoners, to hunt down books,
to rob Juan Potosme of his five pesos.
And I saw these arms going down the Avenida Roosevelt.
And the people in the streets fell silent when they saw
     them passing:
the skinny fellow, the one with no shoes, the one with a
     bicycle,
the Negro, the one with a big nose, the one dressed in
     yellow,
the tall fellow, the blond one, the bald-head, the one with
     a moustache,
the flat-faced fellow, the scrawny one, the curly-head, the
     one with straight hair;
and every one of these people had the face
          of a dead ex-lieutenant.

The music of the mambos goes down toward Managua.
With eyes red and bleary like a shark's eyes,
but a shark with a bodyguard and machine-guns,
(*Eulamia nicaragüensis*)
Somoza was dancing the mambo
                              mambo mambo

355

y siguen. Uno ha oído sus voces.
Es en la esquina. Estarán cambiando de guardia.
Uno ha oído sus risas y sus armas.
El sastre de enfrente ha encendido la luz.
Y pareció que golpearan aquí. O donde el sastre.
¡Quién sabe si esta noche vos estáis en la lista!
Y sigue la noche. Y falta mucha noche todavía.
Y el día no será sino una noche con sol.
La quietud de la noche bajo el gran solazo.

El Ministro Americano Mr. Whelan
asiste a la fiesta de la Casa Presidencial.
Las luces de la Presidencial se ven desde toda Managua.
La música de la fiesta llega hasta las celdas de los presos
en la quieta brisa de Managua bajo la Ley Marcial.
Los presos en sus celdas alcanzan a oír la música
entre los gritos de los torturados en las pilas.
Arriba en la Presidencial Mr. Whelan dice: *"¡Fine
    Party!"*
Como le dijo a Sumner Welles el sonofabich de Roosevelt:
"Somoza is a sonofabich
                but he's ours."
Esclavo de los extranjeros
                y tirano de su pueblo
impuesto por la intervención
                y mantenido por la no intervención:
SOMOZA FOREVER.

El espía que sale de día
el agente que sale de noche
y el arresto de noche:
los que están presos por hablar en un bus
o por gritar un Viva
o por un chiste.
"Acusado de hablar mal del Sr. Presidente . . ."
Y los juzgados por un juez con cara de sapo
o en Consejos de Guerra por guardias con caras de perro;

356

while they were killing them.
And Tachito Somoza (his son) goes up to the Presidential
    Palace
to change his blood-stained shirt
for a clean one.
        Stained with blood and chile.
The dogs in the prison howled with pity.
The people who lived near the barracks heard the cries.
First a solitary scream in the middle of the night,
then more screams and more
and then a silence . . . Then a volley of rifle-fire
and a solitary shot. Then another silence,
        and an ambulance.

And in the prison the dogs are howling again!
The noise of an iron door clanging behind you
and they begin the interrogation
and the accusation, the accusation of conspiracy,
and you make your confession, and then you begin
    hallucinating,
you see your wife's photo lit up like a spotlight
before your eyes; the nights are full of people screaming,
of noises, of silence, a graveyard silence,
and again the same question, the same question,
and the same noise reiterated and the spotlight in your
    eyes,
and then the endless months of waiting.
How good it would be
in your own bed tonight
without the terror of them waking you up and hauling you
    out of your house,
or of knocks on the door and the bell ringing!

Shots ring out in the night, or what seem like shots.
Heavy-laden trucks pass, come to a halt,
and move on again. You have heard their voices.

a los que han hecho beber orines y comer mierda
(cuando tengáis Constitución recordadlos)
los de la bayoneta en la boca y la aguja en el ojo,
las pilas electrizadas y el foco en los ojos.
—"Es un hijueputa, Mr. Welles, pero es de nosotros."
Y en Guatemala, en Costa Rica, en México,
los exiliados de noche se despiertan gritando,
soñado que les están aplicando otra vez la maquinita,
o que están otra vez amarrados
y ven venir a Tachito con la aguja.
". . . Y galán, hombre . . ."
                              (decía un campesino).
"Sí, era él. Y galán, hombre . . .
Blanco, con su camisita amarilla
de manga corta.
                    Galán, el jodido."

Cuando anochece en Nicaragua la Casa Presidencial
se llena de sombras. Y aparecen caras.
Caras en la oscuridad.
                    Las caras ensangrentadas.
Adolfo Báez Bone; Pablo Leal sin lengua;
Luis Gabuardi mi compañero de clase al que quemaron
    vivo
y murió gritando "¡Muera Somoza!"
La cara del telegrafista de 16 años
(y no se sabe ni siquiera su nombre)
que transmitía de noche mensajes clandestinos
a Costa Rica, telegramas temblorosos a través
de la noche, desde la Nicaragua oscura de Tacho
(y no figurará en los textos de historia)
y fue descubierto, y murió mirando a Tachito;
su cara lo mira todavía. El muchacho
al que encontraron de noche pegando papeletas
            SOMOZA ES UN LADRÓN
y es arriado al monte por unos guardias riendo . . .
Y tantas otras sombras, tantas otras sombras;

They're at the intersection. They must be changing the
    guard.
You hear their laughter and the clash of their rifles.
The tailor who lives opposite has switched his light on.
And you thought they were knocking here. Or at his door.
Maybe tonight they have your name on their list!
And the night wears on and the hours till dawn are
    endless.
And the day will only be a sunlit night.
The silence of night under the sun at noon.

The American Minister Mr. Whelan
has gone to a banquet at the Presidential Palace.
You can see the lights of the palace anywhere in Mana-
    gua.
The music is wafted from the banquet to the prisoners'
    cells
on the quiet breeze of Managua under martial law.
The prisoners can hear the music in their cells
mingling with the cries of men being tortured in the
    water-troughs.
Upstairs in the palace Mr. Whelan says: "Fine party!"
As that sonofabitch Roosevelt said to Sumner Welles:
"Somoza is a sonofabitch
                but he's ours."
Lackey to the foreigners
                and a tyrant to his own people
imposed by intervention
                and kept there by a policy of
                        nonintervention:
SOMOZA FOREVER.

The spy who walks by day
the secret agent by night
and the arrests at night:
those who are arrested for talking on a bus
or for shouting a Viva

las sombras de las zopiloteras de Wiwilí;
la sombra de Estrada; la sombra de Umanzor;
la sombra de Sócrates Sandino;
y la gran sombra, la del gran crimen,
la sombra de Augusto César Sandino;
Todas las noches en Managua la Casa Presidencial
se llena de sombras.

Pero el héroe nace cuando muere
y la hierba verde renace de los carbones.

or for a joke.
"Accused of slandering Mr. President . . ."
And those who are sentenced by a judge with a face like a
  toad
or in the Councils of War by cops with faces like dogs;
those who have been made to drink piss or eat shit
(when you have a constitution remember them)
those with bayonets in their mouths and needles in their
  eyes,
electrocuted in water-troughs with spotlights in their
  eyes.
—"He's a sonofabitch, Mr. Welles, but he's ours."
And in Guatemala, in Costa Rica, in Mexico,
the exiles wake up in the middle of the night and cry out
dreaming they were being tortured again,
or that they were being tied up with cords again,
or that they were being tied up with his needle.
". . . And he was a nice-looking fellow, y'know . . ."
     (said a *campesino*).
"Yes, that was him. And nice-looking, y'know . . .
Fair-skinned and wearing a little yellow shirt
with short sleeves.
    Nice-looking, the prick."

When night falls in Nicaragua the Presidential Palace
fills with ghosts. And faces appear.
Faces in the gloom.
     Faces that drip with blood.
Adolfo Báez Bone; Pablo Leal with his tongue ripped out;
Luis Gabuardi my classmate whom they burned alive
and who died shouting "Muera Somoza!"
The face of the sixteen-year-old telegraph operator
(even his name is forgotten)
who sent secret messages at night
to Costa Rica, telegrams trembling across
the night, out of the dark Nicaragua of Tacho
(and he will not be remembered in the history textbooks)

361

and who was caught in the act and died staring at
    Tachito;
his face stares at him still. The kid
who was caught one night sticking up posters that said
        SOMOZA IS A GANGSTER
and who was dragged off out of the city by guards who
    laughed as they shot him . . .
And hundreds of other ghosts, so many ghosts;
the ghosts whose bones were picked by the vultures of
    Wiwilí;
the ghost of Estrada; the ghost of Umanzor;
the ghost of Socrates Sandino;
and the greatest ghost of them all, the ghost of the
    greatest crime,
the ghost of Augusto César Sandino.
Every night in Managua the Presidential Palace
is filled with ghosts.

But the hero is born the moment that he dies
and green grass springs again from the ashes.

[*Translated by Donald Gardner*]

Anonymous

La cortina del país natal

Mis amigos demócratas,
comunistas, socialcristianos,
elogian o denigran

La Cortina de Hierro
La Cortina de Bambú
La Cortina de Dólares
La Cortina de Sangre
La Cortina de Caña

Son unos excelentes cortineros.
Pero nadie se refiere
a la Cortina de Mierda
de Mi Nicaragua Natal.

The Curtain of the Native Land

My democratic, communist,
christian-socialist friends
eulogize or denigrate

> The Iron Curtain
> The Bamboo Curtain
> The Dollar Curtain
> The Curtain of Blood
> The Curtain of Cane

They are excellent curtain makers.
But no one ever mentions
the Curtain of Shit
of My Native Nicaragua.

[*Translated by Robert Márquez*]

Peru

Of the younger poets currently writing in Peru, **Antonio Cisneros** (1942–   ) is undoubtedly the one who enjoys the greatest amount of national and international prestige. This recognition is well earned. Finding much of his inspiration in the historical and anthropological themes suggested by the Peruvian landscape and collective experience, Cisneros writes with the studied precision, concern for structure, and understated passion that mark the fine craftsman, without simultaneously depriving his verse of its immediacy and imaginative vitality, of its distinctly original personality.

Cisneros was born in Lima in the same year as Javier Heraud (1942). After studying at the Catholic University, he took his Doctorate in Literature at the University of San Marcos. He was later a member of the faculty at San Marcos and at the University of Huamanga.

In 1965 he was awarded the National Prize for Poetry for his *Comentarios Reales*. Three years later he won the coveted Casa de Las Américas poetry prize for *Canto ceremonial contra un oso hormiguero*, from which the poems included here are taken. His other published works of poetry are *Destierro* (1961), and *David* (1962). His poems have been translated into several languages and his work has appeared in several magazines abroad. He is a member of the editorial staff of the Peruvian journal *Amaru* and currently lives in London.

Karl Marx Died 1883 Aged 65

Todavía estoy a tiempo de recordar la casa de mi tía
    abuela y ese par de grabados:
"Un caballero en la casa del sastre," "Gran desfile militar
    en Viena, 1902."
Días en que ya nada malo podía ocurrir. Todos llevaban
    su pata de conejo atada a la cintura.
También mi tía abuela—veinte años y el sombrero de paja
    bajo el sol, preocupándose apenas
por mantener la boca, las piernas bien cerradas.
Eran los hombres de buena voluntad y las orejas limpias.
Sólo en el music-hall los anarquistas, locos barbudos y
    envueltos en bufandas.
Qué otoños, qué veranos.
Eiffel hizo una torre que decía, "Hasta aquí llegó el
    hombre." Otro grabado:
"Virtud y amor y celo protegiendo a las buenas familias."
Y eso que el viejo Marx aún no cumplía los veinte años de
    edad bajo esta yerba—gorda y erizada, conveniente a
    los campos de golf.
Las coronas de flores y el cajón tuvieron tres descansos al
    pie de la colina
y después fue enterrado
junto a la tumba de Molly Redgrove "bombardeada por el
    enemigo en 1940 y vuelta a construir."
Ah el viejo Karl moliendo y derritiendo en la marmita los
    diversos metales
mientras sus hijos saltaban de las torres de Spiegel a las
    islas de Times
y su mujer hervía las cebollas y la cosa no iba y después sí
    y entonces
vino lo de Plaza Vendôme y eso de Lenín y el montón de
    revueltas y entonces
las damas temieron algo más que una mano en las nalgas
    y los caballeros pudieron sospechar

Karl Marx Died 1883 Aged 65

I can still remember my great aunt's old house & that pair
    of etchings:
"A gentleman at the tailor's," "Great military parade in
    Vienna, 1902."
Days when nothing bad could happen. Everyone carried a
    rabbit's foot tied to their belts.
My great aunt too—twenty years old in a straw hat for
    the sun, scarcely worrying about more
than keeping her mouth shut & her legs closed.
The men were of goodwill & kept their noses clean.
Anarchists could only be found in the music-halls, crazy
    & bearded, wrapped in scarves.
What summers! What autumns!
Eiffel built a tower that said: "Man has reached this
    height." Another etching:
"Virtue, Love & Zeal protecting decent families."
And yet it was less than twenty years since old Marx had
    been put six feet under grass—tough & stiff, fit only
    for golf courses.
The wreaths & coffin rested three times at the foot of the
    hill
& then he was buried
next to the tomb of Molly Redgrove ("bombed by the
    enemy in 1940 & rebuilt").
And old Karl melting & grinding different metals in the
    pot
while his children jumped from the towers of *Der Spiegel*
    to islands of the *Times*
& his wife boiled onions & things didn't go well & later
they did & came the Place Vendome & Lenin & a whole
    lot of revolts then
the ladies were scared of more than a pat on the arse &
    gentlemen suspected
that the steam engine was no longer the symbol of
    universal happiness.

que la locomotora a vapor ya no era más el rostro de la felicidad universal.

"Así fue, y estoy en deuda contigo, viejo aguafiestas."

"That's the way it was & I'm in your debt, old spoilsport."

[Translated by Maureen Ahern and David Tipton]

In Memoriam

Para Mario Sotomayor

Yo vi a los manes de mi generación, a los lares, cantar en
    ceremonias, alegrarse
cuando Cuba y Fidel y aquel año 60 eran apenas
un animal inferior, invertebrado.
                Y yo los vi después
cuando Cuba y Fidel y todas esas cosas fueron peso y
    color
y la fuerza y la belleza necesarias a un mamífero joven.
Yo corría con ellos
                y yo los vi correr.
Y el animal fue cercado con aceite, con estacas de pino,
    para que ninguno conociera
su brillante pelaje, su tambor.
Yo estuve con mi alegre ignorancia, mi rabia, mis plumas
    de colores
en las antiguas fiestas de la hoguera,
                Cuba sí, yanquis no.
Y fue entonces que tuvimos nuestro muerto.
(Los marinos volvieron con su cuerpo en una bolsa, con
    las carnes estropeadas
y la noticia de reinos convenientes.
Así les ofrecimos sopa de acelgas, panes con asado,
    betarragas,
y en la noche
                quemanos su navío.)

Quién no tuvo un par de manes, tres lares y algún brujo
    como toda heredad
—sabios y amables son, engordan cada día.
Hombres del país donde la única Torre es el comercio de
    harina de pescado,
gastados como un odre de vino entre borrachos.
                Qué aire ya nos queda.

In Memoriam

For Mario Sotomayor

I'd seen the manes & lares of my generation singing at
    celebrations, making merry
when Cuba & Fidel & that year of 1960 were just
a lower, invertebrate animal.
                And I saw them afterward
when Cuba & Fidel & all those things had weight & color
& the strength & beauty necessary to a young mammal.
I ran with them
            & watched them running.
And the animal was encircled with oil & pine stakes, so
    that no one should know
its brilliant coat, its drum.
With my gay ignorance, my rage, my colored feathers
I was there at the ancient bonfire feasts,
           Cuba sí, yankees no.
And it was then we had our death.
(The marines came back with his body in a bag, with the
    ravaged flesh
& news of convenient kingdoms.
So we offered them onion soup, beef sandwiches, beet-
    root,
& in the night
           burnt their ship.)

Who's not had a pair of manes, three lares & some
    witchdoctor as all their inheritance
—wise & kindly, they grow fatter every day.
Men of the land where the only Tower is the fish-meal
    business,
spent like a wine-butt among drunks.
           What air is there left to breathe.
And we were given an old wreath from the hands of Virgil
    himself & from Erasmus

Y recibimos un laurel viejo de las manos del propio
    Virgilio y de manos de Erasmo
una medalla rota.
Holgados y seguros en el vericueto de la Academia y las
    publicaciones.
Temiendo algún ataque del Rey de los Enanos, tensos al
    vuelo de una mosca:
Odiseos maltrechos que se hicieron al agua
aun cuando los temporales destruían el sol y las manadas
    de cangrejos, y he aquí
que embarraron con buen sebo la proa
hasta llegar a las tierras del Hombre de Provecho.
(*Amontonad los muertos en el baño, ocultadlos, y pronto
    el Coliseo*
será limpio y propicio como una cama blanda.)

Hay un animal noble y hermoso cercado entre ballestas.
En la frontera Sur la guerra ha comenzado. La peste, el
    hambre, en la frontera Norte.

a broken medallion.
Well-placed & safe in the tricky ground of the Academy &
    publishing.
Fearful of some attack from the King of Dwarves, tense at
    the buzzing of a fly:
battered Odysseuses who put to sea
even when storms were destroying the sun & the throngs
    of crabs, & behold
they daubed the prow with good tallow
until they reached the lands of Opportunity.
(*Heap up the dead in the lavatory, hide them away, & in
    no time the Coliseum*
will be clean & propitious like a soft bed.)

There's a noble & beautiful animal encircled with cross-
    bows.
On the Southern frontier war has begun. In the North,
    plague & hunger.

[*Translated by William Rowe*]

Crónica de Chapi, 1965

Para Washington Delgado

"Lengua sin manos, ¿cómo osas hablar?"
Poema de Mío Cid

Oronqoy. Aquí es dura la tierra. Nada en ella
se mueve, nada cambia, ni el bicho más pequeño.
Por las dudosas huellas del Angana
—media jornada sobre una mula vieja—
bien recuerdo
a los 200 muertos estrujados
y sin embargo frescos como un recién nacido.
Oronqoy.
La tierra permanece repetida, blanca y repetida
hasta las últimas montañas.
Detrás de ellas
el aire pesa más que un ahogado.
Y abajo,
entre las ramas barbudas y calientes:
Héctor. Ciro. Daniel, experto en huellas.
Edgardo El Viejo. El Que Dudó Tres Días.
Samuel, llamado el Burro. Y Mariano. Y Ramiro.
El callado Marcial. Todos los duros. Los de la rabia
entera.
(Samuel afloja sus botines.) Fuman. Conversan.
Y abren latas de atún bajo el chillido
de un pájaro picudo.

"Siempre este bosque
que me recuerda al mar, con sus colinas,
sus inmóviles olas y su luz
diferente a la de todos los soles conocidos.
Aún ignoro
las costumbres del viento y de las aguas.

Chronicle of Chapi, 1965

For Washington Delgado

"Tongue without hands, how durst thou speak?"
Mío Cid

Oronqoy. Here the earth is hard. Nothing
moves, nothing changes, not even the smallest beast.
Along the faded tracks of the Angaga
—half a day's journey on an old mule—
           I well remember
the 200 dead crushed
yet fresh as a newborn child.
           Oronqoy.
The land continues repeated, white & repeated
up to the furthest mountains.
           Behind them
the air is heavier than a drowned man.
           And below,
between the hot & bearded branches:
Hector. Ciro. Daniel, the expert in tracking.
Edgardo The Old Man. The One Who Doubted Three
    Days.
Samuel—called the Ass. And Mariano. And Ramiro.
Marcial, the quiet one. All the hard men. The men of
    complete rage.
(Samuel undoes his boots.) They smoke, & talk.
And open tins of tuna beneath the shriek
of a sharp-beaked bird.

"Always this wood
which reminds me of the sea, with its hills
its immobile waves & its light
unlike that of any known sun.
           I still don't know

Es verdad,
ya nada se parece al país que dejamos y sin embargo
es todavía el mismo."

Cenizas casi verdes,
restos de su fogata ardiendo entre la nuestra:
estuvieron muy cerca los soldados.
                    Su capitán,
el de la baba inmensa, el de las púas
—casi a tiro de piedra lo recuerdo—
en pocos días ametralló
            a los 200 hombres
                    y eso fue en noviembre
(no indagues, caminante, por las pruebas:
para los siervos muertos no hay túmulo o señal)
                    y esa noche,
en los campos de Chapi,
hasta que el viento arrastró la Cruz del Sur,
se oyeron los chillidos de las viejas,
                    ayataki,
el canto de los muertos,
pesado como lluvia
                    sobre las anchas hojas de los plátanos,
duro como tambores.
            Y el halcón de tierras altas
sombra fue sobre sus cuerpos maduros y perfectos.

(En Chapi, distrito de La Mar, donde en setiembre,
Don Gonzalo Carrillo—quien gustaba
moler a sus peones en un trapiche viejo—
fue juzgado y muerto por los muertos.)
"El suelo es desigual, Ramiro, tu cuerpo
se ha estropeado entre las cuevas y corrientes submari-
    nas.
Al principio, sólo una herida en la pierna derecha,
                    después
las moscas verdes invadieron tus miembros.

the customs of the wind & the waters.
                    It's true
now nothing resembles the country we left & yet
it's still the same."

Ashes almost green,
remains of their fire glowing within ours:
they got very close, the soldiers.
                    Their captain,
the one with the barbs & the great slobber
—I remember him at just a stone's throw away—
in a few days
machine-gunned
            the 200 men
                    & that was in November
(don't inquire, passerby, for the proofs:
for dead slaves there's no tumulus or sign)
                    & that night
in the fields of Chapi
until the wind dragged away the Southern Cross
old women's screams were heard
                    ayataki
the song of the dead,
heavy as rain
                    on the wide banana leaves
hard as drums.
                    And the hawk from the high lands
cast his shadow on their mature & perfect bodies.

(In Chapi, district of La Mar, where in September
Don Gonzalo Carrillo—who liked
to grind his peons in an old mill—
was judged & sentenced to death by the dead.)
"The ground is rough, Ramiro, your body
has been maimed in undersea caves & currents.
At the beginning, just a wound in the right leg,
                    afterward

Y eras duro, todavía.
                    Pero tus pómulos no resistieron más
—fue la Uta, el hambriento animal de 100 barrigas—
y tuvimos, amigo, que ofrecerte
como a los bravos marinos que mueren sobre el mar."

Ese jueves, desde el Cerro Morado se acercaban.
                    Eran más de cuarenta.
El capitán—según pude saber—
sólo temía al tiempo de las lluvias
y a las enfermedades que provocan
las hembras de los indios.
                    Sus soldados
temían a la muerte.
Sin referirme a Tambo—5000 habitantes y naranjas—
doce pueblos del río hicieron leña tras su filudo andar.
Fueron harto botín hombres y bestias.
                    Se acercaban.
Junto a las barbas de la ortiga gigante
cayeron un teniente y el cabo fusilero.
                    (El capitán
se había levantado de prisa, bien de mañana
para combatir a los rebeldes.
Y sin saber que había una emboscada,
marchó con la jauría hasta un lugar tenido por seguro y
        discreto.
Y Héctor tendió la mano, y sus hombres
se alzaron con presteza.)
                    Y así,
cuando escaparon, carne enlatada y armas recogimos.
El capitán huía sobre sus propios muertos
abandonados al mordisco de las moscas.
                    No tuvimos heridos.

Los guerrilleros entierran sus latas de pescado,
recogen su fusil, callan, caminan.
                    Sin más bienes

green flies invaded your limbs.
And you were strong, still.
                    But your cheekbones could bear no more
—it was Uta, the hungry animal with 1000 bellies—
& we had, friend, to offer you up
like a brave sailor who's died at sea."

That Thursday, they came up from the Cerro Morado.
                    There were more than forty of them.
The captain—as far as I could tell—
feared only the time of the rains
& the diseases caused by
Indian women.
                    His soldiers
feared death.
Without speaking of Tambo—5000 inhabitants & or-
    anges—
twelve riverside villages turned firewood behind his knife-
    edged march.
Men & beasts made plentiful booty.
                    They came up close.
Beside the giant nettle's beard
fell a lieutenant & the corporal gunner.
                    (The captain
had hurried to get up early in the morning
to fight the rebels.
And not knowing there was an ambush,
he marched with his pack to a place held to be safe &
    discreet.
And Hector stretched out his hand, & his men
rose up rapidly.)
                    And so,
when they got away, we picked up meat & guns.
The captain fled over his own dead
abandoned to the nibbling of the flies.
                    We had no wounded.

que sus huesos y las armas, y a veces la duda como grieta
en un campo de arcilla. También el miedo.
                     Y las negras raíces
y las buenas, y los hongos que engordan y aquellos que
        dan muerte
ofreciéndose iguales.
                     Y la yerba y las arenas y el pantano
más altos cada vez en la ruta del Este, y los días
más largos cada vez
                     (y eso fue poco antes de las lluvias).
Y así lo hicieron tres noches con sus días.
                     Y llegados al río
decidieron esperar la mañana antes de atravesarlo.

"Wauqechay, hermanito, wauqechay,
es tu cansancio
largo como este día, wauqechay.
Verde arvejita verde,
wauqechay,
descansa en mi cocina,
verde arvejita verde,
wauqechay,
descansa en mi frazada y en mi sombra."
Daniel, Ciro, Mariano, Edgardo El Viejo,
El Que Dudó Tres Días, Samuel llamado El Burro,
Héctor, Marcial, Ramiro,
                     qué angosto corazón, qué reino habitan.

Y ya ninguno pregunte sobre el peso y la medida de los
        hermanos muertos,
y ya nadie les guarde repugnancia o temor.

The *guerrilleros* bury their tins of fish,
pick up their guns, fall silent, walk on.
                    With no belongings
but their bones & guns, & sometimes doubt like a cleft
in a field of clay. Also fear.
                    And the black roots
& the good ones, & the fungi which fatten & those which
        bring death
proffering themselves identically.
                    And the grass & the sands & the swamp
getting higher on the eastern route, & the days
getting longer
                    (& that was a little before the rains).
And they kept on like this for three days & nights.
                    And arriving at the river
they decided to wait for morning before crossing.

"*Waukechay*, little brother, *waukechay*,
it's your weariness
long as this day, *waukechay*.
Green little green pea,
waukechay,
rest in my kitchen,
green little green pea,
waukechay,
rest in my blanket & in my shadow."
Daniel, Ciro, Mariano, Edgardo The Old Man,
The One Who Doubted Three Days, Samuel—called the
        Ass,
Héctor, Marcial, Ramiro,
                    what narrow heart, what kingdom do
                    they inhabit.

And now let no man ask about the weight & height of our
        dead brothers,
let no one nurture fear or hatred for them now.

[*Translated by William Rowe*]

Arturo Corcuera (1935–   ) was born in the seaport of Salaverry. He studied at the University of San Marcos, in Lima, and has since traveled extensively throughout Europe and Latin America. When his poems began to appear for the first time in journals, newspapers, and magazines in and around Lima, it was immediately apparent that here was an aggressively social poet, technically competent and broadly versatile, whose touchstone was a directness of statement and the familiarity of colloquial speech. He is a great admirer of his compatriot and fellow poet Javier Heraud, seeking the same transparency without naiveté, the simplicity and accessibility that is neither patronizing nor simple-minded. "In the falling leaves / of autumn," he writes to his now dead younger contemporary, "I seem to hear your footsteps."

Corcuera has won several prizes for his poetry over the years, among them the University Floral Games prize for poetry (1956), the National Prize for Poetry (1963), and the César Vallejo Prize (1968). He is among the most productive poets of his generation: his many books include *Cantoral, El grito del hombre, Sombra del jardín, Territorio libre, Poesía de clase,* and, more recently, *El arca y sus ojos de buey.*

Fábula de Tom y Jerry

Plantas de goma
(Goodyear)
sobre la alfombra,
Tom.

Jerry,
como el Che,
fuma habano.

Ojos de diamante,
Tom,
bigote y olfato,
él un tigre de papel
faziendo papel de gato.

Mínimo Jerry,
en las narices de Tom,
trasmutándose en lagarto,
en largo, largo, lagarto.

Tom and Jerry: A Fable

Rubber soles
(Goodyear)
on the rug,
Tom.

Jerry,
like Che,
smokes a havana.

With diamond eyes,
Tom,
moustache and a nose,
a paper tiger
assuming the role of a cat.

Little Jerry,
under Tom's nose,
turning into a lizard,
a long, long, lizard.

[*Translated by Robert Márquez*]

Fábula del Lobo Feroz

"San Tío Lobo
con cara de Cordero Pascual:
¿y el Radar que tienes, dime?"

"Para detectar tus pasos
ocultándote en el bosque."

"¿Y tu Cámara de Rayos
Infrarrojos, Tío?"

"Para detectar por el olor
el fiambre de tu mochila."

"¿Y tu rayo Láser, San Tío Lobo?"

"Para cocinarte y comerte
mejor."

"¡Que te parta un rayo,
torvo Tío de la muerte!"

Fierce Wolf: A Fable

"Saint Uncle Wolf
with the face of paschal lamb:
what is the radar for?"

"To detect your footsteps
when you hide in the forest."

"And your infrared camera, Uncle?"

"To detect by the smell
the cold meat in your knapsack."

"And your laser beam, St. Uncle Wolf?"

"The better to cook and
to eat you."

"You can go to hell,
fierce uncle of death!"

[*Translated by Robert Márquez*]

Cow-boy y fábula de Buffalo Bill

Winchester y Colt 45
de Cara Pálida
embistiendo en el Oeste.

Lo mira,
mirada de águila,
el Indio Toro Sentado.

Civilizado Buffalo
Bill,
animal bravo ostentado
estrella de Sheriff.

A Piel Roja,
a Piel Negra,
a Piel de Bronce,
a Piel Amarilla acosando
el traficante de pieles,
Buffalo Bill.

Cowboy and Fable of Buffalo Bill

A Winchester and Pale
Face Colt 45
attack in the West.

Watching,
with an eagle eye,
is the Indian Sitting Bull.

Civilized Buffalo
Bill,
a wild animal wearing
a sheriff's badge.

Hunting
Red Skins,
Black Skins,
Bronze Skins,
Yellow Skins
the trader in skins,
Buffalo Bill.

[*Translated by Robert Márquez*]

Javier Heraud (1942–1963) was born in Miraflores, a fashionable residential district of Lima. A precocious youth, he began his studies at the age of sixteen at the Catholic University of Lima; from there he went on to the National University of San Marcos. For a time he taught English and literature in local technical and secondary schools. His public career as a poet began in 1960 when, with his compatriot César Calvo, he won first prize in a national poetry contest for his poem "El viaje" and was named "Young Poet of Peru." A short time later he represented the Movimiento Social Progresista at the World Youth Congress and so traveled to Moscow and various other European capitals.

In 1961 Heraud went to Cuba to study cinematography. The Revolution's impact on him was immediate and lasting, and solidified his militant convictions. He joined

the Peruvian Army of National Liberation, then strug-
gling in the Peruvian Andes. In 1963 he was shot and
killed by government troops as he was attempting to
re-enter Peru clandestinely by crossing the Río Marañon
on a raft. In that same year *Estación reunida*, his last
book, was posthumously awarded the first prize for
poetry in a contest sponsored by the University of San
Marcos. The poems included here are from the collection
Poemas published in Cuba in 1967.

Heraud's poetry shows a remarkable maturity and
self-assurance for a man whose career was only begin-
ning when he was cut down. His is a fluid and transparent
verse which has earned him a large following in Peru,
where he remains a symbol of the revolutionary poet's
commitment.

Alabanza de los días
destrucción y elogio de las sombras

Nos prometieron la felicidad
y hasta ahora nada nos han dado.
¿Para qué elevar promesas si
a la hora de la lluvia sólo
tendremos al sol y al trigo muerto?

¿Para qué cosechar y cosechar si
luego nos quitarán el maíz,
el trigo, las flores y las frutas?

Para tener un poco de descanso no
queremos esperar las promesas y
los ruegos:
Tendremos que llegar al mismo
nacimiento del camino, rehacer todo,
volver con pasos lentos desparramando
lluvias por los campos,
sembrando trigo con las manos,
cosechando peces con nuestras
interminables bocas.
Nada queremos aprovechar,
¡oh, alegría!
Mejor hubiera sido naufragar
y no llegar,
porque ahora todo tenemos
que hacerlo con las manos:
construir palabras como
troncos, no implorar ni
gemir sino acabar,
terminar a golpes con la tierra muerta.

In Praise of Days
Destruction and Eulogy to Darkness

They promised us happiness
and we still have nothing.
Why promises
if when the time for rain comes
we have no more than sun and the dead wheat?

Why harvest and harvest again
if afterward they take the corn,
the wheat, the flowers, the fruits?

To have our bit of rest
we don't want to wait on promises
and pleas:
We'll have to go back to the
beginning, start over again,
come back slowly spreading rain
over the fields, planting wheat
with our own hands, harvesting fish
with our unending mouths.
We don't want to take anything
we're not entitled to,
O happiness!
Better to have been sunk
and never have arrived,
for now we must do everything
with our own hands:
build words
like the trunks of trees,
neither beg nor weep
but end,
put an end to the dead earth with blows.

[*Translated by Robert Márquez*]

397

Palabra de guerrillero

Porque mi Patria es hermosa
como una espada en el aire
y más grande ahora y aún
y más hermosa todavía,
yo hablo y la defiendo
con mi vida.
No me importa lo que digan
los traidores
hemos cerrado el paso
con gruesas lágrimas
de acero.
El cielo es nuestro.
Nuestro el pan de cada día,
hemos sembrado y cosechado
el trigo y la tierra,
son nuestros
y para siempre nos
pertenecen
el mar,
las montañas
y los pájaros.

A Guerrilla's Word

Because my country is beautiful
as a sword held in the air
and bigger now and even
more beautiful still,
I speak and defend it
with my life.
I do not care what may be said
by traitors
we have blocked the way
with heavy tears of steel.
The sky belongs to us.
The daily bread is ours,
we have sown and harvested
the wheat and the land,
and the wheat and the land
are ours,
and the sea,
the mountains and the birds
belong to us forever.

[*Translated by Robert Márquez*]

Arte poética

En verdad, en verdad hablando,
la poesía es un trabajo difícil
que se pierde o se gana
al compás de los años otoñales.

(Cuando uno es joven
y las flores que caen no se recogen
uno escribe y escribe entre las noches,
y a veces se llenan cientos y cientos
de cuartillas inservibles.
Uno puede alardear y decir
"yo escribo y no corrijo,
los poemas salen de mi mano
como la primavera que derrumbaron
los viejos cipreses de mi calle.")
Pero conforme pasa el tiempo
y los años se filtran entre las sienes,
la poesía se va haciendo
trabajo de alfarero;
arcilla que se cuece entre las manos,
arcilla que moldean fuegos rápidos.

Y la poesía es
un relámpago maravilloso,
una lluvia de palabras silenciosas,
un bosque de latidos y esperanzas,
el canto de los pueblos oprimidos,
el nuevo canto de los pueblos liberados.

Y la poesía es entonces,
el amor, la muerte,
la redención del hombre.

Madrid, 1961   *La Habana, 1962*

Ars Poetica

In truth, and frankly speaking,
poetry is a difficult job
that's won or lost
to the rhythm of the autumnal years.

(When one is young
and the flowers that fall are never gathered up,
one writes on and on at night,
at times filling hundreds and hundreds
of useless sheets of paper.
One can boast and say:
"I write without revising,
poems leave my hand
like Spring discarded
by the cypresses on my street.")
But as time passes
and the years filter in between the temples,
poetry becomes
the potter's art:
clay fired in the hands,
clay shaped by the quick flames.

And poetry is a marvelous lightning,
a rain of silent words,
a forest of throbbings and hopes,
the song of oppressed peoples,
the new song of liberated peoples.

So poetry, then,
is love, is death,
is man's redemption.

Madrid, 1961   *Havana, 1962*

[*Translated by Elinor Randall*]

401

Puerto Rico

Pedro Pietri (1944–   ) was born in Ponce, Puerto Rico, but grew up in the streets of Spanish Harlem. Synthesizing the experience of a generation, he writes of himself: "Uneducated in three public schools. Worked on and off for ten years in various jobs (menial). Got drafted in 1966, blew two years in military service. Returned to odd jobs, last one as an orderly for helpless men in Brooklyn state mental institution. In these ten years, wrote many things in the downtown train."

Puerto Rico is a nation isolated and unnaturally divided by a colonialism which also threatens the extinction of its language—the language of Spanish America—and its cultural integrity. Those, mostly poor, who were forced to immigrate by the realities of life in a dependent economy are doubly victimized and alienated. It is to them that Pedro Pietri addresses his poetry; it is from them that it springs. His lines come, with an uncommon immediacy and authenticity, "From the nervous breakdown streets / where the mice live like millionaires / and the people do not live at all / are dead and were never alive"; in defiance of "the white supremacy bibles," he celebrates his specifically Puerto Rican identity, exulting in a culture in which "to be called negrito / means to be called LOVE."

Deeply committed to the struggle of the Puerto Rican nation, Pietri's work has appeared in *Palante*, the Young Lords Party newspaper, in *Unidad Latina*, and in the *Revista del instituto de estudios puertorriqueños*, of Brooklyn College, New York. He has also recorded a public reading of his verse, *Pedro Pietri en Casa Puerto Rico*, and made a film, *A Serious Monster Picture* (1971). His only book of collected poems to date, *Puerto Rican Obituary*, written mostly in English, was published in 1973. The following is the title poem to that volume.

Obituario puertorriqueño

Trabajaron
Llegaron siempre a tiempo
Nunca llegaron tarde
Nunca se reviraron
cuando los insultaban
Trabajaron
Nunca tomaron días libres
que no marcara el calendario
Nunca hicieron la huelga
sin permiso
Trabajaron
diez días a la semana
por el pago de cinco
Trabajaron
Trabajaron
Trabajaron
y murieron
sin un centavo
Murieron endeudados
Murieron sin saber el aspecto
que tenía la entrada principal
        del banco nacional

Juan
Miguel
Milagros
Olga
Manuel
Todos murieron ayer hoy
y mañana de nuevo morirán
dejando cobradores
y deudas como herencia
Todos murieron
esperando que abriera

Puerto Rican Obituary

They worked
They were always on time
They were never late
They never spoke back
when they were insulted
They worked
They never took days off
that were not on the calendar
They never went on strike
without permission
They worked
ten days a week
and were only paid for five
They worked
They worked
They worked
and they died
They died broke
They died owing
They died never knowing
what the front entrance
of the first national city bank looks like

Juan
Miguel
Milagros
Olga
Manuel
All died yesterday today
and will die again tomorrow
passing their bill collectors
on to the next of kin
All died
waiting for the garden of eden

405

otra vez el Paraíso
con nuevos directores
Todos murieron
soñando con que américa
los despertara en medio de la noche
gritando: ¡Mira! ¡Mira!
su nombre está en la lista de ganadores
del premio de cien mil dólares
Todos murieron
odiando las bodegas
que les vendían carne de mentira
y frijoles y arroz a prueba de balas
Todos murieron esperando soñando y odiando

A los puertorriqueños muertos
Que no supieron nunca que eran puertorriqueños
Que nunca se tomaron un descanso
de los diez mandamientos
para MATAR MATAR MATAR
a los tenientes de sus cráneos rotos
y comunicarse con sus almas latinas

Juan
Miguel
Milagros
Olga
Manuel
Salidos de calles deprimentes
donde las ratas viven como millonarios
y el pueblo no vive en absoluto
han muerto y no vivieron nunca

Juan
murió esperando que saliera su número
Miguel
murió esperando que el cheque del subsidio

to open up again
under a new management
All died
dreaming about america
waking them up in the middle of the night
screaming: Mira Mira
your name is on the winning lottery ticket
for one hundred thousand dollars
All died
hating the grocery stores
that sold them make-believe steak
and bullet-proof rice and beans
All died waiting dreaming and hating

Dead Puerto Ricans
Who never knew they were Puerto Ricans
Who never took a coffee break
from the ten commandments
to KILL KILL KILL
the landlords of their cracked skulls
and communicate with their latino souls

Juan
Miguel
Milagros
Olga
Manuel
From the nervous breakdown streets
where the mice live like millionaires
and the people do not live at all
are dead and were never alive

Juan
died waiting for his number to hit
Miguel
died waiting for the welfare check

viniera y se fuera y volviera
Milagros
murió esperando que sus diez hijos
crecieran y trabajaran
para poder dejar de trabajar
Olga
murió esperando un aumento de cinco dólares
Manuel
murió esperando que su superior muriera de una vez
para lograr un ascenso

Es muy larga la tirada
desde el Barrio
al cementerio de long island
donde los enterraron
Primero el tren
después la guagua
y los fiambres para el almuerzo
y las flores
que alguien robará
al terminar las horas de visita
Es muy caro
Es muy caro
Pero ellos comprenden
Sus padres comprendieron
Una larga tirada improductiva
desde el Barrio
al cementerio de long island

Juan
Miguel
Milagros
Olga
Manuel
Todos murieron ayer hoy
y mañana de nuevo morirán
Soñando

408

to come and go and come again
Milagros
died waiting for her ten children
to grow up and work
so she could quit working
Olga
died waiting for a five dollar raise
Manuel
died waiting for his supervisor to drop dead
so he could get a promotion

Is a long ride
from Spanish Harlem
to long island cemetery
where they were buried
First the train
and then the bus
and the cold cuts for lunch
and the flowers
that will be stolen
when visiting hours are over
Is very expensive
Is very expensive
But they understand
Their parents understood
Is a long non-profit ride
from Spanish Harlem
to long island cemetery

Juan
Miguel
Milagros
Olga
Manuel
All died yesterday today
and will die again tomorrow
Dreaming

Soñando con queens
Amplia barriada blanca como un lirio
Paisaje sin puertorriqueños
Hogares de treinta mil dólares
Los primeros spics en la cuadra
Orgullosos de ser de una comunidad
de gringos que los quieren linchar
Orgullosos de estar a gran distancia
de la sagrada expresión: *¿Qué Pasa?*

Estos sueños
Estos sueños vacíos
desde los cuartos ilusorios
que sus padres les dejaran
son los efectos secundarios
de los programas de televisión
sobre la ideal
familia blanca americana
con criadas negras
y conserjes latinos
que están bien entrenados
para hacer a cualquiera
como a sus cobradores
reírse de ellos
y del pueblo que representan

Juan
murió soñando con un carro nuevo
Miguel
murió soñando con nuevos programas contra la pobreza
Milagros
murió soñando con un viaje a Puerto Rico
Olga
murió soñando con joyas de verdad
Manuel
murió soñando con el premio de la lotería oficial

410

Dreaming about queens
Clean-cut lily-white neighborhood
Puerto Ricanless scene
Thirty-thousand-dollar home
The first spics on the block
Proud to belong to a community
of gringos who want them lynched
Proud to be a long distance away
from the sacred phrase: Que Pasa

These dreams
These empty dreams
from the make-believe bedrooms
their parents left them
are the after-effects
of television programs
about the ideal
white american family
with black maids
and latino janitors
who are well train
to make everyone
and their bill collectors
laugh at them
and the people they represent

Juan
died dreaming about a new car
Miguel
died dreaming about new anti-poverty programs
Milagros
died dreaming about a trip to Puerto Rico
Olga
died dreaming about real jewelry
Manuel
died dreaming about the irish sweepstakes

411

Todos murieron
como muere un pan con timba
en el distrito comercial obrero
a las doce del día
números del seguro social vueltos a la ceniza
recibos del sindicato vueltos al polvo

Sabían
que habían nacido para trabajar
y dar empleo a los sepultureros
mientras juraban su fidelidad
a la bandera que los quiere destruir
Vieron sus nombres en la lista
del directorio telefónico de la destrucción
Fueron entrenados para ofrecer
la otra mejilla por los periódicos
que deletrearon mal y pronunciaron
mal y entendieron mal sus nombres
e hicieron una fiesta cuando llegó su muerte
a robar su última ropa en la tintorería

Nacieron muertos
y vivieron muertos

Es hora
de ver de nuevo a la hermana lópez
la curandera y cartomántica
número uno
del Barrio
Puede comunicarse
con los parientes muertos
a un precio razonable
Se garantizan buenas nuevas

Crece Mesa Sube Pronta
no es la muerte torpe o tonta

412

They all died
like a hero sandwich dies
in the garment district
at twelve o'clock in the afternoon
social security number to ashes
union dues to dust

They knew
they were born to weep
and keep the morticians employed
as long as they pledge allegiance
to the flag that wants them destroyed
They saw their names listed
in the telephone directory of destruction
They were train to turn
the other cheek by newspapers
that mispelled mispronounced
and misunderstood their names
and celebrated when death came
and stole their final laundry ticket

They were born dead
and they died dead

Is time
to visit sister lopez again
the number one healer
and fortune card dealer
in Spanish Harlem
She can communicate
with your late relatives
for a reasonable fee
Good news is guaranteed

Rise Table Rise Table
death is not dumb and disable

Los que te aman quieren ver
a qué número apostar
Ven a hacérnoslo saber
Crece Mesa Sube Pronta
no es la muerte torpe o tonta
Ahora que tus cuentas saldas
y no hay peso en tus espaldas
a quien sufre da esperanzas
y da paz a sus finanzas
Crece Mesa Sube Pronta
no es la muerte torpe o tonta
Cuando el número acertamos
ya problemas no tendremos
y a su tumba en procesiones
iremos en vacaciones
Los que te aman quieren ver
a qué número apostar
Ven a hacérnoslo saber
Tu luz hace adelantar
No es la muerte torpe o tonta
CRECE MESA SUBE PRONTA

Juan
Miguel
Milagros
Olga
Manuel
Todos murieron ayer hoy
y mañana de nuevo morirán
Odiando luchando y robándose
ventanas rotas uno al otro
Practicando una religión sin techo
El viejo testamento
El nuevo testamento
según el evangelio
de la renta pública interna
juez y jurado y verdugo
y protector y eterno cobrador

414

Those who love you want to know
the correct number to play
Let them know this right away
Rise Table Rise Table
death is not dumb and disable
Now that your problems are over
and the world is off your shoulders
help those who you left behind
find financial peace of mind
Rise Table Rise Table
death is not dumb and disable
If the right number we hit
all our problems will split
and we will visit your grave
on every legal holiday
Those who love you want to know
the correct number to play
Let them know this right away
We know your spirit is able
Death is not dumb and disable
RISE TABLE RISE TABLE

Juan
Miguel
Milagros
Olga
Manuel
All died yesterday today
and will die again tomorrow
Hating fighting and stealing
broken windows from each other
Practicing a religion without a roof
The old testament
The new testament
according to the gospel
of the internal revenue
the judge and jury and executioner
protector and eternal bill collector

Mierda de segunda mano para vender
Aprenda a decir *Cómo Está Usted*
y se hará millonario
Han muerto
Han muerto
y nunca volverán de entre los muertos
hasta que dejen de olvidar
el arte de su diálogo
por las lecciones de un precario inglés
con el que impresionar al míster amo
que les da sus empleos
de lavaplatos cargadores mensajeros
obreros sirvientes empleados de almacén
recaderos asistentes de correos
asistentes del asistente del asistente del asistente
del asistente del asistente del lavaplatos
y porteros automáticos con sonrisa artificial
por el más bajo precio de los siglos
y la rabia cuando piden un aumento
pues no es costumbre de la empresa
promover SPICS SPICS SPICS

Juan
murió odiando a Miguel porque Miguel
tenía un carro de uso en mejores condiciones
que su carro de uso
Miguel
murió odiando a Milagros porque Milagros
tenía un televisor a colores
y él no podía aún comprarse uno
Milagros
murió odiando a Olga porque Olga
ganaba cinco dólares más por el mismo trabajo
Olga
murió odiando a Manuel porque Manuel
adivinaba números más veces

Secondhand shit for sale
Learn how to say Como Esta Usted
and you will make a fortune
They are dead
They are dead
and will not return from the dead
until they stop neglecting
the art of their dialogue
for broken english lessons
to impress the mister goldsteins
who keep them employed
as lavaplatos porters messenger boys
factory workers maids stock clerks
shipping clerks assistant mailroom
assistant, assistant assistant
to the assistant's assistant
assistant lavaplatos and automatic
artificial smiling doormen
for the lowest wages of the ages
and rages when you demand a raise
because its against the company policy
to promote SPIC SPICS SPICS

Juan
died hating Miguel because Miguel's
used car was in better running condition
than his used car
Miguel
died hating Milagros because Milagros
had a color television set
and he could not afford one yet
Milagros
died hating Olga because Olga
made five dollars more on the same job
Olga
died hating Manuel because Manuel

de las que ella adivinaba números
Manuel
murió odiándolos a todos
Juan
Miguel
Milagros
y Olga
porque todos hablaban en su precario inglés
con más fluencia que él

Y ahora están juntos
en el vestíbulo principal del vacío
añadidos al silencio
Más allá de los límites del viento
confinados a la supremacía del gusano
en el cementerio de long island
Este es el glorioso después
del que la alcancía protestante
hablaba tanto y con tanto orgullo

Aquí yace Juan
Aquí yace Miguel
Aquí yace Milagros
Aquí yace Olga
Aquí yace Manuel
quienes murieron ayer hoy
y mañana de nuevo morirán
Siempre arruinados
Siempre endeudados
Sin saber nunca
que son gentes hermosas
Sin saber nunca
la geografía de su complexión

PUERTO RICO ES UN BELLO LUGAR
Y LOS PUERTORRIQUEÑOS UNA RAZA EJEMPLAR

had hit the numbers more times
than she had hit the numbers
Manuel
died hating all of them
Juan
Miguel
Milagros
and Olga
because they all spoke broken english
more fluently than he did

And now they are together
in the main lobby of the void
Addicted to silence
Off limits to the wind
Confine to worm supremacy
in long island cemetery
This is the groovy hereafter
the protestant collection box
was talking so loud and proud about

Here lies Juan
Here lies Miguel
Here lies Milagros
Here lies Olga
Here lies Manuel
who died yesterday today
and will die again tomorrow
Always broke
Always owing
Never knowing
that they are beautiful people
Never knowing
the geography of their complexion

PUERTO RICO IS A BEAUTIFUL PLACE
PUERTORRIQUEÑOS ARE A BEAUTIFUL RACE

Si sólo hubieran
desconectado los televisores
y encendido su propia imaginación
Si sólo hubieran
usado las biblias de la supremacía blanca
como papel sanitario
y hecho de sus almas latinas
religión única de su raza
Si sólo hubieran
vuelto a la definición del sol
después de su primer tormenta psíquica de nieve
en el verano de sus sentidos
Si sólo hubieran
mantenido los ojos abiertos
en el entierro de sus compañeros
que vinieron a este país a hacer fortuna
y bajaron al hoyo en camiseta

Juan
Miguel
Milagros
Olga
Manuel
estarán ahora haciendo ya lo suyo
donde la gente hermosa canta
y danza y trabaja unida
donde el viento es un extraño
para las miserables condiciones del tiempo
donde nunca hace falta un diccionario
para comunicarse con el pueblo
Aquí Se Habla Español a toda hora
Aquí saluda uno primero su bandera
Aquí nunca hay anuncios de jabón
Aquí toda la gente huele bien
Aquí para la cena instantánea no hay futuro
Aquí admiramos el deseo
y nunca nos cansamos uno de otro

If only they
had turned off the television
and tuned into their own imaginations
If only they
had used the white supremacy bibles
for toilet paper purpose
and make their latino souls
the only religion of their race
If only they
had return to the definition of the sun
after the first mental snowstorm
on the summer of their senses
If only they
had kept their eyes open
at the funeral of their fellow employees
who came to this country to make a fortune
and were buried without underwears

Juan
Miguel
Milagros
Olga
Manuel
will right now be doing their own thing
where beautiful people sing
and dance and work together
where the wind is a stranger
to miserable weather conditions
where you do not need a dictionary
to communicate with your people
Aqui Se Habla Espanol all the time
Aqui you salute your flag first
Aqui there are no dial soap commercials
Aqui everybody smells good
Aqui tv dinners do not have a future
Aqui the men and women admire desire
and never get tired of each other

Aquí es todo el poder en español *Qué Pasa*
Si *aquí* te dicen negrito o negrita
te están diciendo AMOR

[*Traducción por David Fernández Chericián y Robert Márquez*]

Aqui Que Pasa Power is what's happening
Aqui to be called negrito
means to be called LOVE

Iván Silén (1944–) belongs to the new generation of militantly anti-imperialist Puerto Rican poets who, in an attempt to revitalize the cultural and political atmosphere of the island under United States colonial control, have congregated around the journals *Mester*, *Guajana* and, more recently, *Penélope* and *Zona: carga y descarga*.

Silén is an ex-seminarian whose poetry frequently uses biblical imagery and a prophetic stridency. He is the advocate of "neosurrealism," a "new" form of surrealism that is an attempt to reconcile anarchist individualism with the collective philosophy of revolutionary communism. Clearly an heir to the rebellious tradition of the decadent poets, Silén defines neosurrealism as "an automatic creation of violent metaphors . . . in which one tries to express all the socially repressed poetry there is in the unconscious. . . . In the last analysis, the final reality of neosurrealism will be the very search with which each poem begins." "The revolution," he continues, "will be neosurrealism's supreme act, because the angels of the new poetry are armed."

Silén, who has so far published two books of poetry—*Después del suicidio* (1970) and *El pájaro loco* (1972)—is currently living in Spain where he is at work on a third, *El ángel extraviado*, on his first novel, and on his first film script.

The poems included here are taken from *Después del suicidio*.

Los he mandado a llamar

Los he mandado a llamar
porque hay que aclarar un problema,
porque hay que aclarar algunas posiciones,
los he mandado a llamar
para que oigan lo que voy a decir,
para que luego no digan que no fueron convidados.

Los he convidado a todos,
a los políticos,
a los moralistas,
a las putas,
y para que todo el mundo esté contento
he hecho una excepción,
he invitado,
qué remedio,
también a los religiosos.

No,
no se apuren,
es muy corto lo que tengo que decir,
tal vez lo han oído antes,
en algún bar,
a lo mejor en la cárcel,
lo pudo haber dicho
un borracho,
un comunista,
un pillo,
o tal vez un maricón.

Lo que voy a decir no tiene importancia
aunque puede escandalizar a muchos,
pero se puede publicar,
desde luego,
en la última página,

I sent for you

I sent for you
because we have a problem to clear up,
because some positions have to be clarified,
I sent for you
so you can hear what I have to say,
so later you won't say you weren't invited.

I've invited all of you:
the politicians,
the moralists,
the whores,
and to make everybody happy
I've made an exception:
I've also invited
—why not?—
the pious.

Oh,
don't worry,
what I have to say is very brief,
you might have heard it before,
in some bar,
maybe in a jail,
it could have been said
by a drunk,
a communist,
a thief,
or perhaps a queer.

What I have to say is not important
though many may be scandalized,
still it can be published,
on the last page,
needless to say,

porque yo todavía
creo en el amor
o en el sexo,
en el placer,
creo también en Cuba,
y en la revolución,
en el sabotaje,
y en las ilusiones de los niños,
creo en el prójimo,
especialmente
los que odian la clase media,
creo también en algunos sacerdotes,
sobre todo
los que están en las montañas,
creo en todas las cosas
que ustedes desean olvidar
porque yo soy un inquisidor,
aunque sé que todo lo que he dicho
no tiene gran importancia,
porque lo puede decir cualquiera,
por ejemplo,
un borracho,
un comunista,
un pillo,
o tal vez un maricón.

because I still believe
in love
or sex,
in pleasure,
I also believe in Cuba,
and in the revolution,
in sabotage,
and in the dreams of children,
I believe in my fellow men,
particularly
those who hate the middle class,
I believe also in some clergymen,
above all those
in the mountains,
I believe in everything
you want to forget
because I question,
though I know what I have said
is not very important,
for anyone at all can say it,
for example,
a drunk,
a communist,
a thief,
or perhaps a queer.

[*Translated by Robert Márquez*]

Voy a escribir un poema

Voy a escribir un poema
(aunque no tengo tinta roja)
voy a escribir un poema de acero
que sepa a fábrica,
a metal,
a fusil,
voy a escribir un poema
para cambiarlo por los militantes
         los inconformes
         los químicos
               (los fantasmas del imperio)
los que se llaman . . .
         marcianos
         "traidores"
         o comandos,
voy a escribir un poema que sepa a molotov
         al Che
comandante en armas de la poesía de guerrilla,
voy a escribir un poema con sangre
que grite:
        ¡PATRIA O MUERTE!
a lo puertorriqueño:
        Albizu
        Albizu
        Albizu.
             Padre nuestro que estás en los
            fusiles,
voy a escribir un poema que sepa a patria.
Patria se escribe con puños
        puños se escribe con sangre
sangre se escribe con muertos,
        muerto está Fefel
(que terminó de escribir su poema)
        muerto están los muertos,

I am going to write a poem

I am going to write a poem
(though I haven't got red ink)
I am going to write a poem of steel
with the feel of a factory,
metal,
a gun,
I am going to write a poem
and exchange it for the militants
    the nonconformists
    the chemists
       (the ghosts of the empire)
they call
    Martians
    "traitors"
    or commandos,
I am going to write a poem with the taste of a Molotov
    to Che
comandante in arms of guerrilla poetry,
I am going to write a poem with blood
that will scream:
    PATRIA O MUERTE!
Puerto Rican style:
    Albizu
    Albizu
    Albizu.
       Our father who art in the guns,
I am going to write a poem with the taste of the
  homeland.
Homeland is written with fists
    fists is written with blood
blood is written with dead
    Fefel is dead
(who finished writing his poem)
    dead are the dead,

431

los que dicen sí cuando hay
que decir NO,
los que siguen el letrero . . .
ONE WAY . . .
los que se quitan el sombrero
y dicen "thanks"
y no entienden la locura
ni por qué Camilo se fue
a la montaña,
por eso santificado sea tu nombre:
Albizu
Albizu
Albizu
por eso decimos ¡ALELUYA A LOS COMANDOS!
y vénganos la república
ahora y por los siglos
mientras yo sigo escribiendo mi poema,
mientras la caña crece agria,
y los puños,
y los crepúsculos no existirán más hasta que
resucite Albizu
(y Fefel)
en todas las manos que escriben,
en todas las manos que sabotean,
en todas las manos
el pan nuestro
de cada día
y en todas las bocas que dicen NO,
ahora y por los siglos
esperamos que nos libres de la inseguridad
y de la queja
y también de la Coca-Cola
Albizu
Albizu
Albizu

de los débiles
y los distraídos

those who say yes when
we have to say NO,
those who follow the sign . . .
ONE WAY . . .
those who take their hats off
and say "thanks"
and don't understand the madness
nor why Camilo went
to the mountain
because of it; hallowed be thy name:
Albizu
Albizu
Albizu
that's why we say HALLELUJAH FOR THE COMMAN-
DOS!
the republic come
now and at the hour of our death,
while I keep writing my poem,
while the cane grows bitter
and the fists,
and the sunsets cease to exist until
Albizu
(and Fefel)
are resurrected
in every hand that writes,
in every hand that sabotages,
in every hand
our daily bread
and in every mouth that says NO,
now and at the hour of our death
we will wait to be delivered from insecurity
and complaint
and Coca-Cola too
Albizu
Albizu
Albizu
of the weak

y que nos podamos vengar de nuestros deudores
ahora y para siempre
                                    AMÉN

and the distracted
and may we be able to revenge ourselves on those who
    trespass against us
                now and at the hour of our death
                                        AMEN

[Translated by Robert Márquez]

A veces estoy aburrido

A veces estoy aburrido
y me entero
de que han quemado un Kay Mart,
y oigo por la radio
que en Guatemala
han matado dos militares yanquis,
y que Corea capturó
un barco en aguas territoriales,
y que un documental cubano
fue premiado en Europa,
entonces comprendo
que la vida no es tan aburrida,
porque todavía existen guerrilleros,
poetas,
y amantes que vierten sangre,
que todavía hay hombres en esta tierra,
pero no me acusen,
no me critiquen,
porque yo todavía sueño un poco más,
porque yo quiero,
anhelo,
oír por la radio,
desde Cuba
hasta Argentina,
que en San Juan hundieron
un acorazado,
que mataron dos marinos
un domingo por la noche,
que en vez de haber arrestado,
(aunque eso no es nada nuevo)
nueve jóvenes esta semana,
por ellos surjan cientos,
a sesenta,
y a treinta por uno,

I am sometimes bored

I am sometimes bored
and learn
that a Kay Mart has been burned,
and hear over the radio
that in Guatemala
two Yankee soldiers have been killed,
and that Korea captured
a ship in territorial waters,
and that a Cuban documentary
won a prize in Europe,
then I understand
that life is not so boring,
because guerrillas still exist,
poets,
and lovers who spill blood,
that there are still men on this earth,
but don't accuse me,
don't criticize me,
because I dream yet a little more,
because I love,
and want,
to hear over the radio,
from Cuba
to the Argentine,
that in San Juan they sank
a battleship,
that they killed two marines
one Sunday night,
that instead of having arrested
nine youths this week
(though that is nothing new),
hundreds will surge forth,
at seventy
and thirty to one,

entonces tomaremos,
aunque usted ahora no lo crea,
todos los diccionarios del mundo
y tacharemos,
borraremos con alegría
y con orgullo,
la palabra aburrimiento,
por todos los siglos
de los siglos . . .
¡VENCEREMOS!

then we will take
—though now you don't believe it—
all the dictionaries in the world
and cross out,
erase with joy
and pride,
the word "boredom"
for all time . . .
VENCEREMOS!

[Translated by Robert Márquez]

Iris M. Zavala (1936–   ) is a critic and historian of ideas as well as a poet. One of the most wide-ranging talents of her generation in Puerto Rico, her articles and essays have appeared in journals in Europe, the United States, and throughout Latin America. A native of Ponce, on the southern Puerto Rican coast, she studied first at the University of Puerto Rico and later at the University of Salamanca, Spain. She is a member of the faculty at the State University of New York at Stonybrook, where she teaches Hispanic Literature.

Zavala's poetry bears the stamp of her wide interests and experience. It also reflects a militant internationalism not at all surprising in a historian of radical movements and ideas. Hers is a spare and polished verse, with a linguistic sensitivity and dream-like aura that seeks to join the best of the classical Spanish lyric tradition to the more recent surrealist avant-gardism of a Buñuelesque stream of consciousness. She says of herself: "I can only conceive of poetry as the expression of the shouts in the streets—those that are muffled, that are felt. It is placing your feet firmly on the ground and blowing up the White House, making Wall Street, Brazil, and Argentina tremble, and having the tremor reach all the way to Spain. A poem is . . . an immense Yes! to the wretched of the earth, with words and metaphors ('in the beginning was the word') that challenge and confront each other, in tension and struggle . . . to write a poem is to convert the language of the world into a legitimate instrument."

Zavala's published works include *La literatura de la angustia* (1965), *Masones, comuneros y carbonarios* (1971), *Ideología y política en la novela española del siglo XIX* (1971), and two books of poetry, *Barro doliente* (1964) and *Poemas prescindibles* (1971). The poems included here are from the latter volume.

Duelo I

A George Jackson

Brilla en negro un sol
aguerrido
en Ática
que tigres y águilas muerden
humillantes
forjan cadenas
y grillos
para Jackson
y Robinson y Pérez
majestuosos
gigantes
sobre el faro.
La ciudad y su humo
los siguen de lejos
cuerpos
del cielo
y las sombras.

Lament I

For George Jackson

A sun shines in black
embattled
in Attica
that tigers and eagles bite
humiliatingly
forging chains
and shackles
for Jackson,
Robinson, Pérez
majestic
giants
towering over the searchlight.
The city and its smoke
pursue them from afar
flesh
of the sky
and the shadows.

[*Translated by Robert Márquez*]

Nunca conoceré tu rostro

Nunca conoceré tu rostro
mis palabras no apagarán
el ruido de los aviones y las bombas
no veré el mundo que defiendes
     guerrillero de Viet-Nam
     de Cuba
     de Bolivia
Miguel Cruz, Eric Zamora, Li Tuan Quyhn.

Muchachos como tú
con sus jóvenes manos
y palabra sencilla
levantan sus geografías diversas
transforman su piel en una sola
su grito en uno solo.

No, no conoceré tu rostro
(tampoco conocí el de Samuel Leví en Auschwitz
ni le hablé a Pedro Gómez en Jarama)
pero me llegaron su dolor y su muerte
y el gusto de mi boca aún es amargo.

No oiré nunca la voz de tus compañeros
ni sabré sus nombres
que acaso tú mismo ignores
pero tú, sin conocerlos,
hoy te has unido a ellos
cargando tu fusil y tu certeza.

I'll never know your face

I'll never know your face
my words will never squelch
the noise of planes and bombs
I'll never see the world that you defend
      guerrilla of Vietnam
      of Cuba
      of Bolivia
Miguel Cruz, Eric Zamora, Li Tuan Quyhn.

Young men like you
with youthful hands
and simple words
construct their diverse geographies
transform their skin into one skin
their scream into one scream.

No, I'll never know your face
(I didn't know the face of Samuel Levi in
    Auschwitz either
nor did I speak to Pedro Gómez in Jarama)
but I felt their pain and death
and the taste in my mouth is still bitter.

I'll never hear the voice of those you walk with
nor know their names
which even you perhaps don't know
but you, not knowing them,
today have joined them
taking up your gun, your certainty.

[*Translated by Robert Márquez*]

445

Palabras y palabras

Palabras y palabras
que dijo el inmenso burócrata
de ojos pardos
como gatos inmensos
o fauces de rinoceronte
quizá cañones
tal vez Migs
pero eso fue en
1936
ahora Dow Chemical
con sus fuegos
que no son fatuos
arde en Asia Africa
y América
y hasta en Avenue A
de Chicago
en 157 y Lenox Avenue
donde no se baila al son
tom-tom
sino que gente como yo
no carga ya su miseria
ni esconde su
odio al burócrata
o técnico que construye
grandes avenidas y máquinas
y fábricas
donde la Dow Chemical
produce sus fuegos no fatuos.

Words words

Words words
said by an immense bureaucrat
with gray eyes
big as cats
or the jaws of rhinoceri
cannons perhaps
or Migs
but that was
1936
now Dow Chemical
with its
nonfatuous flames
burns in Asia Africa
America
even on Chicago's
Avenue A
on 157th and Lenox Avenue
where they don't dance to the
drum
but where people like me
no longer bear their misery
nor hide
their hate of bureaucrats
or technicians who build
great avenues machines
and factories
where Dow Chemical
produces its nonfatuous flames.

[*Translated by Robert Márquez*]

Uruguay

"I have the impression," **Mario Benedetti** (1920–   ) wrote over five years ago, "that even though many intellectuals are not convinced of this, the era of the pure, uncontaminated writer has ended once and for all in Latin America. Of course, this constitutes a certain risk, but at the same time it offers a beautiful opportunity to feel the invigorating presence of one's neighbor."

By his own standards, Benedetti—his early reputation established with his masterful dissections of Uruguay's conformist, complacent urban bourgeoisie—has always managed to take that risk, to be impure. Besides a half-dozen volumes of verse (collected in *Inventario 70*), he has written novels, collections of short stories, plays, and a large number of excellent critical essays and interviews dealing with Latin American politics and literature. During the past decade he has traveled to Cuba a number of times, most often to serve on juries for the literary prizes awarded by the Casa de Las Américas. From late 1967 until early 1969 he lived in Havana, where he organized and directed the Casa's newest branch, the Center for Literary Research.

Benedetti's novella in diary form, *La Tregua*, was published in English as *The Truce* (Harper and Row, 1969). His most recent work, *El Cumpleaños de Juan Angel*, published in 1971, is a short biographical novel in free verse narrated through a sequence of flashbacks by an urban guerrilla in Montevideo. Benedetti now lives in Montevideo. He contributed to and was an editorial staff member of the recently banned left weekly *Marcha*. Committed to radical change in a country he describes as a place where "basic liberties are totally curtailed, prisons and concentration camps overflow with political prisoners, and torture has reached extremes of sadism comparable only to what is practiced in Brazil," he was a leader of the Movimiento de Independientes 26 de Marzo, part of the leftist Frente Amplio, a coalition formed in opposition to Uruguay's present regime.

Con permiso

Está prohibido escribir sobre cierta violencia
así que voy a hablar de la violencia permitida

el violento autorizado asiste comprensivo y curioso
    a tus cartas de amor acaricia contigo los muslos
    de tu novia escucha tus murmullos tus
    desfallecimientos
duro e infeliz se introduce doméstico en tu casa
pobre gendarme de repente promovido al horror
manoseador de secretos y mayólicas
a veces ladroncito sin vocación ni melancolía
recién llegado al crimen nuevo rico del miedo

el violento autorizado ve con preocupación el camello
    que pasa por el ojo de la aguja
y ordena un silencio sin fisuras para poder vociferarte
    en el oído su higiénico entusiasmo por
    la libertad
deja el corazón en el hogar junto a los nenes o en
    el apartamento de su hembrita tercera a fin de
    no comprometerlo cuando ultima a los heridos
    de ojos abiertos

el violento autorizado poro a poro te odia pero sobre
    todo se aborrece a sí mismo y como todavía no
    puede reconocerlo sabe que en el espejo ha de
    encontrar puntual su arcada indivisible su
    minifundio de vergüenza

tortura así con la boca seca malbaratando de ese
    modo sus insomnios sus poblados y resecos
    insomnios y sabiendo muy en el fondo que todo
    es una gran postergación inútil porque la
    historia no es impaciente pero mantiene sus ficheros
    al día

With Your Permission

It is forbidden to write about a certain class of violence
so I will speak only of that violence which is permissible

authorized violence is present comprehensive and curious
      in your love letters caresses with you the thighs of
      your sweetheart listens to your whispers your
      expirations
crude and wretched he insinuates himself tamely into
      your house
poor gendarme promoted suddenly to horror
handler of secrets and majolica
at times a minor thief without vocation or melancholy
a parvenu to crime and nouveau riche with fear

authorized violence watches with deep concern the camel
      passing through the eye of a needle
and ordains an imperforate silence so he can vociferate
      in your ear his hygienic enthusiasm
      for liberty
he leaves his heart at home with the kids or in the
      apartment of his third mistress so it will not be
      compromised when he goes out to finish off his
      wide-eyed victims

authorized violence hates your every pore but above all
      loathes himself and as he still cannot confess this
      knows that in the mirror he will find punctilious his
      chronic retching his minifundio of shame
so he torments with his mouth parched squandering
      insomnias desiccated well-populated insomnias
      knowing deep inside it is all a great futile
      postponement because history is not impatient but
      does keep its files up to date

el violento autorizado tiene una descomunal tijera
      para cortar las orejas de la verdad pero después
      no sabe que hacer con ellas
no entiende de símbolos y lo bien que hace porque
      todo las calles las ventanas los ojos las paredes
      el cielo los puños los dientes son mercados de
      símbolos son ferias donde el futuro se ofrece
      como pichincha inesperada

el violento autorizado se mete en sus metales en sus
      fortalezas semovientes en su noche expugnable
      pero como deja un huequito para respirar por
      ahí se cuela no la bala perdida sino el guijarro
tiene miedo y lo bien que hace

el violento autorizado posee una formidable computadora
      electrónica capaz de informarle qué
      violencia es buena y qué violencia es mala y por
      eso prohibe nombrar la violencia execrable

la computadora por ejemplo advirtió que este poema
      trataba de la violencia buena.

authorized violence owns an extraordinary pair of
    scissors for cutting off the ears of truth but after he
    has no idea what to do with them
he cannot understand symbols and good for him because
    everything the streets windows eyes walls sky fists
    teeth are marketplaces of symbols fairs where the
    future is offered like an unexpected bargain

authorized violence plunges deep into his self-moving
    laminated strongholds expugnable nights but leaves a
    little chink for breathing through which not a stray
    bullet but a small boulder can pass
he is afraid and good for him

authorized violence has a formidable electronic computer
    to inform him which violence is good and which
    violence is bad so that way he can prohibit
    the mentioning of execrable violence

the computer reported for example that this poem
    was about good violence.

[*Translated by David Arthur McMurray*]

453

Holocausto

Usted quiere matarse en nuestro nombre

ahí
en el inestable centro del mundo
solo
frente al espejo avejentado

usted quiere matarse en nuestro nombre
ser el vicario de nuestras cotidianas agonías
el portavoz de nuestro dulce asco

sin embargo se mira francamente a los ojos
tiene presente que ésa puede ser la penúltima mirada
acabado como una noticia

por fin admite que
(a la mierda vicarios
portavoces)
no ha de matarse

por lo menos que no ha de matarse por nadie
que no sea
        usted mismo.

Holocaust

You want to kill yourself in our name

there
in the unsteady center of the world
alone
before the artificially aged mirror

you want to kill yourself in our name
to be the vicar of our quotidian agonies
the spokesman for our sweet nausea

but you look yourself squarely in the eye
and are aware that it could be
the penultimate look
and find yourself old like old enmity
worn out like yesterday's news

once and for all admit
(to hell with vicarial
spokesmen)
you need not kill yourself

that is you need not kill yourself
for anyone
        except
              yourself.

[*Translated by David Arthur McMurray*]

Quemar las naves

El día o la noche en que por fin lleguemos
habrá que quemar las naves

pero antes habremos metido en ellas
nuestra arrogancia masoquista
nuestros escrúpulos blandengues
nuestros menosprecios por sutiles que sean
nuestra capacidad de ser menospreciados
nuestra falsa modestia y la dulce homilía
de la autoconmiseración

y no sólo eso
también habrá en las naves a quemar
hipopótamos de Wall Street
pingüinos de la OTAN
cocodrilos del Vaticano
cisnes de Buckingham Palace
murciélagos de El Pardo
y otros materiales inflamables

el día o la noche en que por fin lleguemos
habrá sin duda que quemar las naves
así nadie tendrá riesgo ni tentación de volver

es bueno que se sepa desde ahora
que no habrá posibilidad de remar nocturnamente
hasta otra orilla que no sea la nuestra
ya que será abolida para siempre
la libertad de preferir lo injusto
y en ese solo aspecto
seremos más sectarios que Dios Padre

no obstante como nadie podrá negar
que aquel mundo arduamente derrotado

Burning the Ships

That day or night when we at last reach land
we shall have to burn the ships

but first we will have stowed inside
our masochistic arrogance
our squeamish hesitations
our disdain no matter how slight
our capacity for being disdained
our false modesty and the sweet homily
of self-pity

besides all that the ships
we burn will also hold
hippopotami from Wall Street
penguins from NATO
crocodiles from the Vatican
swans from Buckingham Palace
bats from El Pardo
and other combustible materials

that day or night when we at last reach land
we shall doubtless have to burn the ships
so no one will be tempted or liable to go back

better make it clear beginning now
that there will be no way to row by night
toward another coast which is not ours
since the freedom to prefer injustice
will be abolished once and for all
and in that one way
we will be more sectarian than God the Father

nonetheless since no one will deny
that world so arduously overcome

457

tuvo alguna vez rasgos dignos de mención
por no decir notables
habrá de todos modos un museo de nostalgias
donde se mostrará a las nuevas generaciones
como eran
    París
    el whisky
    Claudia Cardinale.

had upon occasion some noteworthy
not to say remarkable features
there must be at all costs a nostalgia museum
where future generations can find
out about
    Paris
    whiskey
    Claudia Cardinale.

[*Translated by David Arthur McMurray*]

Contra los puentes levadizos

1

Nos han contado a todos
cómo eran los crepúsculos
de hace noventa o novecientos años

cómo al primer disparo los arrepentimientos
echaban a volar cómo palomas
cómo hubo siempre trenzas que colgaban
un poco sucias pero siempre hermosas
cómo los odios eran antiguos y elegantes
y en su barbaridad venturosa latían
cómo nadie moría de cáncer o de asco
sino de tisis breves o de espinas de rosa

otro tiempo otra vida otra muerte otra tierra
donde los pobres héroes iban siempre a caballo
y no se apeaban ni en la estatua propia

otro acaso otro nunca otro siempre otro modo
de quitarle a la hembra su alcachofa de ropas

otro fuego otro asombro otro esclavo otro dueño
que tenía el derecho y además del derecho
la propensión a usar sus látigos sagrados

abajo estaba el mundo
abajo los de abajo
los borrachos de hambre
los locos de miseria
los ciegos de rencores
los lisiados de espanto
comprenderán ustedes que en esas condiciones
eran imprescindibles los puentes levadizos.

Against Drawbridges

1

We've all of us been told
how the sunsets were
ninety or nine hundred years ago

how at the first shot regrets
would fly like doves
how there were always dangling braids
a little soiled but always beautiful
how there were hatreds old and elegant
that throbbed in their prosperous barbarity
how no one ever died of cancer or of nausea
but of galloping consumption or rose thorns

another time another life another death another land
where the poor heroes always rode on horseback
never dismounting even onto their own statues

another perhaps another never another always another
    way
of stripping a woman of her artichoke of clothes

another fire another fear another slave another master
who had the right and besides the right
the tendency to use his holy whip
below there was the world
below there were the underdogs
those drunk with hunger
those crazed by misery
those blinded by resentment
those crippled by fear
you will understand that under such conditions
drawbridges were indispensable.

461

2

No sé si es el momento
de decirlo
en este punto muerto
en este año desgracia

por ejemplo
decírselo a esos mansos
que no pueden
resignarse a la muerte
y se inscriben a ciegas
caracoles de miedo
en la resurrección
qué garantía

por ejemplo
a esos ásperos
no exactamente ebrios
que alguna vez gritaron
y ahora no aceptan
la otra
la imprevista
reconvención del eco

o a los espectadores
casi profesionales
esos viciosos
de la lucidez
esos inconmovibles
que se instalan

en la primera fila así no pierden
ni un solo efecto
ni el menor indicio
ni un solo espasmo
ni el menor cadáver

2

I don't know if this is the time
to say it
on this dead spot
in this year of affliction

to tell it for example
to those gentle souls
who can't
resign themselves to death
and blindly enroll
the snails of fear
in the resurrection
with what guarantee?

for example
to the harsh ones
not drunk exactly
who once shouted
and now do not accept
the other
the unforeseen
accusation of the echo

or to the nearly
professional spectators
those addicts
of lucidity
the unmovable ones
who take a place

in the front row
to avoid losing
a single effect
or the slightest sign
or a single spasm
or the least important corpse

o a los sonrientes lúgubres
los exiliados de lo real
los duros
metidos para siempre en su campana
de pura sílice
egoísmo insecto
esos los sin hermanos
sin latido
los con mirada acero de desprecio
los con fulgor y labios de cuchillo

en este punto muerto
en este año desgracia
no sé si es el momento
de decirlo
con los puentes a medio descender
o a medio levantar
que no es lo mismo.

3

Puedo permanecer en mi baluarte
en ésta o en aquella soledad sin derecho
disfrutando mis últimos
racimos de silencio
puedo asomarme al tiempo
a las nubes al río
perderme en el follaje que está lejos

pero me consta y sé
nunca lo olvido
que mi destino fértil voluntario
es convertirme en ojos boca manos
para otras manos bocas y miradas

que baje el puente y que se quede bajo

or to the gloomy smiling ones
those exiled from the real
the stubborn ones
forever sunk into their
bell of purest quartz
an insect egoism
the brotherless ones
without a pulse
those with the steely look of scorn
those intellects with knife-sharp lips

in this dead spot
in this year of affliction
I don't know if this is the time
to say it
with the bridge half lowered
or half raised
which is not exactly the same thing.

3

I can stay here in my bulwark
in this or that solitude without any right
enjoying my last
clusters of silence
I can look out look on time
on the clouds the river
vanish in the far foliage

but I'm aware I know
never forget
that my fertile voluntary destiny
is to become the eyes the mouth and hands
for other hands and mouths and eyes

lower the bridge and keep it down

465

que entren amor y odio y voz y gritos
que venga la tristeza con sus brazos abiertos
y la ilusión con sus zapatos nuevos
que venga el frío germinal y honesto
y el verano de angustias calcinadas
que vengan los rencores con su niebla
y los adioses con su pan de lágrimas
que venga el muerto y sobre todo el vivo
y el viejo olor de la melancolía

que baje el puente y que se quede bajo

que entren la rabia y su ademán oscuro
que entren el mal y el bien
y lo que media
entre uno y otro
o sea
la verdad ese péndulo
que entre el incendio con o sin la lluvia
y las mujeres con o sin historia
que entre el trabajo y sobre todo el ocio
ese derecho al sueño
ese arco iris

que baje el puente y que se quede bajo

que entren los perros
los hijos de perra
las comadronas los sepultureros
los ángeles si hubiera
y si no hay
que entre la luna con su niño frío

que baje el puente y que se quede bajo

que entre el que sabe lo que no sabemos
y amasa pan

let love and hate and voice and shouting in
let sadness in with its arms open wide
and hope with its new shoes
let in the germinal and honest cold
and the summer with its scorched sufferings
let resentments with their mists come in
and farewells with their bread of tears
let the dead come and above all the living
and the old smell of melancholy

lower the bridge and keep it down

let rage and its dark gestures in
let in good and evil
and that which mediates
between them
which is to say
the truth this pendulum
let fire in with or without rain
and women with or without a past
let work in and above all leisure
that right to dream
that rainbow

lower the bridge and keep it down

let in the dogs
the sons of bitches
the midwives and gravediggers
the angels if they exist
and if not
let in the moon and her icy child

lower the bridge and keep it down

let in the one who knows what we don't know
who kneads the bread

o hace revoluciones
y el que no puede hacerlas
y el que cierra los ojos

en fin
para que nadie se llame a confusiones
que entre mi prójimo ese insoportable
tan fuerte y frágil
ése necesario
ése con dudas sombra rostro sangre
y vida a término
ése bienvenido

que sólo quede afuera
el encargado
de levantar el puente

a esta altura
no ha de ser un secreto
para nadie

yo estoy contra los puentes levadizos.

or who makes revolutions
and the one who can't make them
and the one who shuts his eyes

in short
to avoid confusion
let in my fellow the insufferable
so strong and fragile one
the necessary one
the one with doubts a shadow face blood
and a life that ends
the welcome one

keep out no one but the man
in charge
of raising the bridge

at this point
it should be no secret
to anyone

I'm against drawbridges.

[*Translated by Robert Márquez and Elinor Randall*]

Carlos María Gutiérrez (1926–) was born in Montevideo. A journalist by profession, he has also tried his hand at writing short stories as well as poetry. He was one of the first journalists to interview Fidel Castro in the Sierra Maestra, and later published his report as *En la sierra y otros reportajes* (1967). Between 1949 and 1950, Gutiérrez was secretary-general of the Uruguayan Federation of University Students. In 1967 he became editor of the Montevideo daily *Época*, which was subsequently suppressed by President Pacheco Areco. In 1969 he was imprisoned and while incarcerated wrote a series of poems about that experience on scraps of paper which were smuggled out and brought together in *Diario del cuartel* (to be published in English as *Prison Diary*), which was awarded the Casa de Las Américas prize for poetry in 1970. This first collection is, in the words of the Cuban poet Cintio Vitier, one of the judges awarding the prize, the work of a nonprofessional poet "who makes use of poetry as one would use an airplane or a gun [and] who was born the day the author discovered Vallejo . . . in a Montevideo bar."

After his release Gutiérrez was on the editorial staff of *Marcha*, a left weekly now banned in Montevideo. A frequent visitor to Cuba, he is currently at work on a biography of Che Guevara. His other works are *El agujero en la pared* (1968) and *The Dominican Republic: Rebellion and Repression* (1973).

The following poems are taken from *Diario del cuartel*.

Condiciones objetivas

Me consuela saber
aunque haga frío para andarse mojando en estos temas
que mi teniente es además dialéctico
y cree como Arismendi como Budin
en las múltiples vías
para efectuar el cambio de estructuras

cuando me dio la orden
le pregunté tan bobo como siempre
mis boberías burguesas ese lastre mis dudas
y mi teniente ha dicho

"con el trapo las manos o la escoba
pero limpie la mierda del retrete
y tiene diez minutos ciudadano"

Objective Conditions

I'm consoled by the fact
though it's cold to be getting wet in such matters
that my lieutenant is also dialectical
and believes along with Arismendi along with Budin*
in a multitude of ways
to effect the change of structures

when he gave me the order
I asked dumb as ever
my bourgeois idiocies that albatross my doubts
and my lieutenant said

"with the rag your hands or the broom
but clean the shit off that latrine
and you've got ten minutes citizen"

[*Translated by Margaret Randall and Robert Cohen*]

---

* Rodney Arismendi is first secretary of the Uruguayan Communist
Party. Stanislav Budin is a Czech journalist who responded to Che's
Tricontinental message by writing in the official party paper in Prague in
1967: "Guevara asks, not for peace in Vietnam but for the extension of
the Vietnam War . . . While socialism's main attraction lies in human-
ity's growing conviction that socialism means peace, Guevara wants to
convince us that socialism means war . . ."—*Trans.*

03:15 AM / −4°

El tiempo es luminoso
con nombre y apellido
su nombre es Automatic Seastar alias PR516
su apellido Tissot
su anatomía acero inoxidable

el tiempo tiene luz
pero no da calor
a cada vuelta entera de sus verdes luciérnagas
la oscuridad desciende un grado escala Celsius
dentro de esta cobija

en las grietas del piso
contiguas a mi oreja recibiendo la gotas de la escarcha
mis cucarachas duermen ateridas soñando que las amo
y despiden a veces el olor de sus sueños

éstas son sin embargo las normas rigurosas
que exige la verdadera observación científica
el cero meridiano pasa por esta celda y por mí mismo
y coinciden aquí privilegiadamente
las condiciones óptimas de humedad atmosférica
temperatura bajo el nivel del hombre
velocidad del viento
y no hay interferencias de la picana eléctrica

éste es mi observatorio del tiempo
al que sólo aporté un pequeño aparato de precisión
y una modesta vocación meteorológica
pero ha sido equipado por la generosa contribución del
    gobierno
debido a lo cual comunico al señor Presidente
que mis investigaciones quedan a su disposición
especialmente el Parte de esta noche

3:15 AM / −4°

Time is luminous
with first and last name
its first name is Automatic Seastar alias PR516
its last name is Tissot
anatomy: stainless steel

time has light
but it gives no heat
each time its green fireflies come full circle
under this blanket
the darkness drops one degree on the Celsius scale

in the cracks on the floor
next to my ear that receives its quota of frost
my frozen cockroaches sleep dreaming I love them
and sometimes they exude the odor of their dreams

nevertheless these are the ideal conditions
true scientific observation demands
zero meridian passes through this cell through me
and the optimum conditions of atmospheric humidity
and temperature below the level of man
and the speed of wind
are privileged to come together here
and there's no interference from the electric probes

this is my time observatory
to which my only contribution has been a small precision
        instrument
and a modest meteorological talent
but it's been equipped with the government's generous
        contribution
in the light of which I report to the President
my investigations remain at his disposal
especially tonight's forecast

475

"Cielo: va a amanecer
Precipitación Pluvial: lavará todo durante cuarenta días y
    cuarenta noches
Vientos: del sur del norte este y del oeste
Pronóstico del Tiempo:
el Tiempo sigue andando en mi muñeca
nadie puede pararlo es automático
y la hora se acerca Su Excelencia"

"Sky: sun's coming up
Pluvial precipitation: there will be rain for forty days and
    forty nights
Winds: from the south the north the east and the west
Forecast:
time keeps running at my wrist
no one can stop it   it's automatic
and the hour approaches Your Excellency"

[*Translated by Margaret Randall and Robert Cohen*]

Cartilla cívica

La única salida está en el voto
y habrá que hacerles caso compañero
nos criaron mamando democracia
vox populi vox dei

> *dei* con minúscula
> como cuadra a un moderno Estado laico

desde la escuela izamos la bandera
y tiranos temblad (a-a-ad recuerde)

la Corte Electoral urnas selladas
cada cuatro noviembres (¿o eran cinco?)
la mayoría construirá el futuro
y sanará la sociedad enferma
con tal que comiciemos que elijamos
lo que el forro del alma nos pronuncia

única condición que sea de prisa
no demoremos a la democracia
a votar a votar antes que todo
se nos vaya a la mierda al Chase Manhattan

en consecuencia tome una botella

> limpia vacía de a litro como ésas
> que cien patriotas dueños de las vacas
> nos venden con el tenue subproducto
> de los subsidios y los contrabandos

llénela en sus tres cuartos de bencina

> use nafta estatal dicen que es nuestra
> nada de Shell ni Esso ni Texaco

Voting Instructions

The only answer is the vote
and we'll have to take their advice compañero
because we haven't weaned ourselves from democracy's
    breast
vox populi vox dei

        dei with small letters
        as befits a modern secular state

in school they raised the flag
and "tyrants tremble" (e-e-emmmmmble, remember?)

the Electoral College ballot boxes
every four (or is it five?) Novembers we're free
the majority will build the future
and the sick society will get well
as long as we assemble as long as we elect
what our heart dictates

only one problem we have to hurry
democracy won't wait
vote   vote   before everything goes to hell
to Chase Manhattan

so take a bottle

        empty and clean a quart like the ones
        a hundred patriots owners of the cows
            sell us
        with the delicate by-product
        of their subsidies and contrabands

fill it three-quarters full of gasoline

sobre todo Texaco con su estrella
de cinco puntas y la T en el medio

ciérrela luego con tapón de diarios

le sugiero una *Acción* buen papel sueco
artículos que tapan cualquier cosa

y con rabia con sebo derretido

el que quedó en el plato de la sopa

dedos pacientes caras de los muertos
nudos dolor miedo de todos hambre
trence una larga una prolija mecha

si no encuentra otros trapos es lo mismo
su única camisa de uruguayo
el sudor qué excelente combustible

venza por fin ese temor tan lógico
de vulnerar la libertad de prensa
y agujereando los editoriales

van a quejarse pero no haga caso

pase la mecha huela la bencina
impregnando su casa su miseria
con el olor a incendio de su voto*

---

* Trabaje de mañana pues de noche
corre el riesgo de que un allanamiento
sin orden judicial alguna puerta
descerrajada a coces o balazos
su hija de doce años en rehén la idea
repentina y exótica de un *tira*
que viene de cobrar sus horas extra

use state naphtha they say it's ours
none of that Shell Esso or Texaco
especially not Texaco with its five-
           pointed star
and the T in the center*

then cork it with paper

           let me suggest a copy of *Action* good
                  Swedish paper
           articles that conceal just about anything

and with rage and with melted grease

           what was left in the soup plate

and with patient fingers and remembering the dead
and with knots and with pain and with everyone's fear
and with hunger
braid a careful wick

           if you have no other rags it doesn't
                  matter
           your only sad man's shirt will do
           sweat is an excellent combustible

overcome that natural fear
of attacking the freedom of the press
and making small holes in the editorials

           they'll complain but don't let it bother
                  you

insert the wick smell the gasoline

---

* Tupamaro sympathizers in Uruguay were putting Texaco T-stickers
on their car windows.—*Trans.*

entonces a votar como nos piden
a cumplir la costumbre de la patria

parado en la vereda tan anónimo
como prescribe nuestra democracia
vote en vez de albergar ideas foráneas
participe en la fiesta ciudadana
con su voto agarrado en una mano
encendiendo la mecha con la otra
con odio firme y con veloz parábola
deposítelo a nombre del futuro
donde haga más efecto en el presente
donde el forro del alma le pronuncie
usted es la mayoría compañero

y más dopado que lo necesario
se le ocurra probar cómo parece
su esposa desnuda y sumergida
en la bañera de Investigaciones
le alteren o interrumpan para siempre
esta preparación de los comicios

flooding the house flooding misery
with the smell of your burning vote*

and then vote just like they ask us to
do your duty to the nation

standing on the curb as anonymous
as our democracy demands
vote don't harbor foreign ideas
participate in the civic celebration

with your vote in one hand
light the wick with the other
with firm hate and good aim
deposit your vote in the name of the future
where it means the most in the present
where your heart dictates
you're the majority *compañero* it's up to you

[*Translated by Margaret Randall and Robert Cohen*]

---

* Do this by day
at night you risk a raid
without warrant
your door kicked in or riddled
with bullets
your twelve-year-old daughter
a hostage
or the sudden exotic idea
a plainclothes pig is coming around
after picking up his overtime
and more doped up than usual
it occurs to him to try your wife out
naked and submerged in that icy bathtub
at Investigations
altering or interrupting
your election day preparations
forever

483

Piedra blanca sobre piedra blanca

Aquí no tengo libros y cito de memoria sobre papel
    higiénico
no sé si habrá llegado el momento de hablar
y tampoco sé bien si les importa
pero la idea ha sido en estos años sucios
como un salvoconducto y ya no me hace falta
el viaje ha terminado

puedo decir ahora resumiendo
desde que era ignorante con lentes y muy joven
descubrí
pido excusas
que este César Vallejo de uso tan mal usado
se parecía a alguien que yo no supe nunca

eso me vino en un bar montevideano
hace como dos Batlles como doce mujeres
hace cientos de amigos y vacunas
y lo leí absorto destripado
con la camisa afuera
con piedad y con miedo repentinos
tragando bocanadas de poesía que se cristalizaba mortal-
    mente
ácido cruel que me comía la boca
y luz no usada y mierda y eras la boina gris y el corazón
    en calma
si un tiempo fuertes hoy desmoronados
y rosas flemas rodajas de cebolla
mientras me bajaban por el esófago flujos dolores de
    parto y el recuerdo
de Rita andina y dulce de junco y capulí

a ustedes les pasó y estoy seguro
y sé que me pasó

484

White Stone on White Stone

No books here and I'm quoting from memory on toilet
    paper
I don't know if the time has come to talk
nor am I really sure it matters to you
but the idea has been like a safe-conduct
through these dirty years and I don't need it anymore
the journey is over

now summing it up I can say
since I was ignorant with glasses and very young
I discovered
excuse me
that used César Vallejo so badly used
looked like someone I never knew

it came to me in a bar in Montevideo
two Batlles twelve women ago
hundreds of friends and vaccinations ago
and I read him absorbed disemboweled
with my shirt out
with sudden pity and fear
swallowing mouthfuls of poetry that crystallized mortally
a cruel acid that ate at my tongue
and *luz no usada* shit and *eras la boina gris y el corazón
    en calma*
si un tiempo fuertes hoy desmoronados
and roses phlegms and onion rings
while flux and labor pains ran down my throat and the
    memory
of *Rita andina y dulce de junco y capulí*

it happened to you too I'm sure
I know it happened to me I still tremble
at each new line

todavía tiemblo
a cada nuevo verso
quedárseles Dios Padre atracado en los dientes
yo por lo menos sí
y con la lengua negra casi paralizada
hacía a un lado carozos de palabras hollejos de palabras
para que jugos gástricos y jugos salivares
pero sobre todo una pena purísima y de cráter lunar
me bloquearan el aire
me empañaran los lentes y me jodieran el mundo
porque yo me volvía créanme al mismo tiempo
cadáver feto amor planta podrida y nuevamente amor
perro con sarna niño extraviado amor o trapo sucio
y el microbio atrocísimo de César

esa noche el peruano
me curtió a bofetadas
escupió en mi cocacola y se cagó en mi sandwich olvidado
iluminando el bar con sus relámpagos
pero su cara estaba debajo del paraguas
debido a que era jueves y llovía
sólo le vi las manos y los zapatos rotos
y entonces los borrachos se escondieron llevándose el
    teléfono
botellas
y un cuadro de Gardel que estaba serio
porque ya no podíamos aguantarnos las lágrimas la risa
porque de tan hermanos
el César refregaba contra mi jeta de auxiliar tercero
los pedazos las entretelas la cuchara
el dedo de Pedro Rojas fusilado
y salimos los dos como en un tango

más tarde cumplí los años de mi edad y al alba
me paré muerto de hambre en una pasarela
tal vez el Pont des Arts pero no sé perdonen
mi francés era escaso

486

those *Dios Padres* caught in my teeth
at least for me
and with my tongue black and half-paralyzed
piling up to one side pits of words peelings of words
so that gastric juices and salivary juices
but above all the purest of moon-crater sorrows
cut off my air
hazed my glasses and fucked over my world
because I became believe me
at once cadaver fetus love rotten plant and once again
    love
mangy dog misplaced child love or filthy rag
and César's heinous microbe

that night the Peruvian
worked me over
he spit in my coke and shit in my forgotten sandwich
illuminating the bar with his lightning bolts
but his face was beneath the umbrella
since it was Thursday and it rained
I only saw his hands and broken shoes
and then the drunks hid themselves
taking bottles the telephone and a picture of Gardel who
    was serious
because we couldn't hold our tears or laughter back
    anymore
because being such brothers
César knocking against my civil servant's jaw
the pieces the padding the spoon
Pedro Rojas' finger up against a firing squad
and the two of us left as in a tango

later I reached the years of my age and one early morning
stood dead from hunger on a bridge
maybe the Pont des Arts I don't know forgive me
my French was scant I admit it rained
and I looked at the black water without a return ticket in

admito que llovía
y miré el agua negra sin pasaje de vuelta en el bolsillo
masticando aquel tango
cenándolo abrigándome disfrutando sus suecas sus
    cigarrillos rubios
hasta que recordé el yeyuno de Vallejo
no su perfil no a quién se parecía
sólo la piedra negra sobre la piedra blanca
y que eligió París para morirse
o tal vez
pensé entonces
sólo la lluvia de París
o tal vez
pienso ahora
sólo la lluvia

no importa ya
César Yeyuno ha muerto ya no le pega a nadie
aquí no tengo nada
hay tres grados es julio
y en San Pedrito a veintiséis dentro de pocos días
usurpé con permiso de la Revolución una vivienda virgen
una novia doncella señorita
que esperaba en silencio
feliz con muebles nuevos
al esposo guajiro con su título

abajo
el claxon de una guagua llamaba periodistas retrasados
pero me quedé allí que era mi casa
había sudado la guayabera
Fidel Castro afirmó bajo el sol que ahora Cuba está sola
y algún guardián de la conciencia crítica
presupuestado en la Sección Metáforas del ICAP o el INIT
o como rayos sea el nombre de la fraternidad con oficinas
había dejado en la mesa
los versos del peruano mi socio buena gente

my pocket chewing that tango
dining on it wrapping myself in it enjoying its Swedish
    women and blend tobacco
until I remembered Vallejo's empty belly
not his profile not who he looked like
just the black stone on the white stone
and that he chose Paris to die in
or maybe
then I thought
only the Paris rain
or maybe
now I think
only the rain

it doesn't matter now
César Yeyuno is dead he won't hit anyone anymore
I have nothing here it's three degrees it's July
and in San Pedrito on the twenty-sixth in a few days
I took with the Revolution's permission a virgin dwelling
a maiden girl señorita
waiting in silence
happy with new furniture
for her *guajiro* husband with his deed

down below
the busses' horns calling lagging journalists
but I stayed that was my house
I'd sweated the *guayabera*
Fidel Castro in the sun declared now Cuba is alone
and some guardian of critical consciousness
—budgeted under the Metaphor Department of the ICAP
    or the INIT
or whatever the fuck that fraternity with offices is
    called—
had left on the table
the Peruvian's poems my partner good man
Vallejo without opening the book throwing me back

Vallejo sin abrir libro que vuelve
de una montevideana torpísima memoria

César Vallejo ha muerto sin embargo
desde hace doce putas dos Batlles otras enfermedades
y la pena de cráter que Rita nunca supo
estaba pelos uñas tejido conjuntivo húmeros a la mala
cal en el cementerio
porque toda la tarde
asándome a este sol
descifrando una tesis que construye doncellas habitables
y ordena la violencia
en batallones verdes que leen a Retamar al pie del cuatro
    bocas
eschuché la poesía verdadera que nos manda vivir
que prohibe morirse simplemente

salvo que sea en el Yuro
y eso ya no es morirse

aquí no tengo libros y han dispuesto que la luz no se
    apague por las noches
ya que Pacheco teme a ciertos sueños
pero si no me muevo y no tirito
tal vez pueda salir y a lo que venga

abajo ya la Trecha ha reventado
y el carnaval
envía sus comparsas y sus ñanigos para sitiar Santiago
con el barraje de la Guantanamera y el retumbar del
    Chori
mi novia se entristece de repente
y la Revolución que también sabe de eso
planta en la noche una guitarra tenue

esto ya no es tristeza es sentimiento
dice Sindo Garay en la ventana

490

to an awkward Montevidean memory

César Vallejo is dead nevertheless
twelve whores two Batlles other sicknesses ago
and the crater's sorrow Rita never knew
it was hair nails conjunctive tissue damp bones
lime in the cemetery
because all afternoon
roasting under this sun
deciphering a thesis that constructs habitable maidens
and orders violence
in green battalions that read Retamar at the foot of
    anti-aircraft guns
I heard the real poetry that commands us to live
that simply prohibits our death

unless it comes in the Yuro
and that's no longer death

I have no books here and they've arranged for the light to
    stay on all night
since Pacheco fears certain dreams
but if I don't move and don't tremble
maybe I'll get out and on to what's ahead

below La Trecha's overflowing
and the *carnaval*
seeds its masqueraders and its *ñañigos* to besiege Santi-
    ago
with the barrage of the "Guantanamera" and the beat of
    Chori's drum
my girl is suddenly sad
and the Revolution that also knows about that
plants a tenuous guitar in the night

this isn't sadness anymore it's sentiment
says Sindo Garay in the window

y el soldado con poncho camina por la escarcha con el
	Garand al hombro

César Vallejo ha muerto
llegó hasta aquí no más
ahora me entero
reconozco la cara que no supe
y a lo mejor no agrego nada nuevo
a lo mejor ustedes ya lo saben
porque César Vallejo
en aquel libro a veintiséis de julio
se pareció por fin a Cuba
como un mapa distinto se parece a otro mapa
pero hay un solo mapa para no equivocarse y caer al agua

antes que venga el oficial de guardia
pidiéndome el cigarro de las cuatro
alcanzándome el mate clandestino
pongo por si les sirve compañeros
que allá en Santiago de Cuba el veintiséis de noche
con guitarras
no hay lluvia nunca es jueves
sólo hay piedras blancas
y decían los guajiros o decía Fidel
vale lo mismo
que hay que usarlas en casas de vivir
con vida para siempre
se dan cuenta

perdonen que los deje viene el hombre
en Minas hace frío y ya amanece

and the soldier with a poncho walks through the frost his
    Garand on his shoulder

César Vallejo is dead
he came this far no further
at last they tell me
and maybe I can't add anything new
maybe you already know all about it
because César Vallejo
in that book on the twenty-sixth of July
finally resembled Cuba
like one map resembles another
but there's only one map so you won't go wrong and fall
    into the water

before the guard comes by
asking for his four o'clock cigarette
handing me the clandestine *mate*
I'm telling you *compañeros* if it's of any use
that there in Santiago de Cuba the twenty-sixth at night
with guitars
it doesn't rain it's never Thursday
there are only white stones
and the *guajiros* or Fidel
it's all the same
said we have to use them   build houses to live in
with life forever   understand

pardon me I'm going   the Man's here
in Minas it's cold the sun's coming up

[*Translated by Margaret Randall and Robert Cohen*]

493

Notes

Batlle: this refers to Luis and his son Jorge. The former was president of Uruguay, the latter the leader of his father's party and a regular aspirant to the same office—a kind of family dynasty covering twenty years of Uruguayan political life.

Chori: a famous Cuban drummer.

eras la boina gris . . . : this is a line from Pablo Neruda's "Poema #6," from *Veinte poemas de amor y una canción desesperada:* "Te recuerdo como eras en el ultimo otoño / eras la boina gris y el corazón en calma" (I remember you as you were in the last autumn / you were the gray beret and the heart at rest).

Gardel, Carlos: a famous singer of tangos, whose smiling portraits customarily hang in Montevideo bars.

Garay, Sindo: a Cuban troubadour who died in 1969 at the age of 101.

guajiro: the Cuban slang equivalent of peasant or farmer.

guayabera: the traditional long white pleated shirt worn outside the pants and often taking the place of a suit jacket in tropical countries.

luz no usada: a line from "Oda a Salinas," a poem by the sixteenth-century Spanish poet Fray Luis de León: "El aire se serena / y viste luz no usada" (The air becalms / and you were virgin light).

Minas: a military stockade three hours from Montevideo.

ñañigos: representatives of an African ritual secret society of men, symbolized by the figure of Ochún. They take an active part in the *carnaval* celebration. In the time of Gustavo Machado they were also paid political assassins, and they still operate on the margin of society.

Pacheco Areco, Jorge: then President of Uruguay.

Rita andina y dulce . . . : this is a line from Vallejo's "Idilio muerto," from the book *Heraldos Negros.* The three poetic references form part of the formal education of Uruguayans of bourgeois cultural orientation.

Rojas, Pedro: a Spanish worker shot in the Civil War. He is described in Vallejo's "Himno a los voluntarios de la República," part III, from the book *España, aparta de mi este cáliz.* Dying, he wrote with his own bloody finger "LONG LIVE THE REVOLUTION!" on one of the city walls.

si un tiempo fuertes . . . : Francisco de Quevedo wrote: "Miro los muros de la patria mía / si un tiempo fuertes hoy desmoronados" (I looked at the walls of my homeland / if once strong now they are in ruins).

La Trecha: Santiago de Cuba's main street.

Yeyuno, César: the word *yeyuno* refers to part of a cow's intestine; Vallejo makes the image into one of hunger, alluding also to the similar word *ayuno*, which means fast. The line is: "Vaca mi estómago, vaca mi yeyuno," from the poem "La rueda del hambriento," in *Poemas humanos*.

Yuro: the ravine in Bolivia that was the scene of Che's last battle.

Venezuela

Edmundo Aray (1936–   ) was trained as an economist and now earns a living as a university professor. He is a writer of short stories as well as an elegantly polished poet and one of the most promising of the younger generation of Venezuelan writers. He was a member of the Sardio literary group and in 1961 became one of the founding editors of the journal *El techo de la ballena*. He is currently one of the editors of the literary journal *Rocinante*.

The following are his published works to date: *La hija de Raghú* (1956), *Nadie quiere descansar* (1961), *Sube para bajar* (1963), *Twist presidencial* (1964), and *Cambio de soles* (1968).

Sin título

Vamos. Ahora comienza.
Ahora comenzamos.
No haya paz para las Soberanas Bolsas.
Donde los asesinos a sueldo
y los asesinos sin sueldo,
donde los señores Presidentes
y los señores generales
y los señores señores
señores hijos de puta
ministros del gabinete,
jefes de partidos democráticos.
Esta es la hora de joderse.
Para ellos
esta es la hora de consumarse.
Que no haya paz,
que no haya paz para la muerte
que no haya luna ni sol para ellos,
la vida pide permiso.
De pie, camaradas,
de pie aquí en la ciudad,
de pie allá en la montaña.
No véis cómo huyen,
no véis cómo se cagan.
Fuera de la mesa,
fuera con todo y mesa.
La pira está encendida,
es un fuego solemne,
es el viejo fuego nuevo
que nos viene quemando,
que desde antes y mucho antes
nos viene quemando.

Untitled

Let's go. Now it begins.
Now we're beginning.
Let there be no peace for the sovereign Stock Exchanges.
Where there are paid assassins
and assassins without pay,
and Mr. Presidents
and generals
and Mr. Misters
and Mr. sons of bitches
cabinet ministers,
and leaders of democratic parties.
Their fucking hour has come.
This is the time for them
to be consumed.
Let there be no peace,
let there be no peace for death
let there be no moon, no sun for them,
life asks for a chance.
Comrades, on your feet,
on your feet here in the city,
on your feet in the hills.
They're on the run—
see how they shit in their pants?
Leave the table,
away with the table and all.
The pyre is lit,
and it's a solemn fire,
an ancient fire made new
that's been consuming us,
since before and long before
has been consuming us.

[*Translated by Elinor Randall and Robert Márquez*]

499

Siete y cincuenta y cinco

Estoy a punto de salir.
Tomo el café y llamo a mi mujer
  —hombre de impecables hábitos—
y me abotono al paltó. Ascensor. Sexto piso.
Llega para bajar. Elena está enferma
y *la grand-mère* no ha salido a recibir sol.
Baja con cuidado. Bajemos. Espera que la máquina
caliente. En L. En ele. Siete y cuarenta y cinco,
¡apura! La oficina—señores, por favor—las consultas,
las clases que dictar,
los libros y el Ministro o el Director
   Livia
la Secretaria—competente y eficaz. Es necesario
andar y andar, golpeando, sosteniendo, golpeando,
   andar,
analizando, señores, silencio, por favor,
de la Planta han salido, en la Planta han declarado,
gritos, pancartas, manifestaciones, ¡Livia!
cárcel y andar, golpeando, hambre, sosteniendo
golpeando, ¡hambre! ¡hambre! ¡hambre!
   ¡hambre!
   ¡ham!
   bre
Andar.
Sosteniendo
   golpeando
     andar.
Vendrá un día mejor. Con la corbata haré
un nudo alrededor de tu cuello. Un año mejor
Algún hecho profundo. ¡Un grito!
Siete y cincuenta y cinco,
puertas doradas, porteros y bedeles,
   noticia y lotería
   por favor,

Seven Fifty-Five

I'm on the verge of leaving.
Drink my coffee, call my wife
        —a man of impeccable habits—
button my overcoat. The elevator. Sixth floor.
It stops on the way down. Elena's sick
and *la grand-mère* hasn't gotten any sun.
Go down slowly. Let's go. Wait till the car
warms up. "L." On "el." Seven forty-five.
Hurry! The office—gentlemen, please—appointments,
classes to be given,
the books, and the Minister or the Director
        Livia,
the Secretary—competent, efficient. You have to
keep moving, moving, hitting, holding on, hitting,
        moving,
analyzing, gentlemen, quiet please,
they've come from the plant, in the plant they've de-
        clared,
shouting, placards, demonstrations, Livia!
jail and keep moving, hitting, hunger, holding on,
hitting, hunger! hunger! hunger!
        hunger!
        hun!
        ger
Moving.
Holding on
        hitting
                moving.
A better day will come. With my necktie
I'll make a noose around your neck. A better year,
some decisive act. A scream!
Seven fifty-five,
gilded doors, porters and doormen,
        the lottery and news,

501

un lujoso auto, magníficas flores y bellas coronas,
      tarjetas tarjetas
un lujoso auto
para los funerales de este pequeño burgués.

please,
a fancy car, magnificent flowers, handsome wreaths,
    cards and more cards,
a fancy car
for the funeral of this petty bourgeois.

[*Translated by Elinor Randall and Robert Márquez*]

Esto leo a mi hija

Río de Janeiro: Yo, Juez militar, predigo
que el sacerdote Alipio de Freitas,
será condenado en distintos procesos
a penas de cien años. Causa:
Subversión e incitación a la indisciplina.

Lima: Yo, Salomón Bolo Hidalgo, sacerdote,
co-presidente del Frente de Liberación Nacional,
pregunto si el hambre y la miseria
se van a solucionar con pactos militares,
con misiones militares,
con pantomimas como la Operación Ayacucho.

La Habana: El sacerdote Camilo Torres Restrepo,
al morir por la causa revolucionaria,
dio el más alto ejemplo
de intelectual cristiano comprometido con el pueblo.
Nosotros, sacerdotes católicos, delegados
al Congreso Cultural de La Habana,
nos comprometemos
con la lucha revolucionaria antimperialista,
hasta las últimas consecuencias,
para lograr la liberación de todo el hombre
y de todos los hombres.

I Read This to My Daughter

Rio de Janeiro: I, a military judge, predict
that the priest Alipio de Freitas
will be sentenced in different trials
to a hundred years in prison. Offense:
Sedition and inciting to disorder.

Lima: I, Salomón Bolo Hidalgo, a priest,
co-president of the National Liberation Front,
ask if hunger and misery
are going to be solved with military pacts,
with military missions,
and pantomimes like Operation Ayacucho.

Havana: The priest Camilo Torres Restrepo,
on dying for the revolutionary cause,
became the supreme example
of the Christian intellectual committed to the people.
We, Catholic priests, delegates
to the Havana Cultural Congress,
commit ourselves
to the revolutionary anti-imperialist struggle,
with all its consequences,
in order to achieve the total liberation of man
and of all mankind.

[*Translated by Robert Márquez*]